SUBMARINE

SUBMARINE
The Ultimate Naval Weapon—Its Past, Present & Future
DREW MIDDLETON

PϞP A Playboy Press Book

FIRST EDITION.

Playboy and Rabbit Head design are trademarks of Playboy, 919 North Michigan Avenue, Chicago, Illinois 60611 (U.S.A.), Reg. U.S. Pat. Off., marca registrada, marque déposée.

Text Design by Bob Antler

Library of Congress Cataloging in Publication Data

Middleton, Drew, 1913–
    Submarine, the ultimate naval weapon.

    Includes index.
        1. Submarine warfare. 2. Submarine boats.
3. Naval strategy. I. Title.
V210.M52   359.8'3   76–7850
ISBN 0–87223–472–X

INTRODUCTION

This book is not a formal history of the submarine. Rather, it is an attempt to trace the development of undersea craft and warfare and to explain their overwhelming importance to contemporary global strategy.

Believers in détente usually are themselves hostile to books dealing with weapons, strategy and power. "Power" is a dirty word in America today. And the epitome of modern military power is the nuclear ballistic missile submarine.

For almost a century men have sought peaceful uses for the submarine. Their successes have been marginal. Submarines have been put to work in underwater exploration, in maintaining off-shore oil rigs, in rescue operations, in scientific expeditions to the deeps. But the submarine has remained primarily a weapon of war. Today it is one of the most powerful weapons in the world, and certainly the most flexible one. Its power, which increased geometrically with the coming of nuclear-powered craft equipped with nuclear ballistic missiles, exerts enormous politico-strategic influence. The history of this strident century is marked with examples of the submarine's influence on rulers, parliaments and peoples.

Any work on submarines, therefore, must deal primarily with their military aspect and political effect. This book, I hope, will provide the layman with a guide to submarines and the increasing complexities of submarine warfare. I make no excuse for discussing so fully the submarine's influence on the strategies of the United States and the Soviet Union. It's a rough world out there. The life or death of our planet may be in the hands of a few hundred young submarine officers. The nuclear-powered, nuclear-missile-armed submarine is today's ultimate weapon. So it is as a weapon that the submarine must be considered.

In writing this book, I had many interviews with American, British and Canadian submarine officers and with their colleagues engaged in antisubmarine warfare. After consideration, I have decided not to identify these officers by name except where their statements are on public record. For the hours they spent discussing submarines and submarine warfare in what they hoped was the simplest language, I am deeply grateful.

Until I began my research, I had no idea how many good books had been written about various aspects of the submarine, its technical development, its role in two world wars and its future. Clay Blair, Jr., in *Silent Victory* and his shorter but still immensely readable work on the development of the *Nautilus* and on Adm. Hyman G. Rickover's part in it has served the navy and his country well. John Bentley and Norman Palmar have written excellent works on the *Thresher* disaster. Siegfried Breyer's *Guide to the Soviet Navy* was the best source work I encountered during my research. I also read widely in Soviet military publications dealing directly or peripherally with submarines.

For an overview of submarine warfare in two world conflicts, Sir Winston Churchill's *The World Crisis* and *The Second World War* are preeminent. Basil Liddell Hart, although chiefly concerned with land warfare, provides illuminating insight into the effect of submarine warfare on the land campaigns of 1914–1918 in his *The Real War*.

The official histories of the American and British sides in World War II are excellent. Samuel Eliot Morison's work on the United States Navy is a more attractive book. But I found *The War at Sea*, Volumes I, II and III, published by Her Majesty's Government, equally informative—although the authors lacked Admiral Morison's enviable touch with the blunt Anglo-Saxon tongue. German histories are long on dramatic anecdotes but short on comprehensive assessments. A pity because the Germans were the pioneers of submarine warfare.

In fact, I encountered so many good books about submarines, naval battles and Soviet sea power that I could not write for reading. Three especially good ones are *The Battle for the Mediterranean* by Donald Macintyre, *A Sailor's Odyssey* by Admiral of the Fleet Viscount Andrew Cunningham and *Russian Sea Power* by David Fairhall.

The submarine's influence on politics and diplomacy is one of the themes of this book. The reader who wishes to explore this aspect further is advised to read *The Road to War*, that forgotten masterpiece by Walter Millis.

Two other sources were important to me and would be important, I expect, to anyone wishing to write seriously about submarines and the general problems of sea power and maritime strategy. *The United States Naval Institute Proceedings*, which published Adm. Sergei G. Gorshkov's articles with commentaries by distinguished American admirals, was one. The second was the files of the *New York Times*, including article after article of clarity and insight by Hanson W. Baldwin, the ablest military commentator America has produced.

Drew Middleton
Westport, N.Y., and
New York City
April 12, 1976

SUBMARINE

> It is an *Automa*, runnes under
> water,
> With a snug nose, and has a
> nimble taile
> Made like an *auger*, with which
> taile she wrigles
> Betwixt the coasts of a Ship, and
> sinkes it streight.
>> Ben Jonson, *The Staple of News*, Act
>> III, Scene II, 1625

1

Man has always displayed a stubborn ambition to do what nature never intended him to do. Daedalus defied the sun and attempted flight. How many similar adventurers in mankind's youth, cramped in a hollow log or a sphere of sticks and skins, sought to submerge beneath the surface of the water and explore the unknown deeps? We do not know, any more than we know the names of the countless others who tried to fly. But the list of would-be submariners must be nearly as long as that of aspiring aviators. The primitive experiments of these seamen were the first steps toward today's submarine, which is at once the world's most formidable weapon of war and mankind's principal tool to explore and exploit the untold resources of the seas.

Nothing in the early history of the submarine and little in its development through World War II prepared us for the dramatic change in the measurement of military strength that grew out of the

3

January 17, 1955, signal that the nuclear-powered submarine USS *Nautilus* was under way and the July 20, 1960, firing of a Polaris ballistic missile from the USS *George Washington*. These two dates mark the emergence of the true submarine; that is, a vessel whose natural environment is underwater and which is armed with the most devastating weapon known to man: the nuclear ballistic missile.

This military advance by the United States, soon to be followed in the navies of the Soviet Union, the United Kingdom and France, was far more spectacular and important than the limited development of the submarine for peaceful purposes. For the submarine run on nuclear power and armed with nuclear-tipped missiles is the most versatile and deadly weapons system yet conceived. The carrier admirals, spawned in the golden days of aircraft carrier supremacy, may not recognize the potential of this weapons system, any more than the battleship admirals of half a century ago recognized the waxing power inherent in the union of carrier and bomber. One hopes they will not have to learn the hard way.

Although the submarine is inextricably linked with war in popular opinion, the first efforts to penetrate beneath the surface of the water were entirely pacific. Alexander the Great, according to legend, had himself lowered into the sea in a glass contraption, and classical and medieval history report similar adventures by less famous figures. But it is not until the 16th and 17th centuries that we encounter men intent not only on submerging in vessels but in moving in them beneath the surface.

That was a great age of theory; men conceived what mankind could do, but their technology was primitive. William Bourne, an Englishman, discoursed on the principles of submerged progress and laid down the basic theory that governs submarines today. In order to submerge and surface, a vessel must be able to vary the amount of water it displaces.

The first ventures underwater demanded a degree of courage that still surprises over the centuries. I recall talking to Adm. Sir Martin Dunbar-Naismith, a submariner who won the Victoria

Cross, Britain's highest military decoration, for his exploits against the Turks in World War I. He did not then consider his feats of a quarter of a century earlier anything extraordinary. Like most authentic heroes he was a quiet man. *His* heroes were the men who had first taken ships underwater.

"Imagine what they went through," he said. "They had nothing to guide them, neither experience nor instruments. Yet they went on. And, really, we don't know much about them."

One was a Dutch doctor living in London, Cornelis Drebbel by name. All that is known about his submarine is that it was made of greased leather stretched over a wooden frame. It was propelled by 12 oarsmen and it fascinated the London of James I. There is a legend that that monarch, "the wisest fool in Christendom," boarded Drebbel's craft for a trip on the Thames, and Ben Jonson talks about a mysterious fluid that enabled the inventor to purify the air inside his craft. The truth is lost. It was a time when fact and fancy went hand in hand and Jonson, hardly a scientist or even an early practitioner of science fiction, may have been romancing.

Yet the idea is intriguing. Had this Dutch physician found some means of releasing oxygen within his craft? Edward Horton, a thorough and scholarly writer, raises the question, in his book, *Submarine.*

Interestingly enough, Drebbel envisioned no military use for his submarine; nor, apparently, did anyone in the crowds that watched it in the Thames. This was odd because that was a day when sea power as we now understand it had become the major factor in war. Less than a third of a century before Drebbel titillated Londoners with his undersea craft, the English, with the timely help of gales, for which the Almighty was given full credit, had defeated Spain's "Invincible Armada." Thus the foundations were laid for the maritime preeminence that, with brief exceptions, was to maintain the islanders as a world power until well into the 20th Century.

The first submarine built as a ship of war was the brainchild of a Frenchman named Le Son, who worked in Rotterdam. What

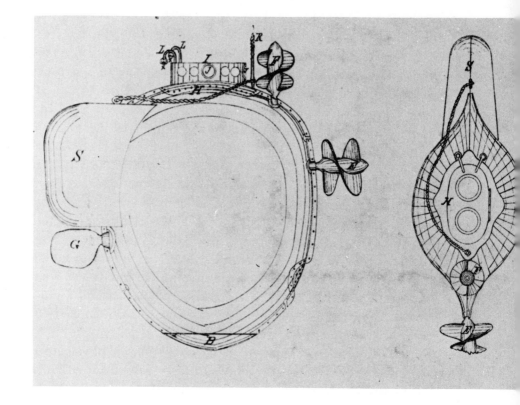

little we know of Le Son's craft is unconvincing. By the standards of the day, she was a large vessel, 72 feet long, and was armed with rams that protruded from both ends. Le Son was not a man to hide his, or his vessel's, light under a bushel. He claimed he could sink 100 ships a day, which would have been inconceivable even for an American submarine captain in the happy hunting ground of the west Pacific in 1944 and 1945. The ship was propelled by a curiously shaped wheel, but unfortunately, this wheel was hardly likely to drive a submarine of the size envisaged by Le Son.

The Frenchman, however, deserves his niche in history. For he was the first to implant the idea of the submarine as a weapon of war in the thinking of admiralties. Had it not been for this concept,

Turtle, *David Bushnell's one-man submarine. Drawing was made by F. M. Barber in 1885 from a description left by Bushnell.*
(*Official U. S. Navy Photo*)

the development of the submarine would have proceeded at a much slower pace.

The year 1776 was memorable both for the birth of the United States and for the first use in war, albeit unsuccessfully, of an underwater craft. The *Turtle* was designed by David Bushnell, a New Englander of an inventive turn, who appears to have made a genuine breakthrough in submarine construction. Today, widely advertised breakthroughs in airplane or ship design are actually the product of years of intensive research development and testing. Bushnell, working without the aid of huge sums of money and with very little encouragement, was the author of a genuine scientific leap ahead.

What he did was to build the first practical one-man submarine. It was egg-shaped, made of wood and sat in the water like an egg. The *Turtle* was strong enough to resist pressure at the depths she was designed to operate in, she carried enough ballast on her bottom to hold her upright, her hatch was truly watertight and her movements, although at times probably erratic, were well beyond anything that had been attempted.

Propulsion was in the form of a screw propeller cranked by a handle inside the vessel. Another screw above the craft, similarly operated, allowed the *Turtle* to submerge. The operator had enough air for about half an hour underwater and two pumps to eject the water ballast that was used in addition to the sand ballast.

The *Turtle*'s weakness was its mode of attack. Bushnell's idea was that the vessel would carry a mine of 150 pounds of gunpowder that would be attached to a ship's bottom by an auger screwed into the planking. The *Turtle*'s operator would then leave the keg of gunpowder floating against the ship and a timing device would explode the charge when the submarine was well out of harm's way.

Bushnell's target was the British squadron then commanding New York Harbor and the surrounding waters. The inventor and the commander of the Continental army, Gen. George Washington, were two Americans who understood the tremendous advantage that superiority at sea gave the British in the Revolutionary War. Bushnell first went to Washington with plans to explode mines under the hulls of British ships, and the general gave him what help he could. When mines proved unsatisfactory, the inventor progressed to the *Turtle.*

If war was the midwife of the submarine, the British fleet was its object from the beginning. The reason was simple enough. From the early 18th until well into the 20th Century, the Royal Navy was probably the world's single most powerful, most successful, instrument of war. British fleets could and did lose isolated engagements, British ships of the line and frigates could and did lose ship-to-ship encounters. But whether the enemy was French, Spanish, Danish, Dutch or American, a war ended with the British still pretty much in control of the seas. Anyone, therefore, who came along with an idea that might lead to the destruction of British sea power expected a warm welcome from the islanders' enemies. Their expectations were not always met.

The *Turtle*'s target was either HMS *Eagle* or HMS *Asia*, ships of the New York squadron. American and British accounts differ. Bushnell, who was ill, entrusted the attack to a Sgt. Ezra Lee. The submarine was towed out into the harbor and Lee, keeping just above the surface, was on his own. Then his troubles began. Tides carried him past his first target. When he found himself beneath the *Eagle*—

USS Turtle *was unsuccessful in its attempt to attach a "torpedo" to the bottom of HMS* Eagle, *Admiral Howe's flagship anchored off Governor's Harbor, New York, September, 1776.* (Official U. S. Navy Photo)

or the *Asia*—he had difficulty attaching the mine to the hull, which was sheathed in copper. His air supply began to run out. At this juncture, a British patrol boat rowing guard on the fleet discovered the strange-looking craft. Lee activated and released the mine and headed for safety. The mine exploded, causing consternation among the captains but no damage in the fleet. However, the British hastily moved their ships out of inshore waters.

Bushnell, although encouraged by Washington, never tried again. But he had accomplished what no man had done before; he had demonstrated the practicality of a submarine as a weapon of war.

Britain's war against the Americans—and the French and Spanish—ended without further attempts at undersea warfare. It was not until the great world convulsion that we call the Napoleonic Wars that the next step took place in the development of the submarine. The inventor was Robert Fulton, one of the most extraordinary and versatile men of his time. Gunsmith, painter, mechanical engineer, Fulton was also a born revolutionary—his background was Irish—and like many of his fellow Americans, he sympathized deeply with the French Revolution. Here were the bloody British, symbolized by the Royal Navy, seeking to defeat a revolution that Fulton, ardent but hardly perceptive, confused with the American Revolution. His target, like Bushnell's, was the Royal Navy.

The basic idea of the vessel was the same. Neither Bushnell nor Fulton planned a submarine in the modern sense, a true underwater craft. What they were after was a craft that could approach a man-of-war unperceived, plant a charge and get away. There was some Scots in Fulton's Irish, however. When, in 1797, he presented the French Directory with his plans for destroying the British fleet, he made it clear that revolutionary sympathy was not his only motivation. He asked for a lump sum for every ship sunk, prize money and other considerations. The Directory, being French, haggled. Fulton, furious, withdrew his offer.

The American's approach, however, was founded on a solid appreciation of British character. He reasoned correctly that the lords of the Admiralty would consider his submarine *hors de loi*, that is, an outlaw weapon, and would summarily hang every crew member they caught. If outlawry was to be the outcome, he wanted to be well paid for his risks. The French reluctance to embrace his idea probably had more to it than financial considerations. In 1797, the French revolutionaries, in common with most of their kind then and now, were suffering from an overdose of confidence. The British, as always, were slow to rearm, and the admirals of the revolution were sure they could sweep the British from the seas with what now would be called conventional forces. So what was the use of this strange craft proposed by the American? He was probably mad.

Fulton's submarine was still in the development stage. He called it the *Nautilus*, the name Jules Verne later bestowed on the most famous fictional submarine, and it represented a considerable advance over Bushnell's *Turtle*. Twenty-one feet long, shaped like a sausage, the *Nautilus* was built of copper over an iron frame. Instead of propeller propulsion on the surface, Fulton fitted the *Nautilus* with a sail and a dismountable mast. There was a glass conning tower and a system for controlling water ballast. A torpedo or mine was attached to the vessel.

By all odds, the *Nautilus* was the most advanced submarine-of-war thus far produced. It is a sad commentary on the vision of the French Directory that no one realized it, but it is not surprising. Although Napoleon, one of the greatest strategists of history, dominated France, the French were singularly lacking in tactical ingenuity. The British had beaten them at Maida ten years before Waterloo and then had defeated them at Waterloo because the imperial army, despite repeated defeats in Spain, had failed to realize that its usual tactic of attacking in column was futile against well-trained infantry.

Fulton persisted. After trials in 1800 he was anxious to employ his craft against the British fleet. He took the *Nautilus* to Brest, acquired a detachable mine and sought a target. The little craft with its scanty sail must have taken a terrible pounding in those unquiet seas. All might have been retrieved by one successful strike. But the

Drawing of Robert Fulton's submarine submerged and under full sail. Plate VII from Fulton's "Drawings and Description." Copied from photos. Reproduced by permission of Mr. John Wyckoff Mettler, owner of the original drawings now in the Wm. Barclay Parsons collection, New York Public Library.
(Official U. S. Navy Photo)

Royal Navy never obliged. Supercilious eyebrows were raised in Paris and Napoleon, the fountain of wisdom, opined that Fulton was just another money-grubbing Yankee.

The American's devotion to the revolutionary cause underwent a swift sea change. Taking an assumed name, which under the circumstances must be considered an ordinary business precaution, Fulton went to London, where he laid his invention before another acute intelligence: William Pitt, prime minister. Pitt liked the idea, although there is little evidence in Admiralty files that he was completely sold. But he did establish a commission to evaluate the scheme, meaning in this case both the submarine and the mine. (In

Robert Fulton's Nautilus. *Copied from a photo. Reproduced by permission of Mr. John Wyckoff Mettler, owner of the original drawings now in the Wm. Barclay Parsons collection, New York Public Library.*
(Official U. S. Navy Photo)

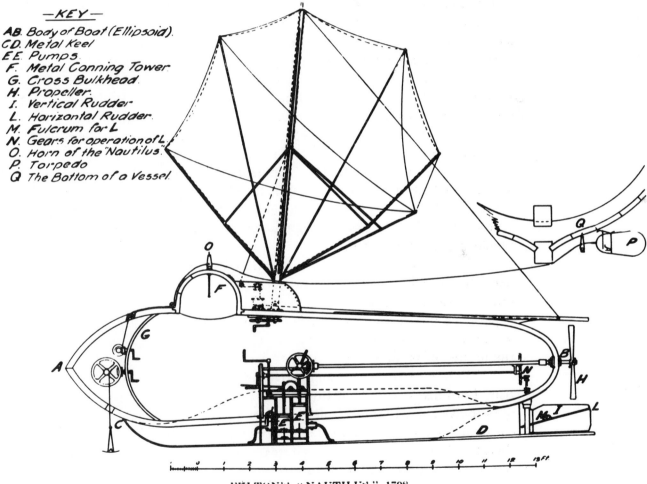

—KEY—

AB. Body of Boat (Ellipsoid).
CD. Metal Keel
EE. Pumps.
 F. Metal Conning Tower.
 G. Cross Bulkhead.
 H. Propeller.
 I. Vertical Rudder.
 L. Horizontal Rudder.
 M. Fulcrum for L
 N. Gears for operation of L.
 O. Horn of the "Nautilus."
 P. Torpedo
 Q. The Bottom of a Vessel.

FULTON'S "NAUTILUS," 1798

those days, and well into the 19th Century, what we call mines were called "torpedoes." David Farragut was talking about mines, not torpedoes, when he uttered his celebrated, "Damn the torpedoes! Go ahead!" at Mobile Bay.)

The commission was more impressed by the military potential of the mine than by the submarine. To prove the mine's effectiveness, Fulton attached one to a captured Danish brig. The brig was blown out of the water, and the American pointed out that such mines would be a relatively cheap form of defense against a French invasion, a danger that threatened England until Adm. Horatio Nelson destroyed the combined French and Spanish fleets at Trafalgar.

The Admiralty was sufficiently interested to offer Fulton 100,000 pounds for his services. But then his luck ran out. Pitt died and a new government was less receptive. Fulton was summoned to the presence of Admiral the Earl St. Vincent, a formidable sea officer but a man of intensely conservative tactical ideas. St. Vincent, however, was not a total fool. His dismissal of Fulton's scheme was shortsighted but there are grains of truth in his remark, "Pitt was the greatest fool that ever existed, to encourage a mode of war which they who commanded the seas did not want, and which, if successful, would deprive them of it."

The crusty earl thus drew attention to a situation that would delay the development of the submarine for decades. The country that had the strongest fleet, the largest reservoir of naval combat experience and the most advanced technology wanted nothing to do with the submarine because it saw in the submarine's development the means of its own destruction.

Fulton's failure was not due wholly to British naval conservatism. Both his *Nautilus* and Bushnell's *Turtle* lacked efficient means of propulsion. Until this problem was conquered, the submarine was consigned to the lunatic fringe of new technologies. Besides, had not this same Robert Fulton harnessed steam power to surface craft? Sail was on the way out, and fleets of steam-driven ironclads lay just over the horizon.

The Diable–Marin, *built by Wilhelm Bauer in St. Petersburg, 1855.*
(The Bettmann Archive)

But the submarine idea would not die. Usually it reappeared when one party to a conflict found itself at a grave disadvantage because of the enemy's superiority at sea. Wilhelm Bauer, a German artilleryman, tried to interest the German states (at war with Denmark, which had a navy in 1866) in a submarine powered by a treadmill. The Danes gave the vessel a wide berth, and it nearly killed Bauer and his crew when it went out of control and got stuck in the mud of Kiel Harbor.

Bauer, like Fulton, was a stubborn man and a believer. He

took his idea to Austria and Britain. No sale. Then he traveled to St. Petersburg where the Russians, at that time proverbial losers in all sea warfare, encouraged him with a grant to build another submarine.

This was the *Diable-Marin*, which was much larger than his German effort, the *Brandtaucher*. She was over 50 feet long, carried a 500-pound mine and, again, was propelled by treadmill. But the resident military geniuses at the court of Alexander II were unimpressed, although Bauer did perform one feat that, so far as research shows, was unprecedented. The story—Russian and German reports are hazy about the details—is that for Alexander's coronation as tsar in 1856, Bauer carried a small orchestra beneath the waters of Kronstadt Harbor, where it played the national anthem. Whether the musicians received danger money is not recorded, but if they did not, they deserved it.

By 1860, then, the submarine could be written off by any normally prudent naval officer as an exciting idea impossible to implement because of the inadequacy of contemporary technology. The concept of a silent, stealthy vessel that would attach mines to ships or distribute them wholesale in the path of a hostile fleet was attractive enough. But that had not been accomplished in war. No submarine had been built that could approach an enemy fleet undetected, with a fair chance of escape.

It took a war on the American continent involving a belligerent without a regular navy but with plenty of ingenuity, for the submarine to score its first real success.

At the start of the war in 1861, the Confederate States of America had a problem rather like that facing France 60 years earlier. The federal navy had blockaded southern ports completely, and although this blockade could be and was "run" by blockade-runners, the northern ships remained in position. Imports and exports dwindled, and the price of cotton on the Liverpool exchange rose to unheard-of heights.

The Confederacy's reasons for experimenting with submarines differed from those of Bushnell, Fulton and Bauer. The South's leaders recognized that in the absence of a decisive strategic victory on land—which Lee's brilliant generalship never provided—a way had to be found to break the Yankee blockade.

The result was a class of ship, called David, built to defeat the blockading squadrons. The South built perhaps 15 of them; nine were captured at the end of the war. They were ironclads, steam-propelled and carried so much ballast that they ran awash with little or no upperworks showing. Their weapon was a mine attached to a projecting spar.

The ships' weakness was obvious: They were steam-driven. Steam engines need air for their boilers. Therefore, a hatch had to be left open. An open hatch in a vessel awash invited disaster; normal seas, the wash from a passing vessel could, and did, swamp the Davids. But the little ships at least scared hell out of the Yankee blockaders one night in October 1863.

David, *Confederate torpedo boat, stranded at Charleston, S. C., in 1865, following the city's capture by federal forces.* (*Official U. S. Navy Photo*)

Confederate torpedo boat David *off the U. S. Naval Academy, Annapolis, Maryland, during the late 1860s. Fort Severn is in the background, with the Naval Academy gashouse behind it. Courtesy of Mr. Elmer Jackson,* Capital Gazette Press, *Annapolis, Md.* (*Official U. S. Navy Photo*)

One of the Davids—they were never given individual names —crept up to the USS *Ironside*, an armored warship off Charleston, South Carolina, and loosed its mine close to the federal ship. The resulting explosion shook the nerves of the seamen aboard the *Ironside* but did little or no damage to the ship. It also came close to swamping the submarine, which, however, made its escape.

The rebels were not daunted. On February 17, 1864, an improved submarine sank the USS *Housatonic*, a corvette in the fleet blockading Charleston. This is the first known example of a vessel built as a submarine sinking a surface vessel. The killer, called the CSS *H.L. Hunley*, was therefore the ancestor of the larger and deadlier boats that roved the oceans in World War I and World War II, sending countless other craft to the bottom.

The *Hunley* differed from her predecessors. She was shaped like a long, thin cigar and was propelled by a crankshaft worked by eight men. The vessel ran awash until she sighted an enemy. Then she submerged with the aid of rudders. Obviously she was difficult to control. The crew working the crankshaft needed a constant supply of fresh air, which was available only when the submarine proceeded awash. Records show that the crew was hesitant about underwater operations. This is understandable. On her trial runs the *Hunley* sank four times. But this did not shake the resolution of her inventors, who were not aboard for the sinkings.

Amidships sections of the Hunley *submarine.*
From sketches by W. A. Alexander.   (*Official U. S. Navy Photo*)

Longitudinal elevation in section and plan view of the Confederate submarine boat Hunley.
(From sketches by W. A. Alexander.   Official U. S. Navy Photo)

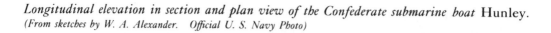

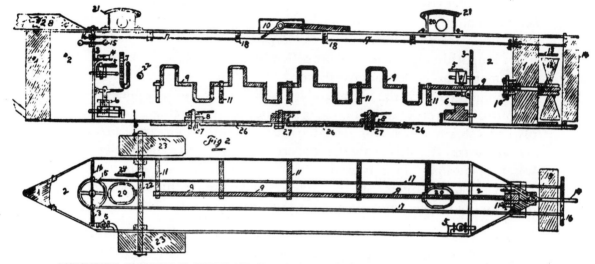

LONGITUDINAL ELEVATION IN SECTION AND PLAN VIEW OF THE CONFEDERATE SUBMARINE BOAT HUNLEY.

From Sketches by W. A. Alexander.

No. 1. The Bow and Stern Castings. No. 2. Water ballast-tanks. No. 3. Tank bulkheads. No. 4. Compass. No. 5. Sea cocks. No. 6. Pumps. No. 7. Mercury gauge. No. 8. Keel ballast stuffing boxes. No. 9. Propeller shaft and cranks. No. 10. Stern bearing and gland. No. 11. Shaft braces. No. 12. Propeller. No. 13. Wrought ring around propeller. No. 14. Rudder. No. 15. Steering wheel. No. 16. Steering lever. No. 17. Steering rods. No. 18. Rod braces. No. 19. Air box. No. 20. Hatchways. No. 21. Hatch covers. No. 22. Shaft of side fins. No. 26. Cast-iron keel ballast. No. 27. Bolts. No. 28. Butt end of torpedo boom. No. 23. Side fins. No. 24. Shaft lever. No. 25. One of the crew turning propeller shaft. No. 31. Keel ballast.

Confederate submarine boat H. L. Hunley, at Charleston, S. C., December 6, 1863.
(Official U. S. Navy Photo)

The Confederacy found it difficult to recruit experienced sea-men for submarine operations. Finally a footloose infantry lieuten-ant named G.E. Dixon was emboldened to take the submarine out in the name of States' Rights and, perhaps, by a modicum of cognac. At any rate, Dixon and his crew loosed the mine, again attached to a spar, against the *Housatonic*. The blast wrecked the corvette. It also wrecked the *Hunley*, which sank with all aboard.

In view of the number of men the Confederacy lost every day, the *Hunley*'s loss probably created no more than a ripple in Rich-mond society, although one must wonder if the death of so gallant and enterprising an officer as Lieutenant Dixon did not create some sorrow among young ladies in crinolines.

The Civil War thus saw the first successful attack by a sub-marine, just as it saw the first battle between ironclad warships. In their day, the *Monitor* and *Merrimac* were the epitome of naval con-struction. But the *Hunley*, deep in the mud of Charleston Harbor, was the precursor of vessels that could destroy the greatest ironclads ever built.

The basic failure of the Davids and the *Hunley* was that they lacked an effective means of propulsion. Drebbel in the 17th Century and the unknown fabricators of the *Hunley* in the 19th thought man power was the only means of propulsion. Steam power had been tried in the Davids and had failed. Men cranking a gear that turned a propeller were equally ineffective. However, the idea lingered of an under-the-surface vessel that could approach men-o'-war unseen and sink them.

Obviously, it was a difficult idea to sell. The late 19th Century was the day of the battleship. The British, the Germans, the French and the Americans turned out ships that seemed the ultimate in war vessels. Each year brought some new development that reinforced the conviction of admiralties that the battleship was *the* weapon of sea warfare. The battleships, or the dreadnoughts, as the most ad-vanced were called, were accorded the same esteem in public opinion that contemporary America gives to attack aircraft carriers.

But some powers, notably the British, could build more battleships than others. The French, whose industrial base and technology in the 19th Century lagged behind that of their neighbors across the Channel, searched for a way to overcome the British advantage. Not unnaturally they examined the submarine.

By the mid Sixties, the Ministry of Marine had turned out a vessel that was extremely advanced for her day. Named *Le Plongeur*, she was the largest submarine yet built: 140 feet long and displacing 420 tons. For the first time, man power was discarded. *Le Plongeur* ran on compressed air. Her problem, like that of her predecessors, was maintaining her balance when she submerged. Admission of the final ballast set her dancing in the depths. A correction in ballast would send her shooting to the surface. The British—who followed the development of *Le Plongeur* with interest, and perhaps with a few thousand discreetly distributed francs—were not alarmed. The battle squadrons of the Royal Navy continued to sail the seven seas in iron precision, and the peace of Europe went undisturbed by this new weapon.

But in all the advanced industrial countries nondescript men in ill-cut coats and derby hats were plotting the downfall of the admirals in gold lace who commanded those squadrons—and those of France, Germany, Russia and, of course, the United States.

Man power had not worked. Well, steam was the great motive force of the 19th Century. It had been tried in the Davids without success—but technology marches on.

George William Garrett, an English clergyman, built a steam-powered submarine that worked. We do not know whether this man of the cloth intended his craft for war. But his example inspired others. Thorsten Nordenfelt, a Swedish cannon builder, designed a twin-screw submarine, also steam-propelled, that was armed with one of the first practical torpedo tubes.

By this time, the two main themes of military submarine construction were fusing: There was a guaranteed means of propulsion and a means of attack less awkward than the mine. The problem was that steam propulsion could not guarantee unobserved progress.

The next step toward the ultimate submarine lay in the use of electricity. In every maritime power people were working on this problem. In 1886 Wolseley and Lyon, a British company, built a submarine that was driven by two 50 horsepower electric batteries operating on a 100-cell storage battery. The submarine moved all right, but the batteries had to be recharged and the vessel's effective range was never more than 80 miles.

Adm. Alfred Thayer Mahan, the demigod of American and British naval theory (the British appreciated him before the Americans, although he was an officer in the United States Navy) published his greatest work, *The Influence of Sea Power Upon History*, in 1890. This book, with its emphasis on the role played by the British blockade in defeating Napoleon, had a powerful influence on the world's navies. The belief of superior navies, like the British, in the efficacy of the blockade was confirmed. Other naval commands sought a means of beating the blockade.

We have seen that both Bushnell and Fulton designed their submarines to humble the Royal Navy—and failed. Now, out of the ruck of the 19th-Century bourgeois, came another with the same idea, the Irish-American John Holland. Whatever his political beliefs, Holland was the archetypal late-Victorian inventor. He was, one feels, more a mechanic than a scientist. He arrived in the United States in 1873 and became a teacher. A good teacher, probably, thorough and patient. But he was an Irish patriot, and he had the brains and energy to turn his patriotism to military use. Barroom orations against "the bloody British" were not Holland's style.

Like Bushnell and Fulton, Holland saw that Britain's position, especially her hold on Ireland, depended on the Royal Navy. Since it was beyond the capabilities of the Irish revolutionaries to build a navy that would challenge Britain's, a way had to be found to reduce the oppressor's strength. (Forty years later a few devoted German submarine captains were to follow the same reasoning, using U-boats that were evolved to a large degree from Holland's genius.)

The derby-hatted Irishman sketched plan after plan for a submarine. Early in his pondering, he hit on the principle of water balance to submerge a vessel and the use of horizontal rudders to make it dive. Propulsion would be by electricity, accepted by then as the best motive power for a submarine—save by certain naval ministries that clung to steam power until long after electric-powered submarines were sinking battleships.

Like most submarine inventors, Holland had a difficult time with shortsighted naval authorities. The United States secretary of the navy rejected his plan in 1875 on the grounds that it would be impossible to man such a vessel.

Holland's tribulations ran the gamut from mechanical to financial. With Washington unimpressed, he raised $6000 from the Fenian Society, a group dedicated to the destruction of British power in Ireland. The $6000 financed the production of the *Holland I,* which sank when she was launched. Recovered and dried out, she went to sea with Holland as the crew, and although the combustion engine failed, the vessel did submerge and rise.

But the *Holland I* was hardly a ship-of-war. So the inventor, encouraged by more Fenian money, produced the *Holland II.* Now he was moving closer to a true submarine. The vessel was propelled by a combustion engine of 15 horsepower, displaced 19 tons and "dove" beneath the surface instead of sinking like her predecessor. This was accomplished by horizontal rudders that, when set down, dove the boat under propulsion. For hitting power, the *Holland II* was provided with a pneumatic cannon that would fire a torpedo. The elements that would make the submarine a weapon of war had finally come together: the ability to dive; to travel submerged and, it was hoped, unseen; and to launch a projectile.

While John Holland pursued his experiments in the Hudson River, others began the development, always secondary, of the nonmilitary submarine. The Reverend Mr. Garrett's craft apparently was intended more for undersea exploration than anything else. Simon Lake, who began building submarines in 1894, produced boats that could travel on the sea bottom. They had an air lock so the crew, if they had diving helmets, could walk on the ocean floor. The first vessel, the *Argonaut Jr.*, was a strange-looking contraption, but Lake was happy enough in it, looking for oysters on the bottom of New York Bay.

Meanwhile, European development continued. Garrett's craft had attracted the attention of Thorsten Nordenfelt, a Swedish arms manufacturer, who built a 60 tonner, 64 feet long, powered by steam. More important to the future military development of the submarine, the Swede was the first to arm a boat with a true torpedo. This was the Whitehead Torpedo developed by Robert Whitehead, a British engineer living in Fiume. An Austrian naval captain had designed a rough model powered by steam or clockwork. Whitehead improved on this and developed a version that traveled on compressed air for 200 or 300 yards and was reasonably accurate.

For once, the British Admiralty was receptive to a new idea. The Admiralty was encouraged by Whitehead's improvements on his first model and brought him back to England, where he opened a torpedo factory in 1872. With the addition of a gyroscope, later torpedoes became more accurate. Ranges were lengthened and the explosive payload was increased.

But neither the British nor anyone else thought of the Whitehead Torpedo as a weapon for submarines. Instead, the naval wisdom of the day installed torpedoes on small, fast vessels that would attack enemy men-o'-war. Such craft had an obvious attraction for poorer nations, and they were built by the hundreds in the Eighties and Nineties. Their menace was believed to be such that a new class of ship, the torpedo-boat destroyer, was designed to cope with them. The modern destroyer is the lineal descendant of the torpedo-boat destroyer. Ironically, the modern ship's chief duty in two world wars was to seek out and attack submarines, not surface vessels armed with torpedoes.

Nordenfelt's vessel came to little, although it attracted much attention. It was finally sold to Greece, where it was never tested in

Submarine built in 1887 by Thorsten Nordenfelt, a Swedish arms manufacturer.
(The Bettmann Archive)

battle and, according to Horton, operated mainly on the surface.

Undeterred, the Swedish arms maker built a second submarine, which he sold to Turkey, Greece's traditional enemy. Like the *Nordenfelt I*, this boat proved difficult to control when submerged and was of slight use to the Turkish navy. Nordenfelt, who believed in keeping rivals happy, sold a third, even less successful submarine to Russia, Turkey's traditional enemy.

Despite the braid-bound conservatism of admiralties and ministries of marine, the development of the submarine was attracting more and more attention in a Europe cautiously choosing up sides for the First World War. The French ordered two submarines from two different inventors in 1886. One of these, the *Gymnote*, was large by the standards of the day—60 feet long—and was promising. Its mild success led to the building of the *Gustave Zédé*, which was launched in 1893. It was the largest successful submarine built up to that time. It was approximately 150 feet long, displaced 260 tons and was powered by electricity.

The first phase of the submarine's development was nearly over. It had been proved that vessels could be built that would move underwater for considerable periods and that they could be armed with a torpedo. In every navy, and especially in numerically inferior navies, young engineers and line officers were taking an increasing interest in the new craft.

Meanwhile, what of John Holland, the most persevering of all the fathers of the submarine? He had broken with the Fenians when some of their bolder hearts stole a Holland submarine that they claimed was theirs. Another of his early models broke up on her first trial. Twice Holland entered competitions sponsored by the Secretary of the Navy for the best submarine design. Twice the Holland entry won. But the navy's specifications were unrealistic, and by 1896, Holland reckoned that the *Plunger*, built to his second design, would prove impractical. He let the work drop and embarked on the construction of a submarine built to *his* specifications. Launched in 1898, the *Holland III*, known simply as the *Holland*, was completely successful. She was 50 feet long (34 feet shorter than the *Plunger*), was propelled by a gasoline engine on the surface and by electricity underwater, carried a crew of five and had one torpedo tube. What put the *Holland* ahead of all previous submarines was her maneuverability when submerged, her speed of dive and her range—about 1000 miles.

The Navy Department may have been stupid about the specifications for Holland's two unsuccessful submarines. But it was not too stupid to know a good thing when it saw one. In 1900, Holland got $150,000 to build more submarines, and the third *Holland* was purchased by the navy. So far as the American navy, slightly swollen with pride after its easy victories over the Spanish at Manila and Santiago, was concerned, the submarine had arrived.

The French continued to move forward. The *Gymnote* and *Gustave Zédé* were followed by the *Morse* and, in 1899, the *Narval* took to the waves. French designers, however, had made the mistake of adopting steam power for this new boat when she was on the surface. This meant that the time necessary to disconnect the steam engine and prepare to dive was overlong. On the other hand, the vessel

The Navy's first submarine was launched and condemned on the same day in 1872. This photo is printed from a copy negative of the original stereopticon taken by Underwood and Underwood Co., presumably on the same day.
(*Official U. S. Navy Photo*)

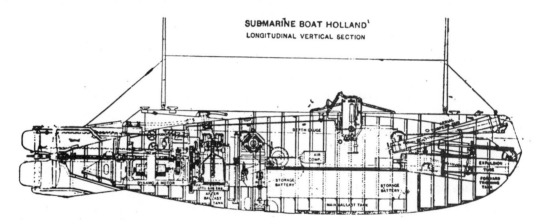

SUBMARINE BOAT HOLLAND¹
LONGITUDINAL VERTICAL SECTION

U. S. Navy submarine, Holland, *invented and designed by John P. Holland. It was built by the Crescent Shipyard, Elizabeth, N. J., in 1898. Accepted by the Navy, April 11, 1900. It had a submerged speed of 2 knots, a crew of one officer and five men, and carried three short torpedoes.* (*Official U. S. Navy Photo*)

boasted one innovation. She had two hulls; the outer one was rather like that of the torpedo boats of the day, the inner one followed the traditional conformation of a submarine. The *Narval* was fast enough on the surface, making 11 knots in her trials.

The double-hull system owed much to earlier work by Simon Lake, whom we last saw guiding his *Argonaut Jr.* over the bottom of New York Bay. Lake had built a larger *Argonaut* in 1897, embodying the double-hull idea. The vessel also carried an air-intake pipe, a forerunner of the German snorkel in World War II. The navy, con-

USS Holland. *(Official U. S. Navy Photo)*

USS Holland *at the New York Navy Yard, October 1901. The Russian Battleship* Retvizan *is in the background.* *(Official U. S. Navy Photo)*

USS Holland. *(Official U. S. Navy Photo)*

Submarine Protector *built by Simon Lake for the U. S. Navy in 1901. Before final acceptance by the Navy, it was sold to Russia.*   (The Bettmann Archive)

tent with Holland, showed little interest in Lake, and he built no ships for America.

So by 1900, the Americans, the French, the Greeks, the Turks, the Russians and even the Spanish all had shown some tangible interest in submarines. But the two maritime colossuses, Britain and Germany, then entering a naval arms race, had displayed little. The reasons lay in geography and naval doctrine.

German naval doctrine expounded by Adm. Alfred von Tirpitz held that the only means of countering Britain's naval might—in 1911, the Royal Navy had 64 battleships available for home defense, divided into the First, Second and Third fleets—was to build battleships. The admiral believed that if imperial Germany could not build as many battleships as Britain, she could build better ones, with greater speed, heavier guns and gun crews with superior marksmanship. The German Naval Law of 1912 sent a tremor through the Admiralty in London and aroused the concern of the first lord, Winston Churchill. He told the cabinet that after reading the law, he had to report that instead of preparing for attacks by 17 battleships, Britain had to reckon that Germany would deploy 25. He also added, almost as an afterthought, that "we may infer that between 50 and 60 submarines" were to be added to the Germany fleet.

Yet the emphasis in Germany, as in Britain, remained on battleships, despite what the *Holland* and the *Narval* had demonstrated. This is easy to understand. For well over a hundred years, the battleship—or as she was originally called, the "line of battle ship," meaning a vessel large enough and powerfully enough armed to be included in a fleet's battle line—had been the decisive factor in naval warfare. Nelson had won Trafalgar and Aboukir with battleships, and recently Adm. George Dewey had humbled the Spanish with battleships. So battleships it must be.

Strangely enough, von Tirpitz, whose name was linked to the submarine in Allied propaganda, was lamentably slow to grasp the new weapon's significance to naval warfare. He did not regard it as a means of countering the British Grand Fleet but as a somewhat dubious weapon for coastal defense. Germany's energies must be devoted to building up the High Seas Fleet: battleships, battle cruisers and cruisers, but especially battleships.

If Germany started late, she caught up rapidly. Noting that the Russians had ordered three submarines to be built to French designs by German yards, the naval authorities ordered Germany's first submarine. She was the *Unterseeboot* U-1, the first in a long line of U-boats that in two great wars were the most effective weapons in the German naval armory. But because Germany was also building major surface combatants, not to mention tens of thousands of guns for its army, the construction of submarines, although steady, was on a minor key compared to the efforts elsewhere in the arms race.

Coming into the game late, the Germans were able to avoid some of the mistakes made by American and French pioneers. They soon decided that steam power was unsuitable. They progressed from this to a decision to avoid gasoline engines, and by 1913, German submarines were powered by the best diesel engines in the world. The Germans also—understandably, in view of their country's preeminence in optical equipment—had the best periscopes.

Yet, as Horton points out, "the Germans were not following any sinister master plan, they were not consciously developing 'the ultimate weapon.' They were getting into the swim with everybody else and they built the type of submarine they did for the logical reason that it was the only one that could be of any use to them. . . . As Europe hurtled toward war, Germany was not looking to the submarine for her salvation any more than Britain was looking to it for her ruin."

Ruin, naval ruin particularly, was not contemplated by the Admiralty in London. But the British suffered from a psychological disadvantage. They had been on top too long. The politicians considered the Admiralty the fountainhead of naval wisdom. And all but a few of the admirals found it impossible to believe that this flimsy, uncertain vessel could be of any real concern to the Royal Navy. Some writers have discerned another reason.

The British navy was supreme and, except for a few brief intervals in the middle of the 18th Century, had been for 200 years. For the British to have thrown their enormous technological and industrial resources into the construction of submarines would have been an admission to the world that the most authoritative naval high command believed there was something to these strange craft. If the British were building them, they must be worth building. Minor navies would be encouraged in their experiments. This is not as strange as it sounds. British naval thought exercised a commanding influence in the field of naval construction. Britain built ships not only for the navies of her overseas dominions but for all who wished to buy, including the Turks, who were soon to be enemies. The British, therefore, did not ignore the submarine through most of its formative years because they thought it would go away and stop bothering them. They ignored it because they thought that if they did, others, who respected their naval leadership, would do the same.

Obviously, none of this would work. The French were building submarines. The Germans were entering the race. The British had better learn about this new weapons system. So the Admiralty ordered five from the Electric Boat Company in the United States, which then commanded Holland's services. And like the Germans, the British, having waited so long, splurged. They decided to build the boats in England under American instruction. Even this wasn't enough. The British employed their technological resources to build a submarine, the A-1, that was larger and more powerful than anything Holland had constructed for the Americans. But the Admiralty's basic idea of the submarines' use hadn't changed. The A-1's were employed in fleet maneuvers to test the navy's antisubmarine weapons and tactics.

Still, the race between the two greatest naval powers in the world was on. On their side of the North Sea, the British went on to 1906 and the D class, diesel engine boats displacing about 500 tons. By 1914 the Royal Navy had developed the E class of about 700 tons, armed with four 18-inch torpedo tubes, capable of 16 knots on the surface and about 10 knots submerged and with a range of 1500 miles. These were oceangoing warships. By the first autumn of the war, Mr. Churchill at the Admiralty was planning the construction of 40 more oceangoing submarines and 22 coastal submarines and was deep in talks with Charles Schwab of the Bethlehem Steel Company about the prospect of building 12 of the larger vessels in the United States.

Across the North Sea, as the war clouds piled on the horizons, the Germans were doing even better. Their bigger boats were equipped with larger, more accurate torpedoes, and although their submarines' speeds were about the same as those of the British D and

E classes, the German boats had greater range. Above all, when the war finally came, the German submarines were more modern than either the British or the French. It was, as it so often is in war, a question of having the right weapon at the right time. The most relative modern instance in the long 20th-Century duel between Britain and Germany is in the field of aircraft construction. The British started to build advanced fighter aircraft later than the Germans. When World War II began, the Royal Air Force Spitfire was superior to any German fighter. Had the war begun in 1937 instead of 1939, the British, without the Spitfire, would have lost the Battle of Britain to the Luftwaffe. So it was in 1914; the Germans had twice as many modern submarines as the British did. It was a tremendous, if largely unappreciated, factor in Germany's favor.

The submarine was on the eve of its first test as a weapon in a major war. Just as naval ministries had been dubious about its usefulness and parsimonious with funds for its development, now naval general staffs were largely ignorant of its tremendous potential. Officers who believed in submarines as weapons were considered cranks. Politicians who urged their greater employment obviously were uninstructed in naval strategy. Such attitudes, like so many others held by general staffs at the start of World War I, were soon proved obsolete.

Basil Henry Liddell Hart, perhaps the foremost military historian of that war, points out that the Germans were less stuffy on the subject of submarines than the British, although they still pursued the idea of defeating the British fleet with surface ships. He criticizes Britain's "comparative neglect of the potential menace of the submarine.

"It is to Germany's credit," he continues, "that, though lacking a sea tradition, her fleet an artificial rather than a natural product, the technical skill of the German Navy made it a formidable rival to the British. . . ."

So the war began with the greatest naval power in history largely oblivious to the military potential of the submarine and with that power's principal challenger unable to recognize how undersea craft could be used to break the blockade that would soon be imposed upon it.

In his old age, H.G. Wells was fond of lecturing young reporters on the abysmal failure of governments to understand the uses of weapons that science had provided. His principal example was the submarine. But in retrospect, it is clear that even Wells's transcendent imagination had failed to foresee the political and diplomatic, as well as the military, uses to which the submarine soon would be put.

> On February 1st, 1917, the "unrestricted" policy—of sinking all ships, passenger or cargo, without warning—was proclaimed—with the full realization that it involved the weight of America being thrown into the scales against Germany.
>
> Basil H. Liddell Hart, *A History of the World War*

2

It is apparent that the submarine has had a greater impact on the troubled history of this century than any other weapon. Consider one salient fact. The submarine, as employed in Germany's campaign of unrestricted undersea warfare, must be accounted the instrument that brought the United States into World War I, with all the consequences that followed that action.

From America's entry flowed the gradual movement of the United States into the center of international affairs, a movement accelerated by the experience of the Second World War. Here again, the submarine played a major role. The navy had begun to escort convoys to Europe well before Pearl Harbor because of the German submarine threat to American shipments to Britain and the Soviet Union.

Bombing and the bomber certainly have played important

military roles in 20th-Century history. The advent of the atomic bomb and its use against Japan ended a war that to all intents and purposes had been already won. But bombing has not forced great nations into war nor has it forced them out of war. Japan was beaten when the first atomic bomb was dropped. The history of World War II shows that, despite the heaviest air attack in history, German arms factories were turning out *more* matériel at the end of the war than they were in 1940 and 1941. The deployment of remotely piloted munitions, "smart bombs," may give the bomber in another war an accuracy it has lacked thus far. But in retrospect, it has been the submarine, not the bomber, that has had the greatest political and military impact on this century.

To be sure, there were other causes for America's action in 1917. But most students of history agree that if the Germans held their hand in 1917, President Woodrow Wilson would not have had a cause for war.

The historical point is not whether or not American intervention won the war. It is that America's entry drastically changed the history of this country and the world. For that entry committed the United States to an international position that, despite subconscious yearnings for the simpler life of isolation, it has maintained ever since.

In a very real sense, the submarine campaign changed the American outlook. For decades, the United States had viewed the great powers of Europe and their struggles with mixed feelings. We had been ready to imitate the Europeans' grab for colonial territories, most notably in our war with Spain. This began over Cuba's fight for independence and ended with the United States, in a righteous chorus of high-minded explanation, crushing the movement for independence in the Philippines, halfway around the world from Cuba. In retrospect, the Philippine rebels appear to have been far more worthy and ready for freedom than those Cubans we went to war to free.

This rather inexpensive imitation of European imperialism was highly popular with Theodore Roosevelt, Sen. Cabot Lodge and other eastern politicos who had long envied Britain's global role and wished to emulate it. It was, however, highly unpopular with Populist forces in the Middle West, who wanted nothing to do with imperialism, American or European. Indeed, large numbers of them, or their fathers, had fled Europe to escape imperialism. Among them, and among many Americans in the East, there existed a strong strain of suspicion of the great European powers and an equally strong aversion to involvement in their quarrels. The first three years of World War I, which saw a bloodletting unparalleled in history, confirmed those fears.

Yet, impelled by submarine attacks, President Wilson in April 1917 went down to Congress to call on America to spend her "blood and treasure" in war. From that day the United States was inextricably involved in that greater world it had by turns imitated and feared.

How did this come about? The answers lie in the naval strategies and operations of the great war that started in August 1914.

The Germans began the naval war in a position of marked numerical inferiority. Their battleships and battle cruisers, on which sea battles were believed to depend, were too few to break the blockade that the Royal Navy established at the outbreak of the war. The German High Seas Fleet withdrew to the Heligoland Bight in the hope that the British would come in after it. In war it is always risky to believe that your enemy will do what will serve you best. The British maintained their blockade and, at considerable effort and cost, rounded up the surface raiders the Germans thoughtfully had deployed around the world before the outbreak of hostilities.

There remained the submarines. But German naval strategists had discounted the importance of submarines in their contest (*Der Tag* they called it in German wardrooms) with the Royal Navy. So the submarines, which as the war progressed imposed their own blockade on Britain, played a minor role at the start. Still they were there, they were the best ships of their kind afloat, and it was thought they might be usefully employed.

On August 6, 1914, ten U-boats left their base to find Britain's

Grand Fleet. Their objective was to sink as many battleships as possible and thus reduce the numerical superiority of the British, rather than to break out into the Atlantic and attack the merchantmen steaming toward English ports with supplies.

The submarines did what they could. They got close enough to the main British battle line to fire one torpedo at a battleship. It missed. The U-boats withdrew and, on their homeward run, ran into trouble. The cruiser HMS *Birmingham* spotted one of the vessels on the surface and promptly rammed and sank her, thus becoming the first surface ship to sink a submarine. Another of the ten was lost for unknown reasons on the return voyage.

Although the U-boats' sally proved unproductive, it encouraged those German planners who always had thought that the submarine, properly used, could cut British numerical advantage. These same planners, however, still had not grasped that the submarine's most valuable role was as a commerce destroyer. And when the next sortie brought unexpected success, their belief in the U-boat as a weapon against enemy surface combatants was reinforced further.

U-boats sank a destroyer, HMS *Pathfinder*, while she was on patrol off the Firth of Forth. She was the first warship sunk in World War I. Worse was in store for the British. On September 22, an elderly U-boat sank three equally elderly British cruisers, the *Cressy*, *Hogue* and *Aboukir*, off the Dutch coast. The loss of three obsolescent ships did not upset the naval balance, although the death toll of approximately 1300 was a serious blow to national morale. There were frantic consultations in the Admiralty and harsh words in the House of Commons. And the sinkings created something close to panic in the Grand Fleet. The chief impact was there. Let Churchill tell it:

The Grand Fleet was uneasy. She could not find a resting place except at sea. Conceive it, the *ne plus ultra*, the one ultimate sanction of our existence, the supreme engine which no one had dared to brave, whose authority encircled the globe—no longer sure of itself. The idea had got round— 'the German submarines were coming after them in their harbors.' . . . Now, all of a sudden, the Grand Fleet began to see submarines in Scapa Flow. Two or three times the alarm was raised. The climax came on October 17. Guns were fired, destroyers thrashed the waters and the whole gigantic armada put to sea in haste and dudgeon.

And for what reason? Because of a weapon only tentatively tried in war, scorned by the lords of the Admiralty and doubted by their German opposite numbers. The submarine had come of age as a weapon. Henceforth, it would be an increasingly important influence on naval affairs.

But although the Grand Fleet now was forced by fear to exercise off the north coast of Ireland, the danger from U-boats was exaggerated. They never sank one of the Royal Navy's dreadnoughts. They played almost no part in the Battle of Jutland, the only encounter between the Grand Fleet and the High Seas Fleet.

But if the British were overly sensitive to the submarine as a weapon, the Germans stubbornly refused to recognize the U-boat's potential in a wider field. The naval high command in Berlin clung to its belief that the best use for submarines was against enemy battleships; a belief reinforced by a relatively unknown submarine campaign that the British conducted in the Baltic Sea. In the autumn of 1914, five British E class boats slipped into the Baltic—no mean feat in view of the German defenses—and sank a number of German merchantmen and many German warships operating on the northern flank of the armies fighting the Russians.

The British followed these underwater successes with others in Asia Minor in the spring of 1915. Perhaps the only real glory won by the British in the brilliantly conceived—Churchill was the instigator and, ultimately, the sacrificial lamb—but badly botched Dardanelles campaign was garnered by their submarines. Defying the Turkish defenses—mines, patrols, shore guns, antisubmarine nets—submarines from the Royal Navy and the coltish Royal Australian

Cross section of a British World War I submarine. (*The Bettmann Archive*)

Navy slipped into the Sea of Marmara and raised hell with Turkish shipping. Down to the bottom went the Turkish battleship *Messoidieh*, dozens of smaller war vessels and merchantmen. Gunners on submarines shelled Turkish troops marching along the shore. Shore parties from submarines blew up Turkish communications.

The Germans replied to the impassioned calls for help from their Turkish allies by sending one of their newest U-boats. She more than repaid the investment and reconfirmed the view of the traditionalists in the German navy department that submarines were useful mainly to counter enemy warships. The U-21 sent two British battleships, the *Triumph* and *Majestic*, to the bottom. Again, as in the case of the three cruisers sunk off the Dutch coast, these were old ships, considered unsuitable for the main battle line. But they had been sunk by submarines.

Yet despite all these successes by both sides, the submarine had not been employed in the role that was to make it famous and was to have the most dramatic effect on the global balance of power. It had not been used to destroy commerce. However, the course of the war in its first year began to impel the Germans toward that end. When, with many misgivings, including those of the kaiser himself, the Germans used submarines properly, they changed the shape of naval history.

The Germans of World War I, unlike their successors in supreme command a generation later, paid some attention to what were loosely called the "laws of war." One of these was that in war, a blockading power could seize war matériel—that is, contraband—regardless of its destination; but conditional contraband—material indirectly helpful to a war effort, such as fuel and food—could be seized only if it was headed for enemy ports. These distinctions had been drawn in the Declaration of London in 1909. The British had signed the agreement but had failed to ratify it for the very good reason that it would limit any blockade of Germany in the event of war. Once the war started, the Royal Navy intercepted both contraband and conditional contraband. The latter was important to Germany for, although at that period of the conflict she had sufficient war materials, she urgently required the fuel and food moving through neutral ports. The British blockade began to nibble at the German war effort. Four years later, the blockade helped bring Germany to her knees.

The Germans had no counterweapon at first. The cruisers and armed merchantmen that had terrorized British shipping in the early months of the war, much as the *Graf Spee* did in 1939, were found by the Royal Navy and either sunk or bottled up in neutral harbors. The British blockade continued. The Germans were in an awkward position. They wanted to meet the blockade with one of their own. But their surface raiders had been chased from the sea. And under the usages of the time, the submarine was an inefficient blockading weapon.

From the Napoleonic Wars onward, a blockading ship overtook a merchantman, halted her with a few well-placed rounds and boarded a prize crew or, if necessary, sank her after allowing her crew to leave in lifeboats. The program was suitable enough for a cruiser or a destroyer. They had sufficient men and were large enough either to put aboard a prize crew or to sink a victim and accommodate her crew. Clearly, this was impossible for the sweating steel box of a World War I U-boat, with its limited living quarters.

While the British Admiralty was occupied with what its master called "the great sea battle," those German admirals who had not concentrated exclusively on that battle began to consider a means of breaking the British blockade. In their eyes, the British were breaking the rules of blockade by seizing conditional contraband and by establishing routes that merchant ships had to follow up the English Channel.

The answer was the submarine. But again the Germans had second thoughts. How could a submarine, operating on the surface, interfere with British shipping and impose a blockade? Obviously, a submarine running on the surface was vulnerable even to an armed merchantman. She was even more vulnerable to any warship in the neighborhood. Admiral von Pohl, chief of the naval staff, was confident that the way out lay in allowing German submarines to torpedo merchantmen and doing what they could to save their crews. Due warning would be given; the crews would be allowed to get away in lifeboats. But the ship itself was to be sent to the bottom.

All this has a strange sound to the modern world, which has grown so accustomed to unrestricted and unrelenting warfare. But von Pohl, no less than Churchill and his sea lords, was the product of a century in which there had been no general European war and in which civilians, unless they happened to be black, brown or yellow, were left in peace. The crass enormities of modern war were strange to them, almost as strange as the power of the submarine. But under the stress of war, the Germans slowly and reluctantly came around to the idea of all-out submarine warfare; that is, British or French merchant ships could be attacked without warning and without anything more than a cursory attention given to their crews. Von Pohl and his colleagues recognized the political risk. But it is doubtful if, in 1915, they understood just how big the risk was.

The U-boats were sent out to sink British merchantmen. But there was no guarantee that these ships would not carry neutrals, especially American citizens.

The United States had greeted the onset of the war with vehement protestations of neutrality. The State Department had asked all belligerents to accept the Declaration of London, and President Wilson had warned his fellow countrymen "against that deepest, most subtle, most essential breach of neutrality which may spring out of partisanship, out of passionately taking sides.

"The United States," he continued with an assist from Tom Paine, "must be neutral in fact as well as in name during these days that are to try men's souls. We must be impartial in thought as well as in action, must put a curb upon our sentiments as well as upon every transaction that might be construed as a preference of one party to the struggle before another."

"Every transaction"—there was the rub. It was not long before men like J.P. Morgan and Mr. Schwab, already noted as negotiating with the British Admiralty, were making transactions. As Walter Millis noted, by the spring of 1915, "J.P. Morgan and Company were getting their Allied purchasing bureau in running order. Mr. Morgan himself had run across to England in March to discuss, it was thought, the big loans which would soon be necessary, with sterling dropping so fast, if the bureau was to continue to purchase and so continue to shower its blessings upon the American wage earner and capitalist."

Initially, the German decision to use the U-boat in unrestricted warfare was not influenced by American arms shipments to Britain and France, although as time wore on and the amount and value of such shipments rose, these became a consideration. But at the start, the principal idea was to counter the British blockade with a German blockade of the British Isles. On December 15, 1914, von Pohl laid before von Tirpitz the draft of a letter to the Foreign Ministry in which he requested approval to open a submarine campaign at the end of January. The English Channel and all the waters surrounding the United Kingdom would be declared a war zone. Von Pohl noted that the British already had created a war zone in those waters and were happily halting neutral ships and seizing their cargoes.

This was true. It was also true that American protests had had singularly little effect on the British.

The State Department, presided over by the earthily emotional William Jennings Bryan, had sent a lengthy and angry protest: "Note to Great Britain Protesting Against Seizures and Detentions Regarded as Unwarrantable." The note objected to the illegal methods by which the contraband lists were enforced, the division of ships, the seizure of food cargoes upon the mere suspicion that they might be for German armies in the field rather than for civilians and the refusal to pass conditional contraband unless it was consigned to Allied control organizations in neutral European nations.

"The present policy of His Majesty's Government," the American note asserted, "toward neutral ships and cargoes exceeds the manifest necessity of a belligerent and constitutes restrictions upon the rights of American citizens on the high seas which are not justified by the rules of international law or required under the principle of self-preservation."

As Mr. Millis observes, this was strong language. But it did not seriously affect British policy. This was observed in Berlin, and von Pohl's faction in the naval ministry benefited. On February 4, von Pohl "took the kaiser by storm" and the All Highest agreed to the submarine campaign.

Popular history sees the sinking of the *Lusitania* as the start of the submarines' attack on British shipping. This is understandable. The disaster looms as large in naval military annals as does the loss of the *Titanic* in civil. But the Germans had picked off a number of less prestigious ships before the *Lusitania* was sunk and they were to get many, many more in the months after they had sent her to the bottom.

However, the Allied and neutral losses to U-boats in the weeks preceding the sinking of the great Cunarder were not sufficient to harm the British home economy, which was the reason for the exercise. The submarine attacks gave the British an excuse to tighten their blockade. The political effect of the attacks in the United States was not particularly damaging to the Germans. The *New York Times* and others of the eastern press denounced the strikes as a new form of barbarism, and insurance rates rocketed. But there is no evidence that the mass of Americans was seriously concerned. The sinking of the *Lusitania* changed that.

The *Lusitania* was one of the best known, fastest and most luxurious transatlantic liners of her time—a day when people in the Atlantic community argued as hotly over the merits of ocean liners and their parent companies as they do now over aircraft and airlines. The Germans could not have picked a better target on which to demonstrate the deadliness of the submarine or one more calculated to arouse American public opinion against them.

The German government had done its best to warn travelers.

For days before the *Lusitania*'s sailing, New York newspapers had run a box in boldface type:

NOTICE

Travellers intending to embark on Atlantic voyage are reminded that a state of war exists between Germany and her allies and Great Britain and her allies; that the zone of war includes the waters adjacent to the British Isles; that, in accordance with the formal notice given by the Imperial German Government, vessels flying the flag of Great Britain,

The Cunard liner, Lusitania, *departing from New York on her last trip, in 1915.*
(The Bettmann Archive)

or of any of her allies, are liable to destruction in those waters and that travellers sailing in the war zone on ships of Great Britain or her allies do so at their own risk.

Imperial German Embassy, Washington, D.C., April 22, 1915

One of the curious aspects of the *Lusitania* incident is that no one appears to have taken this warning seriously. The *Lusitania* had been following her regular schedule almost since the outbreak of war; indeed, Col. Edward M. House, Mr. Wilson's peripatetic and largely ineffectual liaison officer with the warring governments, had sailed on her earlier. The public on both sides of the Atlantic was more ingenuous then. The idea that an embattled navy would sink an unprotected ocean liner was unthinkable. People didn't do such things! The American attitude was a queer precursor of the reaction to Pearl Harbor: Nations just didn't surprise other nations and sink their ships.

Lt. Comdr. Walther Schweiger was bringing his U-20 home after a rather unsuccessful Atlantic patrol off the south coast of Ireland. Pickings should have been good; this was a well-traveled sea-lane. But the U-20 had accounted for only two small steamers and a sailing ship. Now, on May 7, 1915, off the Old Head of Kinsale, Commander Schweiger saw a large liner through his periscope. She was proceeding eastward without taking the zigs and zags laid down in Admiralty instructions to merchantmen. The *Lusitania* was in sight of land. Her passengers were enjoying the fresh breeze from the shore. The voyage was about over, and many were packing their trunks in preparation for the landing at Liverpool a few hours hence.

The U-20 hit the *Lusitania* amidships at a range of about 897 yards. There was an initial explosion, followed by a second, even larger, explosion. The *Lusitania* sank in about 20 minutes with a loss of more than 1100 lives.

A generation hardened to war and its casualties will find it difficult to understand the outcry that arose. This was expectable in Britain, which was a combatant and where the potential effect of the *Lusitania*'s sinking on seaborne supply lines could be readily understood. But nothing had prepared the Germans for the reaction in the United States.

The *New York Times* accused the Germans of making war "like savages drunk with blood." The *Memphis Commercial Appeal*'s editorial was prepared to "consider a declaration of war." The pulpits of some of the Northeast's most fashionable churches rang with denunciations. Theodore Roosevelt, the aging lion at Oyster Bay, condemned the sinking as "piracy on a vaster scale of murder than old-time pirates ever practiced."

There are two interesting points in the American reaction. The first is the apparent inability of the more excitable to grasp the nature of war. War *is* murder, as Mr. Roosevelt must have known. What made the sinking of the *Lusitania* so heinous to the former president and the editorial writers was that it had been accomplished by a novel weapon whose use opened hideous prospects for destruction at sea and for the defeat of the British, to whom American big business and big publishing were becoming more and more attached.

The second point is that the fiery indignation over the *Lusitania*'s loss was strongest in the Northeast and the South. It was far less evident in the Middle West and on the Pacific Coast. The term "Boston-Washington Axis" had not been invented then, but it is clear from the records of the time that this area included the most pro-Ally and bellicose publications and politicians, just as it did at the start of World War II.

Interestingly enough, even the most indignant shied away from demanding war. There were plenty of calls for "action," but action was almost never precisely defined. Mr. Wilson, pondering the editorials, the sermons and the speeches, kept his own counsel. His most notable public utterance in response to the *Lusitania*'s sinking was that "There is such a thing as a man being too proud to fight. There is such a thing as a nation being so right that it does not need to convince others by force that it is right."

The post-*Lusitania* period was a difficult one for German strategists. They realized that once they had sufficient U-boats at sea, they could turn the tables and blockade Britain. They did not contemplate a close blockade in the Nelsonian sense, but one operating on the high seas, where submarines could pick off isolated merchantmen. Britain had enormous maritime resources; the largest merchant marine in the world. But Britain, increasingly the motive power of the anti-German coalition, was an island more and more dependent on supplies, especially munitions, from the United States.

Reinforcing the arguments for unrestricted submarine warfare was the Germans' obvious stalemate on land. They had occupied most of Belgium and much of northern France. Their armies had inflicted appalling casualties. The British-conceived Dardanelles adventure had ended in an Anglo-French withdrawal. The Russian armies had been severely mauled, and revolution was brewing in the workers' quarters of St. Petersburg. Yet despite all this, the Germans were farther from victory in the field in 1916 than they had been in 1914. After Verdun, their own forces began to feel the strain of heavy casualties.

The imperial government, however, could not bring itself to resume unrestricted U-boat warfare. Taken aback by the worldwide protests over the *Lusitania*'s sinking, the government had instructed submarine commanders to avoid attacks on large passenger liners, although they were likely to carry large cargoes of munitions, and to concentrate on the smaller merchantmen.

This half measure, like all such measures in war, proved unsatisfactory. It did not stop necessary cargoes from reaching Britain nor did it lead to any easing of the British blockade. On the contrary, the British were more convinced than ever that their blockade was effective and should be intensified. Nor, granted the rudimentary identification procedures of the day and the submarines' need to approach and attack unobserved if they were to maintain a margin of operational safety, was the German restriction likely to guarantee that large passenger liners would not be attacked and sunk. The *Arabic*, a White Star liner, was torpedoed and sunk in August 1915 with the loss of two American lives. Other Americans were killed when the cross-Channel packet *Sussex* was torpedoed but not sunk in March 1916.

By the beginning of 1917, the pressures on the imperial government to return to unrestricted submarine warfare were rising. The German armies still dominated the battlefields of France and Flanders and had beaten the Russian armies into a state of mutiny. But at that moment, the high command could see no way by which the war on the ground could be won by a single stroke. The submarine campaign appeared the most promising alternative. The Germans would have been bolder had they known just how much the submarine had worried the British when employed in comparative moderation.

Although there is no record of a German submarine penetrating a British harbor in the first world conflict, the Grand Fleet's admirals were all too aware that one might do so. Six months after the outbreak of war, Mr. Churchill conceded that "The enterprise and skill of submarine commanders had greatly grown, and all sorts of possibilities never previously envisaged came successively into view."

As early as November 1914, the first lord was making strenuous efforts to strengthen antisubmarine defenses: gathering and arming trawlers, increasing destroyer patrols, building booms and laying minefields that included the new electric contact mines.

All this activity, it should be remembered, was generated by the first, incoherent German attacks on the Grand Fleet and not by the later, and far greater, menace of a general offensive against merchant shipping.

The Imperial German Navy began the war with 33 submarines in commission and another 28 under construction. This was much less than the British total of 74, but the Germans' advantage, as noted earlier, lay in their possession of a greater number of modern boats, built for long-range patrols. By the spring of 1915, these submarines had emerged as a major factor in the sea war, so far as the British were concerned, and the efforts to counter them were expanded.

To what extent the Admiralty went can be seen from the first paragraph of a Churchill minute issued after a series of conferences among senior officers:

1. The first step should be the closing of the Straits of Dover by lines of nets drifting to and fro with the tide, and each section watched by its respective trawler and with a proper proportion of armed trawlers and destroyers to attack any submarine entangled. In this moving barrier there should be a gate through which traffic can be passed and it appears necessary that this gate should be in a span not of indicator nets, but of antisubmarine nets. Traffic must be invariably directed to this gate, which should be so arranged as to force a submarine to come to the surface to pass through it. Destroyers and other armed

craft should continually watch the approaches and passages through this gate, and be ready to attack any submarine showing on the surface.

The first year of the submarine campaign brought the Germans some success, mitigated considerably by the uproar in the United States over the *Lusitania*. The Germans had also suffered losses. Four U-boats, including the one that had sunk the *Cressy*, *Aboukir* and *Hogue*, were sunk by shellfire, ramming or mines. But these losses were in the narrow seas around the British Isles. To the submarine commanders, the safer and more productive battlefield was the North Atlantic.

Both the Germans and the British were well aware that the latter's blockade was being hotly criticized in the United States. The outcry over the *Lusitania* had momentarily obscured this. But as Mr. Churchill noted, "The War of 1812, not forgotten in America, had arisen out of these very questions" of a neutral's right to trade and "The Treaty with Prussia in 1793 in defense of 'the freedom of the seas' constituted the first international relationship of the American Republic."

The German choice was between unrestricted submarine warfare that was certain to inflame American hostility, perhaps to the point of war, and a continuation of a blockade that daily increased the Reich's economic difficulties. The British choice was simpler. They could soothe the Americans (notably Colonel House and Walter Hines Page, the unashamedly Anglophile ambassador in London), hoping that the outcry over the blockade would diminish and that the Germans would make a major mistake. In the last, they were not disappointed. The kaiser ordered unrestricted submarine warfare resumed from February 1, 1917.

The result was an almost immediate increase in shipping lost to submarines and a higher survival rate for the U-boats. In restricted submarine warfare, the vessels had attacked on the surface, using their guns against smaller craft and their torpedoes against larger ships. Surface action and the escape of passengers and crews in life-boats took time, which meant the submarines were exposed to countermeasures. Now, the submarines could attack submerged, without any warning; the U-boat, at last, was being employed as its advocates had long demanded.

The political effect was intense and, in the end, catastrophic for Germany. President Wilson asked Congress for authority to arm American merchant ships and told it that "Since it has unhappily proved impossible to safeguard our neutral rights . . . there may be no recourse but to armed neutrality."

Arming American merchantmen might be a sop to the strident demands for war in Republican party ranks. But it was no "safeguard" against the submarines. An American ship, the *Algonquin,* was sunk off Plymouth. Then three more, the *Vigilancia, Illinois* and *City of Memphis,* were destroyed. As the clamor arose in Congress and in the cities of the Northeast, Mr. Wilson's cabinet came to the reluctant conclusion that, in the words of one of its most pacific members, Secretary of Labor William B. Wilson, "We were at war."

On April 2, the president delivered his war message. We know its purport. But its first reference to the submarine demonstrated the influence of that weapon on one of the gravest decisions ever taken by an American chief executive.

"The German submarine warfare against commerce is a warfare against mankind," said Mr. Wilson. The submarine had come far in 50 years. Those ugly steel cylinders tossing in the long rollers off the Irish coast had brought a great nation to war and set it on the course in international affairs that it still holds.

"The Germans never understood, and never will understand, the horror and indignation with which their opponents and the neutral world regarded their attack," was Mr. Churchill's verdict. But the Germans of 1917 were not thinking about world opinion but about winning the war. The submarine—quite apart from its political effect, which today would be called counterproductive—came very near to doing it for them. By the spring of 1916, the Germans were able to deploy approximately 50 submarines in the Atlantic. Handicapped though they were by their government's promise that they would attack merchant ships only after insuring the safety of passengers and crews, the U-boat captains were taking a very high toll of Allied shipping. During the last few months of 1916 and in January 1917, Allied losses *before* Germany reembarked on unrestricted submarine warfare were about 300,000 tons a month, or double what they had been the previous year. This figure was the rationale for the German navy's argument that if this could be done in restricted submarine warfare, obviously unrestricted warfare would starve Britain into submission. In February, the first month of unrestricted submarine warfare, British, Allied and neutral tonnage sunk was just under 500,000 tons.

The Germans were conscious that a return to unrestricted submarine attacks might bring the United States into the war. But they were not unduly concerned over the prospect. They had a low opinion of the American army and navy, and in any case, or so their sailors said, they would end the war before American weight could be felt in France or on the high seas. They didn't, but as the Duke of Wellington said of Waterloo, "it was a damn close run thing."

Much of the submarines' success in 1916 and 1917 was due to the combination of complacency and lethargy with which the Royal Navy attacked the problem. Mr. Churchill had been replaced at the Admiralty by the less dynamic Arthur Balfour, and although traditionalists were comforted by the thought that the Royal Navy was no longer in the hands of the harebrained Winston, things moved much slower. Churchill had been a little late in recognizing the U-boats' threat to Britain's lifelines, but once he did, he acted. In 1915 he had begun to arm merchantmen as rapidly as possible. The idea was to prevent the submarines from attacking on the surface with their guns and to force U-boats below, where they were slower.

Mr. Balfour, however, moved at a more leisurely pace. It was not until the autumn of 1916 that he began to arm the whole merchant marine. By then, the Germans were sinking ships from the eastern Mediterranean to the mid-Atlantic.

Mr. Churchill's fertile mind was largely responsible for the development of yet another measure against the U-boats, the Q-ship —a novel weapon that has provided material for scores of movies and novels. The British refitted certain merchantmen with concealed guns and torpedo tubes. The ships were then sent on to the principal trade routes to attract German submarines. When a U-boat attacked on the surface by gun fire, which was done frequently to conserve torpedoes for larger prey, the Q-ship absorbed the initial punishment, waited until the enemy was within range and then put her concealed guns into action. These were served not by merchant seamen but by Royal Navy gunners. Consequently, the Q-ships racked up a good toll of submarines: 11 in 1915 and 1916. Then the Germans grew wary. They refused to take chances and used their torpedoes, to which the Q-ship was as vulnerable as any other vessel.

Even without this romantic weapon, the British did reasonably well with armed merchantmen so long as the Germans did "the decent thing" and tried to sink their ships with gunfire. Of 310 armed ships attacked in 1916 and until January 25, 1917, 236 escaped; whereas of 301 unarmed ships, only 67 got away.

The net effect of the armed merchantmen, American as well as British, and of the Q-ships was to confirm the German high command in its belief that the submerged submarine and the torpedo were the most effective combination. But the submerged submarine, which in those days could go down about 250 feet and make a speed of eight knots, then encountered a new and powerful counterweapon, the depth charge. As the war continued, the British improved the size and lethality of depth charges and the means of dropping them. Destroyers were especially adaptable to their use because they were faster and larger than the smaller antisubmarine craft on which the Royal Navy had first depended. British science also developed listening devices to detect the beat of U-boat propellers.

Why then were the submarines still taking such an enormous toll of Allied shipping? April 1917, when America entered the war, was one of the worst months. The British lost more than 350 ships, and the total world tonnage destroyed was 849,000 tons, well above the figure that the Germans had estimated would ruin British trade, starve the islanders and end the war. While it as yet had not, it was apparent to many in the Admiralty in London, mostly the junior officers, that such losses could not be sustained indefinitely. They began to clamor for a convoy system, in which groups of merchantmen would be herded from port to port by escorting destroyers.

But as so often happens in war, the junior officers encountered the entrenched conservatism of their seniors. If warships were used to escort convoys, might not the warships instead of the merchant ships become the submarines' targets? That would never do. For the admirals, then and later, displayed a marked aversion to risking their warships in any encounter except that for which they had been trained: fleet action.

So the submarines continued to prosper. By the end of May, there were less than six million tons of shipping available for the United Kingdom's supplies and trade. About this time it was calculated that one in four merchant ships leaving the British Isles never returned. "The U-boat," wrote Mr. Churchill, "was rapidly undermining not only the life of the British islands, but the foundations of the Allies' strength; and the danger of their collapse in 1918 began to loom black and imminent."

The Admiralty, goaded by a new prime minister, David Lloyd George, stirred. A small planning section that included many younger officers was organized and went to work. It produced three antisubmarine measures: extensive mining operations against submarines; intensive development of mines, depth charges and listening devices; and finally and decisively, the establishment of a convoy system to escort and control all shipping.

Never underestimate the power of negative thinking. The British merchant fleet was suffering ruinous losses. No means of containing the Germans had been devised. Or to be specific, the means—the depth charge and the mine—had been devised. But the brass-hatted reactionaries in Whitehall had refused to couple these weapons with the convoy—the only tactical device that offered salvation. Admiralty opinion on the antisubmarine proposals was delivered in January 1917:

A system of several ships sailing in company as a convoy is not recommended in any area where submarine attack is a possibility. It is evident that the larger the number of ships forming a convoy, the greater the chance of a submarine being able to attack successfully and the greater the difficulty of the escort in preventing such an attack.

It should be emphasized that this twaddle emanated from men who had spent their professional lives preparing for the multiple contingencies of war at sea and who had been aware of the potential of the submarine—even though they regarded it as an unsporting, un-British weapon—for two decades. Yet there was nothing novel in the convoy system. The Royal Navy had employed it successfully during the wars with the French in the 18th and early 19th centuries. Churchill had used it to get the original British Expeditionary Force to France at the start of the war.

To the younger officers in the Admiralty and to the strategists sitting before the world map in Berlin, the convoy system had two manifest advantages.

A convoy of ships, to be sure, is a larger target than a single ship. But convoys have escorts, and an attacking submarine must expose itself to countermeasures. By 1917, such countermeasures in the form of depth charges were becoming more lethal. Faced with a convoy and its escort, a submarine commander could not pick and choose. He had to go for the first target offered, fire his torpedo and make tracks before the avenging destroyers picked up the wake of the torpedo and arrived with their depth charges. What we now call antisubmarine warfare was in its infancy, but the British had made progress in the development of hydrophones and depth charges. They did not sink many submarines when the convoy system was instituted but they did increase the hazards for submarine commanders, brave men but not fools.

To those who know the sea, there is a final argument for the convoy system. The sea, in the Tolstoyan phrase, "is vast." A convoy is a good target. But it must be located. Certainly at the end of its voyage it must make for port. But if U-boats are going to loiter off port, then destroyers and smaller antisubmarine craft will be stationed there as well.

All these arguments, arrayed by Lloyd George in his most vehement style, finally prevailed upon the Admiralty. The first convoy left Gibraltar on May 10, 1917. In June the system was extended to Canadian ports and in July it was expanded to include ships on the South American route. Its success was due to a considerable extent to the entry of the United States Navy into the battle. American destroyers took over about 25 percent of the escort work and American ports were opened for the assembly of convoys.

At its inception, the convoy system was used only for ships bound for Britain. The naval thinkers who had made this decision were brought up short when it was found that the loss of ships on outward voyages continued to rise. By August 1917, it was decided to extend the system to outward-bound vessels. The effect was significant. At the end of October 1917, the Admiralty could announce that 99 convoys bound from Britain with 1500 ships totaling 10,656,000 tons had reached port with the loss of only 24 ships.

The establishment of the convoy system was accompanied by an intensification of British strikes against U-boat lairs. The Royal Navy's submarine commanders had long argued that the best way to attack a U-boat was with another submarine. Long before the idea of "attack submarines" was formalized in naval doctrine, British submarines based on the northern and western coasts of Ireland had begun to hunt and destroy German U-boats, sinking seven in 1917 and six in 1918. This was the first demonstration, now universally recognized, that the submarine can be the most effective submarine killer.

British mining operations, although extensive, were less successful—when the effort and money involved in laying the minefields was compared to the results achieved. It was thought that by combining surface craft with minefields, the U-boats could be destroyed by surface action or mine explosions when they headed for their hunting grounds. One minefield was laid off the Belgian coast; another, of 15,700 mines, in the Heligoland Bight. In 1918, another 1400 mines were laid in the Kattegat, which was one of the Germans' principal exits to the North Sea and the Atlantic Ocean.

All this imposed difficulties on the Germans. More minesweepers had to be employed. The submarines could no longer go and come as they chose. The strain of threading a passage from German ports to the high seas inevitably affected the hitherto high morale of the U-boat fleet. Submarines based at Ostend and Zeebrugge in Belgium found their passages beset not only by mines but by scores of small craft and destroyers. German destroyers deployed from the two ports came under such heavy fire that they were forced to return to their bases. Nine U-boats were sunk in the Strait of Dover area between January and May 1918.

Finally, the British, who have a taste for and a long record of success in amphibious warfare, mounted a major raid on Zeebrugge, with the objective of closing the port permanently. Although the attack was carried out with the greatest gallantry, it was only a partial success. Zeebrugge was blocked for three weeks, at a time when any reduction of U-boat activity for as much as 48 hours was a positive gain, and was not used extensively by the German submarine command for another two months. Shipping losses in the English Channel dropped and the U-boats' minelaying activities were severely restricted.

The submarine was not only dangerous in itself, it was also demanding in the elaborate and costly expedients that the United States and Britain had to use to frustrate it. In 1918, the two navies laid an enormous minefield between Norway and the Orkney Islands. Approximately 70,000 mines were sown, the majority by the United States Navy, which had developed a mine with antennae that exploded the charge when they came in contact with a metal hull. (These were the precursors of the "horned mines" of World War II.)

All these defensive efforts took their toll of the German undersea fleet. Also, the blockade of Germany by the Royal Navy, instituted on the first day of the war and maintained until the last, affected the crews' morale considerably. Submariners coming home after a successful cruise that they believed had contributed to the starvation of Britain found their own families existing on marginal rations. (In 1918, Germany was rife with reports that advancing German armies in their great spring breakthrough had overrun British depots full of foods that Germans had not seen in three years.)

Yet it is important to remember that the Allies did not defeat the German submarine campaign. Until the end, there were U-boats roving the Atlantic, merchant ships were sunk, U-boat commanders developed means of frustrating their hunters and new and improved vessels were joining the undersea squadrons.

By the summer of 1918, those flotillas represented Germany's

A group of World War I German submarines.   (*Official U. S. Navy Photo*)

A German submarine, 1918. *(Official U. S. Navy Photo)*

only means of successful attack. The army's great offensive of the spring had failed. A combined Allied command had been established. In August, the British attacked in strength with tanks; Col. Gen. Erich von Ludendorff called it the "black day" of the war. German surrender was near. Yet the U-boats still harried their enemies.

So historians must conclude that the submarine was not defeated. It failed. It failed because the Germans, a quarter of a century later the apostles of "total war," refused to wage that sort of war from the outset. One of the intriguing "might have beens" of 20th-Century history is what the effect on the Allied war effort would have been if the Germans had continued to use unrestricted submarine warfare after the sinking of the *Lusitania*. There is ample evidence, including Churchill's, that Britain was not prepared to counter such a campaign.

In retrospect, it is clear that the submarine, although it provoked the entry of the United States into the war, came close to winning it for Germany. From an objective standpoint, Germany's fault was not the use of the submarine in war. It was branded a "terror weapon" and called "inhumane," but these epithets have been leveled at every new armament since the crossbow. No, the fault lay in the failure of Germany's political leaders to understand the submarine's potential.

How close was this "close run thing"? In 1955, I sat in Downing Street with Winston Churchill talking, as he liked to do, about the second German war. We were discussing the desperate hours of 1940. Did he, I asked, think that had been the last ditch? After a pull on his cigar, he said no, that 1917 had been far more critical, "I thought those bloody submarines would do us in."

So World War I ended with the submarine firmly established. Its subsequent growth has been phenomenal.

 The most significant develop-
ments in the submarine field dur-
ing the 21 years between the first and second world wars lay in the
politico-military area. Technology was not downgraded. Every navy
sought to increase the speed, both submerged and on the surface, of
its submarines and to devise torpedoes that were more powerful and
more accurate. But it was the impact of Germany's World War I
submarine strategy that was the most important factor in the naval
balance of power. Tokyo and Moscow, as well as London, Paris and
Washington, knew that the British had lost 62 warships, including
five battleships and five cruisers, to submarines between 1914 and
1918, compared with 37 ships lost to shells and 44 to mines.

These military losses, considered in conjunction with Britain's tremendous losses in merchant shipping to the U-boats, were
a powerful stimulus to submarine construction and development

among her allies and, later, her potential enemies.

For the first 15 years of the long weekend between the wars, Germany was a notable absentee from the race to develop stronger submarine services. She had surrendered 176 U-boats to the Allies in 1918, and the majority of these were sunk by the victors. More than 200 other German submarines under construction or repair were destroyed by the triumphant Allies. The Treaty of Versailles stipulated that the Weimar Republic could not keep, buy or construct submarines. Despite these restrictions, the young officers who had served in the imperial navy's U-boats and who had been fortunate enough to stay on in the diminished navy of the republic maintained a lively interest in undersea warfare. They pondered the lessons of the first and second U-boat campaigns, they plagued German naval designers with ideas for improving future submarines, they watched carefully foreign naval developments in submarine strategy and construction.

Some of these followed unusual courses both in politics and in military technology.

The British, who had just barely scraped home in the face of the U-boat campaign, began to agitate against the future use of the submarine. At the Washington Conference in 1921, the United Kingdom delegation proposed a ban on submarines on moral grounds. Of course there was a moral argument; submarines, like all weapons of war, are nasty killers. But it was not lost on the other conferees that Britain, the island power dependent on seaborne raw materials and food, had more to fear from the submarine than any other nation and more to gain from its worldwide prohibition. Successive British governments argued for a ban at international meetings, but no other country appeared interested in the restriction of the submarine or its abolition as a weapon.

Meanwhile, other major powers were experimenting with the submarine. The French built two boats of the Surcouf class; in their day monsters of 4500 tons armed with two 8-inch guns. The Japanese offered a 5000 tonner capable of carrying a small aircraft. The British themselves built a single M class ship armed with a 12-inch gun.

More pertinent to the future of submarine warfare were two British innovations. One was the R class vessel built to attack other submarines, the forerunner of today's attack submarine. All six torpedo tubes were grouped in the bow of these boats and the diameter of the torpedo was increased from 18 to 21 inches.

The second innovation was a significant British advance in submarine detection. The device was called ASDIC, an acronym for the Allied Submarine Detection Investigation Committee that had operated during the first war and had initiated research on the problem of detection. Asdic was an enormous advance over the hydrophones that were the principal and very unreliable means of locating submarines during World War I.

Fitted to the bottom of a destroyer, asdic moved through an arc, transmitting and receiving signals. When the outgoing sound waves struck an underwater object they bounced back, and the echoing "ping" was received on the bridge of the destroyer. The asdic operator could estimate the distance of the ship from the object by calculating the elapsed time between the transmission of his signal and the receipt of the echo. By repeated checks of the echo, the destroyer could be positioned to attack with depth charges, a weapon that was also greatly improved in the interwar years.

Asdic was the British equivalent of the American SONAR (sound navigation and ranging). Between them, the devices drastically altered submarine warfare by stripping the U-boat of the invisibility it had enjoyed. The response to asdic and sonar was a change in submarine tactics and the construction of vessels that were faster and far more maneuverable when submerged.

The end of the Twenties and the early Thirties saw the decline of the global balance of power that had been constructed by the victors of 1918.

The Soviet Union began a major submarine construction program in 1928, an event that caused quite a stir in capitalist navies. There was little need for alarm. The Soviet submarines were small craft built under a national strategy that assigned the navy the important but scarcely glamorous job of coastal defense. Not until Admiral of the Fleet of the Soviet Union Sergei G. Gorshkov took command in 1956 did the Russian navy begin to shed its defensive outlook and develop into the efficient striking force it is today.

By the middle Thirties, the Americans, French and Japanese all had more submarines in commission than the British. With the complacency that was so dominant a part of their national character during those troubled years, the British reckoned that sufficient destroyers plus asdic amounted to immunity against the submarine. Like so many comfortable illusions of that time, this was to vanish under the iron strokes of war.

Indeed, the British and the French by then were deeply concerned about another "terror" weapon: the bomber. The prophets of victory through air power outdid the advocates of the submarine in claiming miracles for their particular weapon. It is fair to say that by 1938 the people of Britain and France were more frightened of what the bomber might do than of what the submarine had done and could do again. British authorities morbidly predicted in early 1939 that 600,000 people would be killed by bombs in the first two months of a war. In all, 60,000 British civilians were killed by bombs, V-1s—or buzz bombs—and V-2s—or rockets—in five years of war.

With some exceptions, this was a period marked by muddled thinking in London and Paris and by hardheaded opportunism by the new rulers of Germany and Italy. The Third Reich began to build U-boats secretly soon after Adolf Hitler came to power in 1933, and two years later the Germans repudiated the Treaty of Versailles. The British, understandably alarmed, opened negotiations with the Germans for a naval agreement. When concluded, it allowed the Germans to build a navy provided it did not exceed 35 percent of the tonnage of the Royal Navy. An exception, a remarkably foolish one from the British standpoint, was made for submarines. That figure was 45 percent, and there was a rather cloudy clause that said that under "extraordinary" circumstances, the Germans could build up to parity with the British in undersea vessels.

For all their "shadow" submarine service training and extensive strategic planning, the Germans had a good deal of ground to make up. Their Axis allies in Italy had built a number of fast, modern submarines served by enthusiastic officers and crews. This fleet played a notable political role in the Mediterranean crises of the Thirties. The British at first exaggerated its strength and efficiency. But during the 1935 Abyssinian crisis, the Royal Navy's command questioned deeply its ability to meet the threat of Benito Mussolini's submarines.

In this and in the Anglo-German negotiations there is a familiar theme. The submarine is not only an instrument of war, it is a political instrument as well. Slowly it has assumed the role in international relations that was once assigned to a battle fleet. And rightly so. For a battle fleet may seek out and destroy your fleet. Or bombard your ports. Or establish a blockade. But the submarine may destroy your commerce and starve your people. Compared to the battleship, it is a relatively cheap weapon. No wonder that when realists in the Thirties reckoned comparative naval strengths they put the submarine high on their lists. No wonder that foreign ministers saw the submarine as the handmaiden of policy.

Around the world, new and improved submarines were slipping into the seas. Under the genial leadership of Franklin D. Roosevelt, the United States Navy had been revived, just in time, after years of neglect. Gazing across the Pacific at the growing naval might of the Japanese empire, American strategists plumped for larger and more powerful submarines, knowing that in any Pacific war, the American submarine service would have to operate far from its bases. The navy was planning submarines of 1500 tons with an extended cruising range, compared to the Nazis' projected VIII-C class of 750 tons and an extended cruising range.

The Germans, of course, did not have to contemplate operations far afield. Led by then Capt. Karl Doenitz, chief of the submarine service, a group of young enthusiasts had studied the World

War I record and had concluded from the submarine campaign of 1917–1918 that the war could have been won had the Germans adapted their tactics to cope with the convoy system. Unfortunately, Doenitz encountered in the beginning a fuzzy thinking in high places remarkably similar to that prevailing at imperial headquarters in 1916.

Hitler and his naval chief, Grand Adm. Erich Raeder, were convinced there would be a war and that the British wouldn't fight. They reasoned that the United Kingdom would not go to war for Poland or France, but only if its own vital interests, such as world trade and seaborne supplies, were threatened. Hence, Britain should not be provoked by a strong U-boat fleet, and Hitler therefore supported the rules against commerce raiding laid down in the London Submarine Agreement of 1936.

All this infuriated Doenitz. He had concluded that the convoy system could have been beaten and would be beaten in a new war by grouping submarines to act in teams. These were to win fame as the wolf packs of World War II. Doenitz campaigned for the construction of 300 Type VII U-boats, which were relatively fast, maneuverable and fitted with five torpedo tubes. Their parish was to be the approaches to the British Isles and the eastern Atlantic. Their quarry, the convoys making for Liverpool and Glasgow.

The high command compromised, the fuehrer assenting. Some of Doenitz's VIIs were built. But the Germans also constructed many "cruiser" submarines armed with a heavy gun. These could be used in compliance with international law. A great deal of money also was spent on some 250-ton craft for the North Sea.

In the mad dash for submarine supremacy that continued until the outbreak of the war, the civilian uses of the undersea craft received little notice. In every maritime country, scientists pleaded for money to build submarines that would bring home knowledge of underwater currents, degrees of salinity, fish and plant life and sea-bottom topography that would benefit man. They got little attention or money for their pains. Their arguments were swept aside as the nations armed.

The war that was to provide the submarine with its second great test came in September 1939. This time, German inferiority in surface ships was even more marked than it had been a quarter of a century earlier. The Nazi navy had 55 operational submarines and a submarine leader of genius. On September 3, when Britain went to war—and the Royal Navy received the signal "Winston is back"— 12 German submarines were on station ready to begin the longest, bitterest and most costly battle of World War II.

 Although we think of them as World War I and World War II, the two conflicts in the first half of this century were dissimilar. The first was confined largely to Europe. The second was really three separate wars: one in Europe, one in the Mediterranean and one in the Pacific and Southeast Asia. In each of these the submarine was a key weapon. The German U-boat campaign in the Atlantic was recognized by Winston Churchill, at long last prime minister, as the gravest threat facing the Allies. British submarines won decisive victories in the Mediterranean and contributed as much as any weapon to the overthrow of the Axis in Africa. In the Pacific, American submariners accomplished what the Germans tried to do and failed; they effectively blockaded the island empire of Japan in a classic demonstration of how the submarine should be used against both commercial and military sea traffic.

For the sake of clarity, let us consider the submarine's role in separate sections devoted to the three wars within the Second World War. First, the longest and, from the standpoint of Great Britain and the United States, the most difficult: the Battle of the Atlantic.

Curiously enough, the Germans began the war by making a strategic mistake very like that of 1914. To Admiral Doenitz's irritation, Hitler directed his submarines not against their natural prey, the merchantmen supplying Britain and France, but against the British surface fleet. This force was not as numerically powerful as it had been in 1914, but nevertheless it enjoyed a vast superiority in numbers over the German surface navy.

Hitler's reasoning at this stage of the war, as it has emerged from the record of his conversations, was primarily that unrestricted U-boat warfare in the style of 1917 and 1918 would have adverse political effects for the Third Reich. He believed in 1939 and through part of 1940 that if Britain's worldwide trade was left untouched and bombing severely restricted, it might be possible to negotiate a peace with the British. He also was highly sensitive to the effect that the sinking of American ships or neutral ships bearing American passengers would have on public opinion in the United States. Consequently he was furious when, on the first day of the war, the liner *Athenia* was torpedoed and sunk with the loss of 112 lives, including those of 28 Americans.

Successful attacks on the British and French fleets, on the other hand, would reduce their numerical advantage and would have great propaganda value in Europe.

There is a striking difference between the German positions in the two wars. In the first conflict the naval blockade of Germany proved highly effective; some military historians consider it the major element in the empire's collapse in 1918. The situation was entirely different in World War II. At the outset, supplies came to Germany through Italy and the Soviet Union, both of whom could be characterized as neutral on Germany's side. After the great German victories of 1940 and 1941, in Denmark, Norway, France, Belgium, the Netherlands, Yugoslavia and Greece, the Third Reich could draw on the agricultural and industrial production of northern, western, southeastern and eastern Europe. At the end of the war, German factories—despite the Allied blockade and bombing—were turning out aircraft and tanks at a higher rate than in the first year of hostilities. The food situation was poor, but nothing as bad as that of 1918.

The U-boat fleet began the war with a series of outstanding successes against the Royal Navy. The aircraft carrier HMS *Courageous* was sunk on September 17 with the loss of more than 500 lives. But a greater exploit was in the offing.

On the rainy morning of October 8, 1939, Comdr. Gunther Prien took his U-47 out of the naval base at Wilhelmshaven to begin one of the most hazardous voyages in the world for a hostile submarine. He was going to attempt to penetrate Scapa Flow, the great British naval base and anchorage in the Orkney Islands, off Scotland's northernmost tip, and attack the warships at anchor there.

The idea had occurred to Doenitz a few weeks before. In his opinion, the submarine service was still desperately short of U-boats. Others felt differently. Herman Goering, chief of the Luftwaffe and at that time Hitler's closest adviser, wanted a larger portion of Germany's resources devoted to the construction of more and better fighters and bombers. Grand Admiral Raeder doubted whether another hundred submarines, or even two hundred as Doenitz demanded (Doenitz had scaled down his original goal of 300 U-boats), would be decisive against the British navy and merchant fleet. Hitler, as we have seen, was still dreaming of a reconciliation with Britain that would be impossible if Germany initiated unrestricted submarine warfare.

To Doenitz, the situation cried out for some spectacular feat by a submarine, one that would dramatize the weapon and convince the fuehrer of its importance to German victory. The motivation for Commander Prien's mission thus was as much political as military.

The commander and his crew were lucky. No Royal Air Force

reconnaissance plane spotted them. No patrolling destroyer picked them up by asdic. By 11:15 P.M. on the night of October 13 they were off Scapa Flow, ready to negotiate the barrier of sunken ships, mines and nets that lay across the entrance. But there was something even more formidable. Through those narrow waters flow some of the strongest currents around the British Isles. The U-47 was thrown off course repeatedly, once crashing into one of the underwater obstacles. By a combination of meticulous navigation and iron nerve, Prien took the submarine through. The U-47 rose to the surface. She was in Scapa Flow. Just ahead lay two enormous ships, their upperworks clearly visible against the northern sky. They were the battleship HMS *Royal Oak* and the battle cruiser HMS *Repulse*.

The U-47 loosed four torpedoes at the *Royal Oak*. Two of them hit, and the battleship sank at her moorings with a heavy loss of life. The Home Fleet came alive. Prien ran for it full speed, on the surface. A destroyer gave chase. Shells fell nearby. Searchlights swept the dark waters. The currents threw the submarine about as they had during her entry. But by 3 A.M., the U-boat was through the passage and submerged for the homeward journey.

This outstanding exploit had a decisive impact on German naval strategy. Commander Prien and his crew were invited to Berlin to be congratulated by Hitler. Doenitz took the opportunity to press his case. Here, he said, was what submarines could do. Here was something that had excited the admiration of the world. Hitler, never the best of listeners, heard him out. Finally he snapped that Doenitz would have his submarines. From that moment, German strategy moved toward the use of U-boats as Doenitz desired; that is, in groups or packs against merchant ships.

The loss of the *Royal Oak* to a submarine that had penetrated the supposedly impenetrable Scapa Flow shook the Royal Navy from First Sea Lord Adm. Sir Dudley Pound to the rawest recruit.

Without detracting from the courage and daring of Commander Prien and his crew, it should be pointed out that he was able to enter Scapa Flow because of a gap in its defenses that the British knew about but had failed to block. They had failed because of the niggardliness of prewar governments.

A 1937 survey had shown the gap through which the U-47 later penetrated. A blockship had been selected, but Neville Chamberlain's government considered the price too high. When the war started, another blockship was found. She arrived at Scapa Flow on the 15th of October, 24 hours after Prien escaped. Had the blockship been in place on October 13, Britain would have saved 831 lives and a battleship.

The U-boat campaign gathered momentum as Hitler's hopes for a negotiated peace faded and his general staff drew its plans for the invasions of Norway and Denmark and of France, Belgium and the Netherlands.

At this point in the autumn of 1939, the Germans unveiled the first of the many new weapons they introduced during the war. This was the magnetic mine, which could be sown by submarine or bomber. Doenitz's submarines slipped across the North Sea to lay mines in British sea-lanes and even in harbors. The mines claimed 115 British ships—395,000 tons. They also damaged the battleship HMS *Nelson* and the cruiser HMS *Belfast.* Farther at sea, the submarines increased their attacks on merchant shipping. They sank 199 ships, 700,000 tons, between September 3, 1939, and February 29, 1940. The strain on Britain was great but not intolerable, although food rationing was introduced in January 1940.

At this critical juncture, the Germans began to have trouble with their torpedoes. The U-39 fired three equipped with magnetic fuses at the carrier HMS *Ark Royal.* All exploded before reaching the warship. The U-56 loosed three at prime targets: the battleships HMS *Nelson* and HMS *Rodney* and the battle cruiser HMS *Hood.* Again the torpedoes failed to explode, although one actually thumped against the *Nelson*'s hull.

However, technical difficulties were overcome in time. And their importance was dwarfed by the tremendous events on land in the spring of 1940, events that dramatically changed the nature of the war and gave the German submarine command a matchless geographical advantage. The French capitulation in June 1940, following the German conquest of Norway, Denmark, Belgium and the Netherlands, opened Atlantic ports from the North Cape to the Bay of Biscay to U-boats. The submarines were two and three days closer to their prey in the Atlantic. On July 7, the U-30 entered Lorient on the southern coast of the Brittany peninsula to load fuel and supplies. That same month the Focke-Wulf Condor 200, a four-engine, long-range reconnaissance bomber, began operations from French airfields. The Condor's mission was to spot British convoys and radio their positions to headquarters. On September 1, Admiral Doenitz assumed command at his new headquarters at 18, boulevard Suchet, Paris, as Befelshaber der Unterseeboot.

What the German captains and crews called "the happy days" were dawning. For three years, the submarines scored a series of striking successes and came very close to winning the war for Germany. British and Allied losses from April 1940 to March 1941 were severe, 2,314,000 tons, but they were only a foretaste of what was in store. Everything was in the German navy's favor: the use of the Atlantic ports, a new percussion torpedo superior to the magnetic weapon, reliable air-scouting, a British destroyer fleet depleted by losses in the Scandinavian and Dunkirk operations.

The Royal Navy had found that ASDIC was not the miracle device it was thought to be. Operators discovered that the instrument could not differentiate between submarines and other underwater objects. Asdic was generally unreliable at night, and this was extremely important. For Doenitz had instructed his captains to avoid convoys and their escorts in the daylight hours and to attack on the surface at night. Wolf packs operating on the surface found good hunting.

The early German successes were reflected in the tonnage losses. In June approximately 300,000 tons were sent to the bottom. In October the figure was up to 352,000. These totals were sure to rise as new German U-boats were deployed. It was not necessary to

A German U-boat
sustains an attack by a
TBF Avenger aircraft
from the escort aircraft
carrier USS Bogue.
April 12, 1943.
(Official U. S. Navy Photo)

Death of a U-boat. When
Liberator PB4Y's
delivered a steady stream
of bombs and machinegun
bullets, this German
U-boat met its end.

Aerial view of captured German submarine underway with U. S. crew aboard. May 28, 1945. (Official U. S. Navy Photo)

possess a profound knowledge of strategy to see that if the curve of losses continued to rise, the British were beaten.

The Royal Navy's desperate situation in the Battle of the Atlantic was brought home to me when I sailed from Liverpool in November 1940 on HMS *Vanquisher*, an elderly V class destroyer built toward the end of World War I. There were two other ships in the escort, a corvette and a Free French *contre-torpilleur*, which rolled like a barrel even in the placid waters outside Liverpool. Three warships escorting 56 merchantmen. There was no air cover.

The practice was to take the convoy about halfway across the North Atlantic and then turn it loose. We were lucky. When the *Vanquisher* signaled good-bye to her charges they were still unharmed. Perhaps the terrible weather had saved the convoy from attack. The sea that rolled us and rocked us, that soaked us with spume, that shook the old destroyer as a terrier shakes a rat was an enemy more unrelenting than the invisible but ever-present U-boats, which could not use their usual tactic of surface attack in such weather.

Some convoys were not so lucky. In October, one was attacked in the western approaches. Out of 35 ships, only 17 made port, and two of them were damaged. In another convoy, 12 out of 49 ships were sunk in a single night; the killing stopped only when the submarines had exhausted their stocks of torpedoes.

How were the Germans doing it? By following one of the first rules of war: concentration of the maximum force at the focal point. A submarine that sighted a convoy did not attack immediately. Instead, it messaged the size, position and direction of the convoy to the U-boat operational control center in France. The center then signaled other submarines in the area and the pack assembled for the attack. As mentioned earlier, the standard tactic was to operate at night. A worried Churchill in London noted that the U-boats "op-

U-58 captured by USS Fanning *and USS* Nicholson. *This was the Navy's first U-boat capture. Photo taken by William A. Wiggins, Blacksmith, USN, who was attached to the USS* Fanning. (Official U. S. Navy Photo)

A small boatload of submarine experts and marines board the U-858 50 miles off Cape May, New Jersey. *(Navy Department. Photo Number 7004.98. In the National Archives)*

erated on the surface at full speed unless detected in approach" and under these conditions "only the destroyers could rapidly overhaul them."

Weighing German advantages against British disadvantages at that time, it is difficult to see why the losses were not higher, why the British were not throttled in 1941 or 1942. The sea is vast, but convoys, many of them with weak escorts, steamed through every ocean. Merchantmen and troopships crossed the Indian Ocean from Australia to Africa. Other convoys emerged laden with oil from the Caribbean and with beef and wheat from Argentina. On almost every day of the year there were more than 1000 ships at sea, moving along sea-lanes that stretched scores of thousands of miles.

The British recognized the gravity of the threat immediately.

A Churchill directive of March 1941 declared, "The U-boat at sea must be hunted, the U-boat in the building yard or in dock must be bombed." The naval high command had reinstituted the convoy system at the outbreak of the war and believed that it was the answer to Doenitz's wolf pack tactics. The difficulty was that the British didn't have the means to do the job. There was an acute shortage of destroyers, sloops, frigates, corvettes and other escort vessels. There was an equally acute shortage of long-range aircraft to take part in the hunt for submarines.

In this situation, the Royal Navy could not use the tactics that later proved decisive; it could not concentrate antisubmarine forces in sufficient strength to counter the U-boat packs. The shortage of long-range reconnaissance planes meant that there was a gap of approximately 400 miles in mid-Atlantic over which no shore-based aircraft operated. Until well into the war, the RAF Coastal Command, employed in antisubmarine warfare, lacked suitable aircraft for this mission. Finally, the Sunderlands were introduced, and depth charges were modified so they could be dropped from the patrol planes. The first result came in the autumn of 1941 when a U-boat was bombed to the surface and driven ashore on Iceland by a coastal command aircraft.

There were other successes in 1941. Prien and his U-47 were sunk on March 8, and nine days later Otto Kretschmer and Joachim Schepke, captains who had each sunk more than 200,000 tons of shipping, were lost to the service when their submarines U-99 and U-100 encountered destroyers escorting a convoy homeward bound from Nova Scotia. Kretschmer was taken prisoner. Schepke died. Five U-boats were sunk that month, but this failed to balance what Churchill called "the grievous loss" of 243,000 tons of shipping. The next month a wolf pack sank 10 of 22 ships with the loss of a single submarine. In the three months ending with May, 818,000 tons were sunk.

That summer reinforcements arrived. The United States, in effect fighting an undeclared naval war against Germany, was using destroyers to escort convoys outward bound from its ports. (One ship, the USS *Greer,* was attacked by a submarine but escaped. Another, the USS *Reuben James,* was sunk during a convoy battle.) The reinforcements were welcome to the battered British, but they were not enough. By the end of 1941, the Germans had 250 U-boats in service, 100 of them operational at any one time, and were adding 15 to their fleet each month.

Pearl Harbor and the full American involvement in the war had an initially disastrous effect on the Battle of the Atlantic. Doenitz, swift to scent new targets, dispatched five of his larger submarines to attack shipping moving up and down the East Coast. It is almost unbelievable, but still true, that the Navy Department had no plans for convoys or escorts along that coast. As one authority has written, "The heaviest concentration of shipping in the world was steaming unconcerned up and down the seaboard." Doenitz boasted, "Our submarines are operating close inshore along the coast of the United States of America, so that bathers and sometimes entire coastal cities are witnesses to that drama of war, whose visual climaxes are constituted by the red glorioles of blazing tankers." The merchantmen sailed with all lights lit and often were silhouetted against the lights of coastal cities and towns. The submarine commanders, enjoying their second period of "happy days," moved in and killed methodically.

By the end of January 1942, 31 ships totaling nearly 200,000 tons had been sunk. In February, 69 ships, 384,000 tons, were sunk in the United States zone of operations. In March the submarines transferred their attentions to the tanker traffic moving from the West Indies to the United States; nearly 450,000 tons were sunk that month, three-quarters of the ships within 300 miles of the American coast. However, as Churchill remarked, "It is much easier to infuriate the Americans than to cow them," and on April 1, the convoy system was instituted. Escorts were in short supply and the British sent over some corvettes and other craft to help. Eventually the losses fell, but not until they had reached shocking proportions.

From January to July, inclusive, the Germans sank 406 ships, 2,175,161 tons, in what the U.S. Navy called the "Sea Frontier," a frontier more hazardous in those months than any other in American history. Another 113 ships, aggregating 658,334 tons, were sent to the bottom in the United States Strategic Area, to the east of the Sea Frontier. In all, the two allies lost 568 ships, 3,116,703 tons, in those months.

The critical period of this tremendous battle came between August 1, 1942, and May 21, 1943. The crisis began with everything going against the two maritime powers. In June 1942, sinkings reached 752,000 tons, very close to the 800,000-ton monthly toll that Doenitz calculated would, if maintained, insure German victory. The number of operational U-boats rose to 196 between January and October 1942. During the first seven months of the year, total sinkings by Axis U-boats were 681 ships, more than 3,500,000 tons. This figure included Allied shipping as well as American and British.

"Until the end of 1942," Churchill wrote later, "the U-boats sank ships faster than the Allies could build them."

Yet there were signs—perceptible on the boulevard Suchet, in the Admiralty at Whitehall and in the Navy Department in Washington—that the tide was beginning to turn. Some uneasiness was noted in U-boat wardrooms. Prien, Kretschmer and Schepke, the "unkillables," were gone. Sixteen U-boats, the highest monthly total until then, were destroyed in October. The American industrial colossus was building merchant ships and escorts at a rate unbelievable to those who had no knowledge of the country's industrial capacity. Still, the November losses to U-boats were well over 700,000 tons, and another 100,000 tons fell to other weapons.

There were 212 U-boats operating in February 1943. They had become so numerous that the wolf packs could no longer be evaded by skillful routing of the convoys.

In April, 235 U-boats were operational, the maximum at any one time during the war. The wolf packs worked in harmonious and effective cooperation with the Condors. Although some of his "aces" were dead, Doenitz had a cadre of officers and noncommissioned officers whose experience and skill in Atlantic undersea warfare were unmatched in any other navy. Between August 1, 1942, and May 21, 1943, they destroyed 3,760,722 tons of Allied shipping.

These sinkings and the inability of the American and British navies to prevent them were a cause of grave concern to Churchill and President Franklin D. Roosevelt. Once again the submarine weapon appeared capable of frustrating a grand strategic design. The Americans and British had planned boldly and massively for their priority objective: the defeat of Germany and Italy. Armadas of troopships would cross the Atlantic for landings in the Mediterranean theater, in Britain and, ultimately, in France. But how could these passages be accomplished in the teeth of the wolf packs? The U-boat was the key element in the war.

Rather suddenly, considering the duration of the Battle of the Atlantic, the balance began to shift toward the Americans, British and Canadians, the three nations that bore the main burden of the defensive battle. The Canadians had been in the Battle of the Atlantic from the outset. But it was not until 1942 that they were able to deploy enough ships to play an effective role in it.

The first factor that contributed to the shift was an improvement in antisubmarine weapons.

The Royal and American navies had long been troubled by the time gap between a ship's final asdic contact and its depth charge discharge over a U-boat and subsequent run out of the explosion area. Now the Royal Navy developed the "hedgehog," a mortarlike device that hurled contact depth charges ahead of a destroyer, thus enabling the ship to hold a U-boat in its asdic beam while "running up" to the area over the enemy vessel. The hedgehog was subsequently improved and became the "squid," a weapon that combined the hitting power of a full depth charge with the firing-ahead device.

At the same time, high-frequency direction finders were fitted to escort vessels. These could take a bearing on a U-boat's signals, and it became easier and quicker to locate attacking wolf packs than it had been when escorts had relied on direction-finding stations ashore. The RAF Coastal Command, now entirely devoted to the anti-U-boat campaign, fitted its long-range reconnaissance aircraft with radar devices that could fix surfaced U-boats at the hitherto inconceivable distances of 40 and 50 miles.

The improvements in U-boat-hunting technology coincided with the increased production of antisubmarine vessels by American and British shipyards. As these ships were put on station, the Allies adopted the tactics the British had evolved but had not implemented because of their shortage of escorts. These tactics consisted of backing up regular escorts with additional support groups to aid in attacking U-boat wolf packs closing in on a convoy.

The Royal Navy's first support group was made up of two sloops, four new frigates and four destroyers, all manned by veteran crews trained to cooperate with aircraft. By the end of 1942, six escort aircraft carriers flying RAF fighters reinforced the operations of the support groups. German reconnaissance aircraft found themselves engaged by British fighters a thousand miles from shore. This deployment of Allied air power had a dramatic effect on the battle. More than half of the 27 U-boats destroyed in March 1943 fell to the air arm.

The U-boats were at their maximum strength in April 1943. Yet that was the month in which the Allies wrested the initiative from the Germans, an initiative they held for the remainder of the war.

Once the Anglo-American antisubmarine forces got on top, they stayed there. Shipping losses fell by nearly 300,000 tons in April, to 241,687. Fifteen U-boats were sunk. Scores of others avoided encounters with the support groups. In May, 40 U-boats were sunk; in June, 17; and in July, 37. In September, October and November, 53 more were sunk, for a loss of 47 Allied merchant ships. Long before that, however, Doenitz had recognized defeat and had pulled most of his submarines out of the North Atlantic, preferring to risk them in less hazardous waters. The Battle of the Atlantic was over. It had been won at great cost. There were an estimated 3500 combat ships and over 1200 aircraft assigned to the battle at the end. How would the course of the war in Europe, in the Mediterranean, and in the Pacific have gone had even half of these been freed for other missions? The U-boats had failed; but the long, bitter campaign fought by their crews had delayed the Allied victory that now appeared inevitable.

Admiral Doenitz remained as intransigently confident as ever.

"The enemy has succeeded in gaining the advantage in defense," he wrote on January 20, 1944. "The day will come when I shall offer the challenge of a first-rate submarine war. The submarine weapon has not been broken by the setbacks of 1943. On the contrary, it has become stronger. In 1944, which will be a successful but hard year, we shall smash Britain's supply [line] with a new submarine weapon."

The Germans produced an advanced submarine in 1944: a larger, faster U-boat with greater range. They also fitted the snorkel apparatus to new and old submarines. This enabled U-boats to recharge their batteries while submerged, with only a small tube sticking above the surface. The U-boats thus were able to escape detection by patrolling aircraft.

But Doenitz's prediction that the U-boats would "smash" the supply lines was not fulfilled. Submarines were a nuisance and occasionally a real danger in 1944 and up to the end of the European war in May 1945. But they never again exerted the influence on the course of the war that they had exerted in 1940–1943.

We have seen how close the German U-boats came to winning the Battle of the Atlantic. The stakes in that battle were so high, the outcome at hazard for so long that Allied submarine operations in the Mediterranean and Pacific tend to be overlooked. Yet it can be argued that in both these campaigns the submarine was an important element in the eventual victory. There was also a curious reversal of roles. The British submarines in the Mediterranean and the American submarines in the Pacific accomplished the mission the Germans had tried and failed. They so successfully attacked the enemies' sea-borne communications that their overseas combat forces were starved of supplies and their civilian populations and industries were deprived of raw materials, fuel and food.

In the Mediterranean, the British position in 1940 was remarkably similar to that confronting the Germans in the Atlantic. The British naval surface forces were inferior to Italy's, and they had to rely on submarines to halt the transports suppling the North African campaign. There, after some preliminary British successes early in 1941, the advantage rested with the Axis forces, led in fact, if not in title, by Field Marshal Erwin Rommel. But his formidable army, spearheaded by the Afrika Korps, had to be fed, needed fuel, replacements for tanks, ammunition, bombs and a long catalog of matériel requirements.

Measured by the standards of the Battle of the Atlantic, the Axis's sea passage from Italy to North Africa was short. But it was threatened by the British possession of Malta, which was used first as a base for destroyers and submarines and then for submarines

British submarine P554 underway in Placentia Sound, Newfoundland.
(Navy Department. Photo Number 80–G–66813. In the National Archives)

alone. During 1941 and the first half of 1942, Axis air supremacy forced the British to abandon Malta as a destroyer base. Then, the job was up to the submarines.

The British fought at long odds; a condition to which they became accustomed in the 18 months between the fall of France and Pearl Harbor. The Malta flotilla of ten submarines set out to harry Rommel's supply lines in the spring of 1941. The names of the submarines began to creep into the headlines, and the very names gave confidence: *Upholder* and *Upright*, *Unbeaten* and *Unique* and *Utmost*. The Malta group's work was supplemented by other submarine flotillas based at Alexandria and Gibraltar, but the craft that slipped in and out of the island's battered harbor, which was attacked day and night by Axis warplanes, were the main instruments in the battle.

On May 25, the *Upholder* sighted a convoy of troopships. With only two torpedoes aboard, her captain, Lt. Comdr. Malcolm Wanklyn, attacked and, despite a hail of depth charges, sank the *Conte Rosse* with more than 1200 troops aboard. The *Unique* got another troopship in August; and in September, the British—with their own version of Doenitz's wolf pack tactics—closed in on a convoy steaming from Taranto to Tripoli. The *Unbeaten*, *Upright*, *Ursula* and *Upholder* attacked. The *Upholder* sank the transport *Neptunia* immediately. Then Commander Wanklyn shadowed the damaged transport *Oceania*, and after a night spent dodging destroyers, sank her at dawn.

The Italian battle fleet, already savaged by the British at the Battle of Cape Matapan, did not escape. The *Unbroken* blew the bow off the cruiser *Muzio Attendolo*.

Meanwhile, the Gibraltar flotilla made life difficult for Italian convoys sailing from Naples and Genoa, and submarines from Alexandria played havoc with German supply arrangements between Greece and the Aegean Islands. But the Malta flotilla's contribution was paramount. In a few months in 1941, the submarines sank 76 ships totaling 350,000 tons.

The Germans did not overlook the targets offered by the British Mediterranean Fleet. In November 1941, when British submarines, bombers and surface ships were sinking three out of every four Axis supply vessels to essay the passage, Berlin sent ten U-boats to the Mediterranean. This diversion of force from the then-critical battle in the North Atlantic was possible only because Hitler himself issued a direct order to the furious Doenitz. It was one of the few instances in which the fuehrer's celebrated intuition paid off. The British lost the carrier HMS *Ark Royal* to the U-81 and HMS *Barham*, a battleship, to the U-331. The German foray thus weakened the British Mediterranean Fleet and encouraged the Italians, who by that time needed encouragement.

The situation on Malta itself grew extremely precarious in the spring of 1942; the island suffered more than 200 air attacks in April. But the submarines hung on until May, when they followed the surface ships to Gibraltar. For the moment, Malta had lost its sting. Then, after the British victory at El Alamein in October and the Allied landings in North Africa in November, the situation changed dramatically. The submarines returned to Malta by midsummer, exactly when Rommel and his Afrika Korps were bracing for the anticipated British offensive. Again, British submarines began to bite into the Axis supply lines. Rommel received less than half of the gas sent to him in October. But worse was yet to come.

After Alamein and the Allied landings in French North Africa, Hitler threw reinforcements into Tunisia and Libya at a prodigal rate. This was an error. The Allies might suffer tactical reverses, as the Americans did at the Kasserine Pass, but strategically, the war in Africa was all but over. Yet the Germans poured more and more men into the field, and these men had to be fed, their tanks and trunks had to have fuel, their guns and aircraft needed ammunition. Again, the British wolf packs set out. By March, Axis shipping losses were almost 50 percent of all vessels attempting the passage. In April they soared to over 60 percent; and in May, when the Allies launched their offensive against the Tunis-Bizerte position, the last Axis bastion in Africa, almost nothing was getting through. During the final drive on Tunis, I found seven German tanks stalled on the road outside the city. Their gas tanks and shell racks were empty. To paraphrase Admiral Mahan, the Afrika Korps had been brought to a standstill by that unseen handful of submarines working in the clear, and consequently, hazardous, waters of the Mediterranean.

In describing the Atlantic and Mediterranean battles, we have been dealing with standard submarines. Yet both theaters were the scene of bold innovations in midget submarines; weapons the Japanese had used without much success at Pearl Harbor.

The Italians employed what the British described as "chariots." They were in fact huge torpedoes whose two-man crews were dressed in diving suits. Six Italian frogmen in three chariots were launched from a fleet submarine on the night of December 18, 1941. They slipped through the outer port defenses of Alexandria and into its inner harbor. There, the frogmen fixed detachable warheads to the hulls of two battleships, HMS *Valiant* and HMS *Queen Elizabeth*, and made off. Both battleships were severely damaged and out of action for three months.

The Italians' feat must be counted as one of the most remarkable attempted by seamen who dared attack in submarines far more hazardous than the conventional boats. And those were hazardous enough. For every Prien sailing home in triumph from Scapa Flow, there was a Prien gasping for air as his thin steel shell collapsed around him and his crew.

As a young submarine captain, Adm. Sir Martin Dunbar-Naismith had taken his vessel through the Turkish minefields and nets into the Sea of Marmara to waylay the warships and merchantmen there. Years after, when he was commander in chief at Plymouth, he discussed the hazards of his trade.

Today's boats—this was in 1940—were better, he conceded. But the dangers, physical and psychological, were still there.

"Kipling used to write about two o'clock in the morning courage," the admiral said. "Well, a submariner has to have that sort of courage the entire time he's submerged. It's always the hour before dawn and the enemy always is going to attack. It requires a special balance, mental and physical. Submariners are a race apart."

This separation from other sailors, this conviction that they, as submariners, faced dangers unknown to the rest of the fleet, developed in the submarine crews of every navy a unique *esprit de corps*. A submariner knew his vessel could wipe out an enemy battleship. But he also knew he was fighting in an eggshell against foes armed with the explosive hammers of depth charges.

An ex-petty officer of the American submarine fleet gave his view of this special separateness of the submariner one night during a casual conversation in a San Diego bar:

I was a kid then in 1942. But even as a kid, I felt we were something special. One thing people forget. After Pearl Harbor, we in the submarines were the only guys who were hitting back. Not much at first. It took a hell of a time. But we did get some Japs.

And, brother, we were alone. You got up on the tower at night and there was that big ocean, and you knew the only other ships around were Japs. And they were looking for you. You got a feeling you were all in that fucking boat together. I read about the navy now, riots and demonstrations. I dunno. That sort of thing would have been impossible on a sub. Every guy's safety depended on every other guy's doing his job. Officers didn't have to enforce discipline. We did that. Because if a guy goofed off, everybody was gonna suffer. And we knew what that was like. It didn't need much imagination. There were enough accidents in those early boats. Any fool could see what would happen if a depth charge came too close. So we sweated it out. Every fucking minute of every cruise. And when we came back, hell, we didn't want to mix with guys from destroyers and cruisers. We was in submarines. We was different.

The British use of midget submarines was prompted by a situation very like the one that had faced the Italians. In 1941 the *Tirpitz*, probably the most powerful battleship then afloat, had holed up in Alta Fjord in northern Norway. The heavy bombers of the RAF could reach her, but at that extreme range, they could not carry sufficient bombloads to damage her. The *Tirpitz* intact was a constant menace to Allied convoys rounding Norway's North Cape en route to the Soviet Union with supplies.

Conventional submarines were suggested first. But Alta Fjord is long and was heavily defended. It was thought that conventional submarines, with their more powerful engines, would be too easy to detect in the narrow waters of the fjord. Something else had to be devised. In 1941, the British evolved a midget submarine, and in the next year successfully tested two prototypes. Six of the new vessels, called X-craft, were delivered to the Royal Navy in January 1943. They weighed 35 tons, were just over 50 feet long, carried a crew of three officers and an engineer rating, could dive to 300 feet and were armed with two detachable charges. Each of these contained two tons of Amatex, a new and particularly powerful explosive. The charges were to be dropped on the sea bottom under the *Tirpitz* and fired by clockwork time fuses. The crews had volunteered for "special and hazardous service," which was not an understatement.

The operation gives the lie to the idea that the British are supreme improvisers. Little was left to chance. The submariners trained in Loch Cairnbawn in Scotland, where the conditions were judged similar to those in Alta Fjord, against British battleships equipped with the same kind of antisubmarine nets used by the Germans.

The mission began on September 11, 1943. The X-craft were towed by conventional submarines. They had a distance of over 100 miles to cover, and from the beginning they were in difficulty. One X-craft broke her tow and was never seen again. Another went adrift, but after a new line was affixed, she resumed the voyage. The next day she ran into further trouble and had to be abandoned.

Four X-craft remained when the towing submarines made landfall on September 19. On the evening of the next day, the four headed toward Alta Fjord. First they had to thread their way through a German minefield. This was done on the surface. Then they were at the entrance to Kaa Fjord, which leads to Alta Fjord. The British, who had counted on the arrival of all six X-craft, had expected three to attack the *Tirpitz;* two, the battle cruiser *Scharnhorst;* and one, the cruiser *Lützow.*

But the force was cut to three when the X-10, after a series of mechanical breakdowns, had to turn back. This left the X-5, X-6 and X-7 at a rendezvous off Bratholme Island, opposite the entrance to Kaa Fjord, on the evening of September 21. It was an overcast night with a fresh breeze. They were six miles from the *Tirpitz.* They recharged their batteries and made minor repairs. At midnight, one went to periscope depth and headed for the battleship. The others followed.

None of the X-craft returned. But they left their mark. Two, the X-6 and X-7, got through the nets and laid their charges. The Germans captured the captain and crew of the X-6. The captain and one other officer escaped from the X-7. The X-5 was sighted outside the antisubmarine nets and sunk by gunfire and depth charges. That is the British side of the story.

The Germans, like the British in Scapa Flow when Prien had entered it four years before, were complacent. But at seven o'clock on the morning of September 22 someone sighted a submarine, the X-6, which ran aground momentarily when her compass failed. Five minutes later, the X-6 broke the surface again. Lookouts on the *Tirpitz* sighted the craft and all the alarm bells rang on the battleship. Divers were sent over the side to search for mines and the captain ordered the ship to proceed to sea. The order was canceled when the X-7 was sighted. To the Germans, the fjord seemed alive with British submarines. This impression was strengthened when the X-5 was spied outside the nets. The decision was made to keep the *Tirpitz* where she was and to swing her away from whatever charges had been planted. While this was going on, the charges from the X-6 and X-7 exploded.

The effect was sensational. The battleship jumped out of the water. All lights went out. Fittings, including the fire extinguishers, fell from their places. Below, the results were more serious. The three main engines were knocked out, severe damage had been done to the rudders and steering engine, and seawater was flooding the *Tirpitz*'s double bottom.

Later, after a close inspection, the German naval high command concluded that the *Tirpitz* would be out of action for six months. It was longer than that.

The *Tirpitz* was never operational again. Allied convoys bound for the northern Soviet Union continued to be attacked by submarines, destroyers and bombers. But they did not have to worry about the *Tirpitz*.

The German U-boat campaign in the Atlantic, despite its triumphs and the appalling tonnage losses it inflicted, ended in defeat. The British submarines' contribution in the Mediterranean was an important factor in that theater, but perhaps not the decisive one. It was left to the United States Navy's submarine service, a relatively untried force, to score the most decisive undersea victory of World War II—one never sufficiently appreciated by the American public but, as we now know, one closely studied by the Soviet Union's naval high command.

The American submariners' victory was the more splendid because the campaign began so badly. First came the traumatic experience of the Japanese attack on Pearl Harbor. The submarines there escaped relatively unscathed. But their officers and men, like the rest of the navy, were badly shaken by the destruction and by the recognition that the Japanese, those half-tolerated, half-despised "little yellow men," had proved themselves as naval planners and as brave and skillful sailors and airmen.

At the time of the attack, the United States had 55 submarines in the Pacific. These were divided between Pearl Harbor and Subic Bay in the Philippines. Nine were at Pearl on December 8, 1941, the day after the Japanese struck. That day, Rear Adm. Thomas Withers, Jr., set the pattern of aggressiveness that continued throughout the Pacific war; he sent seven of his nine boats on patrol, three of them into the home waters of the then-triumphant Japanese empire.

This was a desperate expedient. But the American situation in the Pacific was desperate. Pearl Harbor had been followed by the successful Japanese bombing of Clark Field in the Philippines and by the imperial army's attacks in Malaya and Hong Kong, and the invasion of the Philippines obviously was impending. It was not a time to delicately balance strategic and tactical objectives, but to do the best that could be done in a steadily deteriorating situation. Submarines had to be used where they were needed, not where they would make the greatest contribution to Pacific naval strategy. For at the time, this strategy had hardly been evolved.

Withers might have sent all his boats on patrol in December 1941, but only seven of the nine were seaworthy. Besides the three that went to Japanese waters, four went to the Marshall Islands. On their return to Pearl Harbor, the captains reported sinking some freighters and attacking several destroyers. Officers and men also reported an enhanced respect for Japanese antisubmarine operations and some doubts about their own torpedoes. These doubts lingered throughout the first campaign.

The USS *Gudgeon,* one of the submarines that went to Japan, scored the first American kill of a Japanese U-boat. The I-173 was waylaid and sunk after a brilliant piece of code interception and breaking by shore installations. It was the first serious Japanese naval loss of the war.

In general, however, the record of the early months was unimpressive. The Manila flotilla failed to halt Japanese advances despite attacking 45 times and firing 95 torpedoes. Captains claimed 11 ships sunk, but postwar examination of Japanese records showed that only three actually went down: two big merchantmen and a small freighter.

Clay Blair, Jr., the outstanding historian of the submarine war in the Pacific, says flatly that "The submarine defense of the Philippines was, on the whole, abysmally planned and executed" and lists eight major errors that reflect the poor state of the American submarine service at the start of its most triumphant campaign.

The errors were inadequate peacetime training; poor submarine maintenance; basing submarines in Manila, a site vulnerable to air strikes; failure to deploy for war; ineffective and shortsighted instructions for combat; faulty dispositions for the defense of Lingayen Gulf, the most obvious route for invasion; unnecessary losses in submarines, matériel and men; and the omission of live tests of the already controversial Mark XIV torpedo.

Despite all these weaknesses, the submarines remained the navy's main striking force in the western Pacific. There were 26 boats operational by early February 1942, and they sallied out to attack the Japanese armadas directed at the Dutch East Indies, Malaya and Singapore. It was a crucial month. But the Japanese records disclose that all the Americans did, in contrast to their vastly inflated claims, was to sink two ships: a destroyer and a troopship. March was no better. The submarines of the Asiatic Fleet again sank only two ships: a freighter and an aircraft ferry.

The first three full months of the Pacific war ended with American submarines playing a relatively ineffective part in the tremendous drama being written by Japanese conquests. As things stood in March 1942, the obvious forecast was that although some American boats would chew up any Japanese merchantmen they might come across and pull off some lucky attacks on warships, they would have little influence on the main battle.

Analysis of the submarines' performance up to that time focuses on two major problem areas: personnel and weapons.

It is interesting today, accustomed as we have become to hearing that this weapon or that is the greatest in history, to learn how the submarine service's best weapons fared in the first months of the Pacific war. The standard torpedo was the Mark XIV. The first combat patrols reported that it was a dud. It ran too deep, below its targets, and its Mark VI exploder did not work properly. The submarine captains who reported these failures to both the Asiatic and Pearl Harbor commands did so even when their patrols had been fairly successful. No captain, one said years later, "could be sure his 'fish' would explode."

Beyond this weakness in the basic weapons system were other

disquieting discoveries. The submarines were too noisy, the air conditioning not powerful enough, the surface silhouette too large, the Hoover-Owens-Rentschler engines defective.

Possibly more important were the weaknesses in personnel disclosed by the first attacks. There were numerous instances of submarine captains who were overcome by the strain of combat and turned over their commands to their executive officers. And the strain was not confined to the higher ranks. Crews found the constant tension of long patrols almost intolerable. Many petty officers were in their late fifties. They had not bargained for a war. They found themselves—at an age when they expected comfortable duty at Pearl Harbor or Subic Bay, broken only by routine sea exercises —flung into the teeth of the Japanese destroyers in situations of continuous danger. They were not up to it.

But the principal problem was in command. As the campaign continued, naval headquarters recognized that a considerable percentage of submarine commanders were overcautious. A submarine commander's position is much different from that of a destroyer captain or an army brigade commander. A submarine commander is the be-all and end-all of decision. He is the officer who sights an enemy ship through the periscope. If he determines that an attack should not be made, the decision is his alone. He initiates, continues or breaks off the action. More important, he is the only man aboard who possesses all the data. But all too many, Blair writes, showed a disinclination to attack the enemy boldly and persistently.

The submarine service held itself, and was held by its peers in the navy, in high esteem. Conscious of its unique role, the submarine service had a high morale at the start of the war. The navy and the service were shocked in 1942 when whispers about attacks broken off too soon or never made began to sift through wardrooms and clubs at naval bases. These were followed by harsh command directives that sought to stiffen the morale of crews and officers alike. The navy slowly overcame this personnel problem largely by realizing that in war, submarine duty imposed psychological and physical burdens on commanders that were unforeseen in peace. Inefficient commanders were weeded out. New blood was introduced.

Tactically, the service was fumbling for a doctrine. By December 1941, the naval war in Europe had been going on for more than two years, but there is little evidence that American commanders were influenced by its lessons. Doenitz's wolf packs in the Atlantic were scoring repeated successes with night attacks on the surface. But the Pacific flotillas did not adopt these methods, although the navy had ample evidence from the British of their effectiveness. The Pacific force also clung to the sonar approach, fixing the enemy by mechanical devices rather than by sighting and fixing by periscope.

The submariners, however, did devise one ploy not practiced by either the British or the Germans. This was the "down the throat" shot. Its primary use was against surface vessels pursuing a submarine. The boat under attack fired two torpedoes at its pursuer. The theory was that the enemy vessel would turn one way or another to avoid one of the torpedoes and would be hit broadside by the other. This tactic proved effective throughout the Pacific war; whenever, that is, the torpedoes ran true and exploded.

The Germans never used this stratagem, which was just as well for the British. A British admiral admitted after the war that if the Nazi U-boats had employed such tactics the victories scored by the support groups in 1943 might not have been possible.

The American navy was fighting with its back to the wall. In that situation, it is not surprising that the submarine priority was given to attacks on Japanese surface combatants. It is easy enough to criticize the high command for not employing submarines more liberally against Japanese merchantmen, freighters and supply ships. But it would have been most difficult in early 1942 for the admirals to order a concentration on nonmilitary ships. After Pearl Harbor and Clark Field, the submarines, a few cruisers and destroyers and the aircraft carriers were all the navy had to check the Japanese tide. The submarines had to be used, and in that critical period, the question of whether they were being used correctly appeared wildly irrelevant. So the undersea boats were directed not at the easier and, in the long run, more rewarding targets—the merchantmen, freighters and supply ships—but at the more difficult battleships, cruisers and destroyers. On one Pacific patrol, the USS *Sturgeon* sighted five large Japanese merchantmen escorted by a cruiser and destroyers. The operational doctrine called for an attack on the cruiser. The submarine was driven off by the destroyers after preparing to go after the cruiser. The merchantmen continued on their way.

Adm. Ernest King, the new chief of naval operations, was alive to the importance of cutting Japan's lifelines. But granted his tactical dispositions and shortage of submarines, he was unable to do more than gesture toward this objective. The submarines of the Asiatic Fleet, withdrawn to Australia with the fall of the Philippines, were ordered to attack Japanese shipping moving south from the home islands to the conquered territories in the Dutch East Indies, Malaya and the Philippines. The concept was correct. But the resources simply were not there. The force based in Fremantle, Australia, was so small that it could maintain only about six boats on station at any one time. These had to patrol in sections thick with Japanese antisubmarine forces, and Blair tells us they suffered from a chronic shortage of torpedoes, spare parts, man power and limited overhaul facilities.

This handful of boats was scattered over a tremendous area. Monday-morning quarterbacking a third of a century later suggests it might have been better employed in the Luzon Strait between the island of Taiwan and the island of Luzon. This was the main sea-lane for Japanese warships, troopships and merchantmen sailing between the home islands and the newly conquered lands in South and Southeast Asia.

After four months of war, the navy's position generally and the submarine service's particularly were not good. Making all due allowances for the lingering psychological effects of a series of defeats unparalleled in the navy's history and the almost intolerable physical and mental strain under which both operational and staff officers were working, the conclusion is unavoidable: At this stage in the war there was no coherent submarine strategy. For that matter, as events in the western Atlantic proved, there wasn't any coherent antisubmarine strategy either.

It also was increasingly evident that American submariners were operating under a severe handicap in the weapons field. Captains in the flotillas operating out of Australia and Pearl Harbor knew that neither the Mark XIV torpedo nor the Mark VI exploder was doing its job. The torpedoes were running deeper than the depths set and the exploders were not exploding. A good deal of bitterness arose between the captains and crews who took the weapons into action and the commanders and technicians at the bases, who argued not too diplomatically that there was nothing wrong with the weapons and that consequently the fault must lie with the crews. It took a good deal of courage to challenge the Bureau of Ordnance. But it was challenged.

Six months after Pearl Harbor, a test was organized in Australia. The target was a fisherman's net stretched in the quiet waters of Frenchman's Bay. A torpedo set to run ten feet below the surface was fired at the net. It hit at 25 feet, 15 feet deeper than set. Here was the reason why so many of the 800 torpedoes fired up to that time had not found their targets. Other tests were carried out. They showed that the torpedoes invariably went lower than set, an average of 11 feet deeper. With the ponderous irascibility of a great bureaucratic institution on the defensive, the Bureau of Ordnance, goaded by Admiral King, deigned to make its own tests. The results were the same as those obtained by the harried operational commanders far away in Australia. The bureau conceded that the torpedo ran ten feet deeper than set and admitted that its depth-control mechanism had been improperly designed. Modifications were made to insure that the Mark XIV ran within three feet of the setting.

The sea officers were not entirely satisfied by their victory in this internal technological battle. Some commanders who had been setting their torpedoes to run shallower and so correcting the malfunction they were morally sure existed also believed that the magnetic exploder was defective. Many of them knew that the Germans and British had already discarded magnetic exploders.

The arguments continued, the doubts proliferated from Newport, Rhode Island, to Albanu, Australia—the submarine subbase farthest from Newport. The world's first industrial power was learning that in war, weapons and doctrines that appear attractive in peace often fail the test of combat. Unless something was done, and done fairly soon, the submarine service's contribution to the Pacific war would be far less than expected.

War also has a way of revitalizing weapons deemed too expensive or too revolutionary in ordinary times. This was true of the electric torpedo, with which the Bureau of Ordnance had been experimenting in a desultory fashion since World War I. The electric torpedo's advantage was that since it ran on batteries, it left no trail for enemy spotters. However, it was slower than the Mark XIV weapon.

The Germans were getting good results with the electric torpedo in the Battle of the Atlantic. Several fell into American hands and the navy decided to turn out a similar one. Finally, with the aid of civilian industry, the Mark XVIII electric torpedo went into production. The bureau ordered 2,000. Production holdups and malfunctions uncovered in testing delayed delivery. The hard-pressed Pacific submariners had to make do with the Mark XIV. And they were not doing very well.

In the summer of 1942, 28 submarine patrols went out from Fremantle and only 17 sinkings were recorded. The new depth-setting for the torpedo helped, but the difference in kills was not significant. Strategy still smacked more of expediency than careful assessment of the enemy's situation. Skipper after skipper reported mechanical difficulties. Commanders complained when they were diverted to spectacular but relatively unimportant operations like the marines' submarine-borne raid on Malkin Island.

By autumn, some of the navy's newer boats were reaching the Pacific. The results were encouraging when these submarines penetrated Japanese home waters or the East China Sea. On the whole, however, the first year of the undersea offensive was a disappointing one.

Japanese merchant shipping was clearly the prime target, whether or not this was realized by the strategists in faraway Washington. The three submarine commands, based at Fremantle and Brisbane in Australia and Pearl Harbor, had sunk 180 ships—warships and merchantmen—totaling 725,000 tons in a year of war. The Germans had sunk more than that amount in February and March of that year.

Japan entered the war with 5.4 million tons of merchant shipping, excluding tankers. Of this, she lost only 200,000 tons in 1942 from all causes. The imports that fed Japanese industry—including coal, iron ore and bauxite—continued to reach port in undiminished quantities.

Nor was there any loss of oil imports, and assuring her oil supplies was one of the principal economic reasons Japan began the war. When Pearl Harbor was attacked, Japan had 575,000 tons of tankers and the empire's shipyards were busy building more. By the end of December 1942, the tanker total was 686,000 tons. When one combines the figures of merchant shipping and tankers lost in 1942, the net loss in civilian shipping was approximately 90,000 tons, a tiny reduction in Japan's maritime resources.

This failure to significantly reduce the trade by which Japan lived was unrecognized by the Americans. Had it been known, improvements in weapons, training and command, and the search for an effective strategy might have been pushed much harder. The submariners themselves suffered from the illusion that they had sunk many more Japanese ships than they had; 274 were claimed sunk, compared with 180 actually sunk. The captains are not to be censured. In most instances, after loosing their torpedoes, they were driven so deep by a hail of depth charges that they had no time to observe the damage they had done. The verification of Japanese losses was virtually impossible.

Yet despite the inflated claims, it should have been obvious that the Japanese war machine, far from being slowed by the submarine campaign, seemed largely unaffected. Battles had been won by the United States at Midway and elsewhere. But the road to victory, by sea or land, appeared long and hazardous.

In that desperate year, a large percentage of the American submarine effort was directed against the surface ships of the Japanese navy, just as the first German effort had been directed against the British Home Fleet in 1939. Four Japanese battleships were attacked and minor damage was done to one. Three carriers out of ten "contacts" were hit, none seriously. But in a full year of war, submarines sank only two major Japanese naval combat units: the light cruiser *Tenryu* and the heavy cruiser *Kako*.

Such emphasis, however, cannot be dismissed as a minor factor if Japanese submarine kills of American surface combatants are considered. The aircraft carriers USS *Yorktown* and USS *Wasp* and the cruiser USS *Juneau* were sunk. Another carrier, the USS *Saratoga*, was hit twice and put out of action. The USS *North Carolina*, a battleship, and the USS *Chester*, a cruiser, were severely damaged by torpedoes.

But the Japanese paid heavily for their success. They lost 23 submarines in the Pacific in 1942 compared to the United States's loss of seven. The high enemy toll was due as much to the efficiency of the American code-breaking organization as it was to the navy's skill in antisubmarine warfare.

The submarine service had done little in the first year of war that offered great promise for the future. The service's principal torpedo and that torpedo's exploder were demonstrably defective. Many of its boats had failed to stand up to the demands of long cruises, and this had proved true, too, of many commanders. About 40 out of 135 submarine captains were relieved for nonproductivity, battle fatigue and poor health. All these were contributory, not major, reasons for failure.

"The major reason for the submarine failure of 1942 was not mechanical, physical or psychological," according to Blair. "It was, to put it simply, a failure of imagination on the highest levels by King, Edwards, Nimitz, Hart, Wilkes, Withers, Lockwood, Christie and Fife. All these men failed to set up a broad, unified strategy for Pacific submarines aimed at a single specific goal: interdicting Japanese shipping services in the most efficient and telling manner. The lessons of the German U-boat campaigns against Britain in world wars I and II—the latter in progress almost on Washington's doorstep—had apparently not sunk home. The military and maritime theories of Clausewitz and Mahan were ignored. The U.S. submarine force was divided and shunted about willy-nilly on missions for which it was not suited, while the bulk of Japanese shipping sailed unmolested in empire waters and through the bottleneck in Luzon Strait."

A harsh indictment, but not unduly so when we consider what the submarines accomplished against Japanese shipping later in the war. But that time was still distant. The high commands in Washington and in the Pacific learned slowly. The dispersal of forces continued. A task force was sent to Dutch Harbor in Alaska, where 70 submarine patrols sank only five ships in two years.

Quite obviously, the submarine campaign would continue to be unsuccessful until the Navy Department chose the strategy that was staring it in the face—that is, an all-out war on Japanese shipping —and until it did something to improve submarine weapons. The weapons scandal was rapidly approaching a crisis. Capt. Daniel Daspit reported that on one patrol he had fired 11 torpedoes under ideal conditions and none had exploded. Intensive tests were carried out at Pearl Harbor, where experts fabricated new firing-pin designs for the exploders. These were fitted to the Mark XIV torpedoes. For the second time in the midst of fighting a war, sea officers had diagnosed the faults of their principal weapon and found remedies.

Weapons were not the only problem. The Hoover-Owens-Rentschler engines powering some submarines—they were known as the HOR boats, and it requires little imagination to guess how their crews described them—were unreliable. Boats broke down within sight of Japan's home islands. Attacking submarines suddenly developed engine trouble. One captain called his engines "an extreme danger" during patrols. Again, months passed before action was taken by the Navy Department. The unreliability of the HOR engines, combined with the torpedoes' ineffectiveness and with American industry's delay in replacing spent torpedoes, should warn this generation not to accept Pentagon infallibility on weapons and matériel.

The year 1943, then, was one of waiting: for new and better ships, for improved weapons and, above all, for a coherent submarine strategy. Through March, only 34 ships were sunk by the submarines based at Pearl Harbor, the boats closest to empire waters and the richest targets. There was no lack of enterprise. In the summer, submarines penetrated the Sea of Japan, bounded on the west by the home islands and on the east by the Soviet Union, Korea and China. But the results were disappointing—five ships sunk, for a total of 13,500 tons.

The submarine flotillas based at Brisbane were worrying the flanks of the Japanese supply line to the Dutch East Indies, Malaya and the Indian Ocean and were beginning to show results. Any successes, however, were due more to the brilliant improvisation of the commanders on patrol than to the intelligent direction of their superiors ashore. The latter still refused to adopt the wolf pack tactics that the Germans had found so effective in the Atlantic. But the skippers took the initiative in organizing joint attacks on enemy convoys. In one of these attacks, they sank four ships in a convoy of five. American submarines also began to exact a higher toll of tankers. These sinkings had some effect on Japanese operations out of their base at Truk and on industry in the home islands. In this period of the war, individual commanders were showing senior admirals how the submarine war should be fought and what the proper targets were. But the admirals remained blind to the value of picking off the tanker fleet. Had they seized their opportunities earlier, the drastic slowdown of Japanese transport and industry that took place in 1944–1945 might have occurred much sooner.

The last months of 1943 were the turning point in the Pacific submarine war. This was not because the toll of enemy ships sunk jumped sky-high, although it did rise. Rather it was because the improvements in weapons and the evolution of strategy and tactics coincided then. The stage was set for triumph.

The machine shops at Pearl Harbor were turning out contact exploders for the submarines' torpedoes. The first Mark XVIII electric torpedoes arrived. Adm. Charles A. Lockwood, Jr., commanding submarine operations from Hawaii, swung around and accepted his skippers' arguments for wolf pack tactics. Finally, and perhaps as important as the foregoing, the high command agreed that Luzon Strait—as junior officers had contended for years—could be the American submarines' "happy hunting ground."

Two other developments are worth noting: Although American code breakers were sending the submarines more accurate information, a damaging development for the United States arose from the extension of Japanese air power to cover their convoys. Combat captains' reports emphasized the ubiquity of the enemy bombers and the skill of their pilots.

To some extent, the submarine record for 1943 was a marked improvement over that of 1942. Submarine strikes at last bit into the enemy's shipping resources. American boats sank 335 naval and merchant vessels totaling 1.5 million tons. The separate campaign against tankers, although also improving, still had not developed fully. Japan that year lost 150,000 tons of tankers out of a fleet of 686,000 tons. However, the construction of new tankers and the conversion of merchantmen to tankers enabled the Japanese to end the year with a tanker tonnage of 863,000 or 177,000 tons more than they had deployed at the start of the year. So the net loss in tanker tonnage was small for the year, 27,000 tons.

Any assessment of the undersea campaign must note that a great deal of time and resources were spent chasing Japanese capital ships, carriers and cruisers; more, it appears now, than was justified by the results. There were two attacks on battleships. One, the *Yamato*, was slightly damaged. Of 30 attacks on the fleet carriers, only four inflicted any damage and no fleet carriers were sunk. The USS *Sailfish*, however, did sink the small carrier *Chuyo*.

The Japanese, who had done relatively well against American surface combatants in 1942, failed to follow up in 1943. Their submarines sank only three American warships—a destroyer, a submarine and a small carrier—in return for very heavy losses, 22 submarines. Two of these were sunk by American submarines.

The American weapons situation had improved remarkably by the end of the year. Commanders were reporting more hits with the old Mark XIV torpedo equipped with the improved exploder, and many boats were putting to sea armed with the electric Mark XVIII. More and more submarines were on patrol with improved radar devices. As weapons and engine failures declined, sinkings increased, a more imaginative strategy took over and morale rose. By the end of 1944, the undersea force was ready for its maximum effort and the greatest victory ever won by the submarine.

The reader must keep in mind that the submariners were not fighting the only war in the Pacific, much as they might have wished to. The Gilbert Islands had been taken in 1943, the Marshall Islands were to be the objectives in 1944. All through the Pacific, ships, troops and aircraft were on the move. Beyond the Marshalls lay Truk and the Marianas Islands. Gen. Douglas MacArthur was preparing for a push northward toward the Philippines, which he had left three years before. In Northeast India, the British were assembling forces to retake Burma and Malaya. All these operations, vast in concept and demanding enormous resources, called for submarines. By the beginning of January 1944, the Americans had assembled about 100 fleet submarines, boats of about 1500 tons with a range of 10,000 miles. Their surface speed was approximately 20 knots, and they could do about half that submerged. They were equipped with the new SJ radar sets that enabled them to locate hostile shipping at night, a tremendous advantage because the Japanese had not yet installed radar on their ships and planes.

The American submarines cooperated closely with the invasion forces, implementing the island-hopping strategy. Many of their targets were the troopships and their escorts that were striving to reinforce Japanese garrisons. The number of attacks was high and there were many significant kills. Nonetheless, submarine warfare purists may lament that the boats were not directed more against enemy merchant shipping, already feeling the pinch. The submarines might have had a greater effect had they been concentrated in the East China Sea and Japanese home waters.

The wolf packs were operating in Luzon Strait. One sank seven ships totaling 35,000 tons. Patrols out of Fremantle, refueling at Darwin, took their toll of tanker traffic. The Japanese monthly losses of tankers and freighters climbed toward 200,000 tons. Yet the diversion from merchant shipping continued.

In an effort to halt the American thrust pointing at the home islands the Japanese high command planned to reinforce garrisons on the Palau Islands and the Philippines and to entice the United States into a major air-sea battle near the Palaus. In light of this, the American submarine forces at Pearl Harbor and in Australia were instructed to sink naval units, troop transports and freighters and to reconnoiter the islands that American ground forces were to invade.

The submariners, with considerable help from the code breakers, were highly successful. A light cruiser was sunk in the Palaus, the third in three months. Two infantry divisions intended as reinforcements for New Guinea were intercepted, and the transport *Yoshida Maru I*, carrying a regiment of 3200 men, was sent to the bottom and the soldiers drowned. On May 6, three more troopers bound for New Guinea were sunk, and on the same day a 16,800-ton tanker was destroyed.

These American successes seriously interfered with the Japanese operational plan. Seven enemy warships had been sunk, a carrier and a battleship attacked. In addition, 24 merchant ships, six tankers, four troopships and 14 smaller freighters had been sent to the bottom. At the same time, the American submariners, operating on the code breakers' information, attacked the line of 12 submarines that the Japanese had established on a defensive position from Truk to New Guinea. Nine were sunk.

That was only the beginning. When the Japanese began their retreat from the Palau-Marianas area in June 1944, they left behind a submarine screen to cover their withdrawal. About a dozen submarines were sunk, mostly in the Marianas, bringing the total for that year to approximately 40—about half of the fleet's modern vessels.

Faced with mounting losses of both warships and merchantmen, the Imperial high command had to make a tough decision. Should the lost submarines be replaced, or should priority go to building the merchant ships without which the home islands would strangle? As hard-pressed governments often do in war, the high command compromised. It decided to continue the merchant program, and instead of replacing the lost submarines, to emphasize the production of midget submarines, believing they could be used effectively against the invasion of the home islands that was forecast. The conventional I class submarines that remained were fitted with man-guided torpedoes called *kaitens,* an undersea relative of the *kamikaze* planes.

As the year faded, the American wolf pack patrols in Luzon Strait reaped an increasingly rich harvest. On one patrol, a submarine sank four ships totaling 11,000 tons and a total of 19 ships in four patrols. Another pack got eight ships totaling about 40,000 tons; a third destroyed five ships totaling 39,000 tons.

The effect on the Japanese home economy and war industry was serious. The merchant navy was losing about 50 ships a month, and with the wolf packs roaming Luzon Strait and the East China Sea, it was clear that the losses would rise, not fall. Oil and other imports dwindled. The shipyards could not keep pace with the destruction at sea. The Imperial navy, badly mauled in the summer fighting, was hard pressed to find sufficient escorts for the convoys.

Oddly enough, the Japanese politicians, who had gone to war ostensibly to protect their access to raw materials and oil in Southeast and South Asia, were slow to grasp the magnitude of the American threat and to prepare the population for the hardships it would bring.

The whole tide of the war in the Pacific was turning. United States forces were storming up from the south. Leyte was invaded. Palau and Morotai were occupied. New ships—carriers, battleships, cruisers, destroyers and submarines—were moving westward for the kill. In the sea battles fought to support the Leyte landings, American submarines sank two heavy cruisers and a destroyer and badly damaged two other heavy cruisers.

Operations against Japanese commerce accelerated. Two wolf packs from Pearl Harbor sank 19 ships totaling approximately 110,000 tons. Transports, tankers, merchant ships, an occasional destroyer were hounded across the southern seas. American submarines were fitted with devices that enhanced their effectiveness: short-range sonar, a small electric acoustical torpedo, a decoy device to divert enemy surface craft, a night periscope. These aids, high morale, and veteran crews and captains helped raise the tonnage sunk; 1944 was the vintage year of the American submarine campaign.

The impact was greatest on Japan's civilian economy. American submarines sank 603 ships, about 2.7 million tons—more than had been sunk in the three previous years of the war. As a result, Japanese imports of bulk commodities fell from 16.4 million tons in 1943 to ten million tons in 1944. Total merchant shipping tonnage was halved from 4.1 million tons to two million tons. Japanese shipyards barely kept pace with tanker losses. Japan began the year with 863,000 tons of tankers, built 204 tankers totaling 624,000 tons and ended the year with a tanker tonnage of 869,000 tons. This was a sad achievement for Japanese shipyards. And in addition to the losses due to submarines, Japanese oil supplies were being reduced by other causes. The invasion of Mindoro, for instance, cut tanker traffic from Southeast Asia to the home islands in half.

The U.S. submarine service's battle against the Japanese surface fleet also reached its climax in 1944. One battleship, seven aircraft carriers, two heavy cruisers, seven light cruisers, about 30 destroyers and seven submarines were sunk. Five other major units were severely damaged.

By year's end, Japanese shipping had been driven back into the Sea of Japan and the Yellow Sea. Merchantmen ran close inshore and hurried into harbor at nightfall. In this situation, the main weight of operations against the Japanese home economy shifted from the submarines, who had borne it so long against so many obstacles and under so many handicaps, to the B-29s of the air force.

The submarine service, however, was not content to rest on its hard-won laurels and turn the war over entirely to the air force. Submarine patrols continued, but targets were scarce. Boats from Guam and Pearl Harbor often returned without sighting a single enemy ship. In 87 patrols from January to March 1945, only 51 ships were sunk. Japanese countermeasures were at a minimum. American submarines operated on the surface, knocking off small craft with their deck guns.

In late May 1945, nine submarines sailed into the Sea of Japan, the enemy's last maritime sanctuary. There, the problem was mines rather than surface antisubmarine forces. The nine boats, code-named "Hell Cats," entered the sea through Tsushima Strait and carried out one of the war's most spectacularly successful operations. Eight submarines accounted for 28 ships, including an enemy submarine, and 54,784 tons of shipping. Only one boat was lost.

The submarines continued on the offensive until the Japanese surrender. A transport was sunk on August 11, a submarine the next day, and on August 14, the last torpedoes fired by any naval combatant in World War II sank two small surface warships.

The naval war in the Pacific was over, and for all practical purposes, the Japanese merchant marine had ceased to exist. American submarines had sunk 1314 enemy vessels totaling 5.3 million tons, or 55 percent of all Japanese tonnage lost. These figures included one battleship, eight heavy and light aircraft carriers and eight light cruisers, besides scores of destroyers and smaller warships. The number of merchant seamen lost was staggering. The most objective estimate is 27,000 killed and 89,000 wounded, missing or stranded on Pacific islands, out of a total of about 122,000 at the start of the Pacific war. Of these casualties, the majority—16,200 killed, 54,000 wounded or missing—were attributed to submarine attacks.

By any standards, this was a tremendous triumph. But it should be placed in a numerical perspective by comparing it with German sinkings in the two world wars. Between 1914 and the Armistice in 1918, U-boats sank 5078 merchantmen of approximately 11 million tons plus 10 battleships and 18 cruisers. On their second try, between 1939 and 1945, the bag was much smaller, 2882 ships, 14.4 million tons and 175 warships.

What did the American submarine service accomplish in the Pacific during World War II? Clearly it succeeded in strangling the island center of an empire, while the Germans, faced with the same general problem, failed. This achievement alone would entitle the submariners to claim that they made a substantial contribution to the naval victory. And this claim is enhanced when submarine operations in addition to those against merchant ships and surface combatants are taken into consideration.

From the darkest days in December 1941 until the very end, the submarine service—which was never more than 50,000 strong, or about 1.5 percent of the navy—cheerfully accepted a variety of unconventional and dangerous missions. Key land personnel in the Philippines were evacuated by submarine. Agents were landed on Japanese-held islands. When the air assault against Japan was at its height, submarines on "lifeguard" patrols rescued scores of downed pilots. All this was hard, unremitting, unspectacular work—demanding from the service, and receiving, the greatest coolness and skill.

A later generation tends to believe that the war against Japan was won by mammoth air strikes with conventional bombs, followed by the two atomic bomb raids on Hiroshima and Nagasaki. This is an unbalanced assessment. Anyone who studies the history of the war in the Pacific must conclude that the American submarine campaign against Japanese seaborne commerce was a principal factor, perhaps *the* principal factor, in the victory. Even if the atomic weapons had not been used, Japan's internal collapse, brought about primarily by the submarine blockade, was only a question of time. That blockade had denied Japan oil, iron ore and other raw materials and food. Modern industrial nations cannot continue a war without the means to make war.

So the long war that had begun on the plains of Poland ended aboard the USS *Missouri* in Tokyo Bay. The submarines—German, Italian and Japanese, British and American—had established their role more firmly than ever before. Fantastic new weapons and devices had been developed to fight them. But the undersea craft continued to operate successfully, in defiance of those weapons. The advent of long-range aircraft was a mixed blessing to submariners. Reconnaissance planes made their work easier. But bombers dropping depth charges were a new dimension of danger.

Despite the strides made between 1939 and 1945, some on the Axis's side unknown to the Allies at the war's end, the undersea boats' military potential had not been fulfilled when the shooting stopped. A new design, a new propellant, a new weapon were required to make the submarine what it has since become—the ultimate weapon.

 The dawn of peace in 1945—a false
dawn if ever there was one—
found the United States and Great Britain triumphant on the seven
seas. Granted the magnitude of their ·triumph, the usual postwar
period of neglect and decay should have set in for the western navies.
But the cold war intervened. Starting in the late Forties—the Soviet
blockade of Berlin in June 1948 is the first milestone—Russian pressure rang alarm bells all over the world. Nowhere were they louder
than in Washington. Of the many disadvantages accruing to the
Soviet Union from its duel with the United States, none was more
lasting in its military effect than the stimulus given to American
weapons technology.

From the standpoint of global strategy, the most significant
product of that technology in the Fifties was the development of the
nuclear-powered submarine and its subsequent marriage to the bal-

listic missile armed with a nuclear or a conventional warhead.

But we are running ahead of our story. First let us look at the state of submarine development at the close of World War II. Great victories had been won in the Atlantic, Mediterranean and Pacific. But the victors were amazed to learn that Germany and Japan, the two principal losers, were well ahead of America and Britain in some aspects of submarine development; the Germans more so than the Japanese.

In the Battle of the Atlantic, the Germans had been beaten by the superior tactics of huge forces equipped with more modern search devices. The U-boats were driven from the seas because they could not continue nighttime operations on the surface, where they were picked up by the new Allied radar sets. But Doenitz and German science were not completely defeated. As Horton points out, the Germans went back to first principles. They decided to build true submarines rather than torpedo boats that could submerge. Their estimate was that the Allied antisubmarine forces would lose much of their effectiveness if convoys were attacked by U-boats operating beneath the surface at high speed. Sonar would be no great advantage to antisubmarine forces faced with submarines moving at speeds comparable to their own.

Since 1937, the Germans had been experimenting with a hydrogen-peroxide engine for submarines. By 1943, the year the Germans were defeated in the Atlantic, Dr. Helmuth Walther, who was in charge of the development, had advised the navy that production of submarines equipped with the engine could begin. A crash program was started at Doenitz's urging.

The new engine was based on the principle that hydrogen peroxide passed over a catalyst furnishes oxygen and water. These were fed into a combustion chamber and there sprayed with oil fuel, to produce a mixture that burned at a very high temperature, producing steam. More water produced more steam to power the turbine that drove the submarine. It was expensive. But it was estimated that hydrogen-peroxide-engine submarines would reach a submerged speed of 25 knots, or twice as fast as any submarine then in operation.

The goal was militarily sound. But the situation for attaining it was bad. Allied bombing raids were hampering the transportation of submarine parts to the ports. Some raw materials were scarce. Man power was being drained from the shipyards to fill the gaps torn in the Wehrmacht by the Allied forces. By the end of the war, the Germans had produced only four small Walther boats.

Before the Walthers were ready, the Germans in their pursuit of speed had built a few streamlined submarines with greater underwater capabilities. They had also, as we noted earlier, installed snorkels—telescopic breathing tubes that fed air to the diesel engine and took off exhaust gases. A snorkel-equipped submarine could recharge its batteries while running submerged at a slow speed, thus reducing the prospects of being picked up by Allied radar.

No one was more surprised to discover these developments after the victory than the mandarins of the American navy. They found that German submarines were generally faster on and beneath the surface than their own boats and that they were equipped with superior sonar optics, diesel engines and batteries. The U-boats also could dive deeper and faster. When the navy inspected Japanese submarines, including dozens of midget craft, it got another shock. The Japanese also had installed snorkels, and their torpedoes were more efficient than the American.

The United States and Britain, the principal western naval powers in the early postwar years, incorporated into their submarines the advances in construction and propulsion pioneered by Dr. Walther. American submarines were streamlined and fitted with snorkels; and a new class, the Guppy (for "greater underwater propulsive power") joined the fleet. The navy also designed an entirely new submarine. These Tang class boats were propelled by a new diesel engine and armed with a homing torpedo modeled on the German acoustical torpedo. But the Tangs were not a big success.

The British took the same line, but went a bit beyond the Americans. They laid down two hydrogen-peroxide-fuel submarines of their own design. They experimented with small submarines based on the four Dr. Walther had had built, and they modified fleet submarines with streamlining and by installing larger batteries.

Despite a great deal of effort and expenditure by both governments, the submarine at the end of the Forties remained basically the same weapon that had fought the Second World War. Consequently, the position of undersea craft in naval strategic thinking remained what it had been then. Indeed, it may be said to have receded slightly as a result of the strategic and tactical importance accorded aircraft carriers in contemporary naval doctrine.

The carrier had played a spectacular part in winning the Pacific war. The feats of individual carriers and of their pilots had caught the imagination of the American public. "Carrier admirals," senior officers convinced by their recent experience of the superiority of the carrier as *the* naval weapon, began to dominate naval thought and, more important, commands. Then, the aircraft carrier's importance was inflated by the harsh realities of the cold war. In that premissile period, long-range aircraft were the only means of delivering nuclear weapons. The carrier admirals argued that air bases were vulnerable to Russian counterstrikes. But not the carrier, the mobile airfield protected by its destroyers. The aircraft carrier, they were fond of explaining, could do it all: destroy hostile ships, bomb Soviet targets and support ground operations in Europe. The range of carrier-based fighterbombers increased. The carriers with the Mediterranean Sixth Fleet and with the Atlantic Fleet when it was deployed in the Northeast Atlantic were regarded as definite threats by the Soviets and were so described in their military literature.

While the cult of the carrier throve, the submarine remained about where it had been at the end of the war. But submarine technology was on the threshold of a startling breakthrough that was to alter the balances of naval warfare drastically.

Dramatic advances in technology seldom are accomplished without the leadership of a powerful personality. He may not be a scientist or an inventor. But he sees the potential in a machine or an idea and provides the driving force that wins its acceptance. Usually the man is a maverick, suspect to traditionalists. Churchill and the tank in World War I and Brig. Gen. William Mitchell, United States Army Air Corps, and the bomber after that war are examples. The nuclear submarine that was to transform naval warfare and for the first time bring every American within range of enemy fire found its driving force in Hyman George Rickover.

Nuclear propulsion was not a new idea when, in August 1947, the then Captain Rickover and four other naval officers visited the Los Alamos Laboratory of the Atomic Energy Commission. As early as the spring of 1939, the navy's Bureau of Engineering had sought funds to research nuclear fission and its application to ships. The first governmental advisory commission on uranium had studied the relationship between controlled chain reaction and ship propulsion.

A Manhattan Project committee had suggested in 1944 that the government consider research-and-development studies on the nuclear propulsion of naval vessels "an urgent project." A year later, the Naval Research Laboratory submitted a program for nuclear ship-building research and development, and one civilian scientist suggested details for the construction of a nuclear submarine. It was this suggestion that impressed Rickover, usually a difficult man to impress.

From the standpoint of naval warfare, the possibilities were tremendous. A nuclear-powered submarine would be the first true submarine: a vessel that could live submerged rather than one that submerged for certain functions but that, even with the snorkel, had to spend part of its life on the surface. The nuclear submarine can live under the surface because a nuclear reactor does not require oxygen. A controlled nuclear reaction generates tremendous heat. This turns water into steam to run turbines and, harnessed to turbo-generators, provides electricity. Oxygen, of course, is necessary for the crew. But this can be stored and purified.

So here was a submarine that could remain submerged indefinitely, that would be far faster below the surface than anything yet developed; the nemesis of battleships, carriers and cruisers.

The man who saw the possibilities of the nuclear submarine and brought it to completion through a tremendous effort of will was about as unusual a naval officer as the country has ever seen. Unlike the Royal Navy, the United States service has never coddled eccentrics, if one excepts the founding father, John Paul Jones. I well remember one senior admiral telling me on the eve of World War II that he doubted whether Nelson would have been much good in the United States Navy since he was blind in one eye, one-armed and "had a bad reputation with women."

Before and after 1947, Rickover was a maverick. His background was most unusual for an Annapolis graduate. His father was a Polish tailor who had settled in Chicago in 1906. Hyman Rickover was a product of what our fathers called "the school of hard knocks": a diligent student who worked as a Western Union messenger while in high school and who was classified as a "grind" at the naval academy. Not for Rickover the participation in major sports that established reputations carried into the service years. Not for him the girls from New York or Baltimore for academy dances. He was a rather humorless fellow, immersed in his studies—obviously a prime target for hazing. Even then he was argumentative, peremptory, demanding, a strange type to find in the navy of 1922 into which he graduated.

Yet oddly enough, the navy—despite its, to him, ridiculous customs and traditions, its emphasis on being a conformist and socially "right"—impressed young Rickover. In those days the navy was slowly becoming the machine-oriented service it is today. Rickover had a "feel" for machinery, expressed in what to his brother officers must have been a rather boring desire to see how everything worked, to cut through wasteful procedures, to make engines and weapons more efficient.

There is nothing in the record of the ensign and lieutenant that hints at future greatness. Rickover was a man of attitudes, but unfortunately for him, his attitudes were not those that win the approval of senior officers. He served on a destroyer and then on a battleship, the USS *Nevada*. Aboard the latter he finally attracted attention. He had a ceaseless, consuming curiosity about the *Nevada*'s inner workings, and bit by bit he became familiar with her machinery. In 1925, he was appointed electrical officer.

As such, he was spotted by his captain, C.S. Kempff, as a comer. Kempff himself was not the usual naval captain. His mind ranged well beyond the day-to-day business of his battleship and into international politics, grand strategy and the philosophy of war. Rickover, young and intense, had never encountered anyone like Kempff in the navy, and the older man's encouragement and sympathy extended his range. He enrolled in the Naval War College's course in strategy and tactics. But although he retained sound views on these subjects throughout his service life, Rickover was more interested in the machinery on which the navy ran. He was an odd mixture of mechanic and scholar, and when he got the chance to return to Annapolis for postgraduate work, he did so and took a master's degree in electrical engineering. Then he went on to Columbia University's School of Engineering.

With these academic credits behind him, Rickover's career took a fortunate turn. With his experience on the *Nevada* and his master's degree, he might have disappeared into the navy's technical side. As it was, he was attracted to the submarine service and applied for submarine duty. There were difficulties—he was overage—but Kempff, now an admiral, intervened, and Rickover began his new career.

He did not stay long, only three years, but his experience proved to be of the greatest value to his country. His life in submarines was not easy for him or, one suspects, for his shipmates. He was a prickly, opinionated fellow who never took people, not even the brass, as they came. He was older and more experienced than his fellow students at the New London, Connecticut, submarine school and a classmate recalls that Rickover gave the faculty "pretty average hell."

Then and later, Rickover was heretical about regulations and procedures. When he sensed that something was done in a certain way because it had always been done that way, he rebelled. He did not mind airing his scholastic record to the faculty. He thought the off-duty conviviality of his colleagues boring. He considered many of the lectures a waste of time and of the government's money. Although Rickover has been largely responsible for some of the most costly programs in the navy's history, he has always kept a sharp eye out for needless expenditure.

Rickover's first submarine job was engineering officer on the S-48, a small, elderly boat given to mechanical breakdowns and fires, one of which Rickover put out. She was not, by any stretch of the imagination, a glamorous or even a lucky craft, the type to attract an ambitious officer. But for all her faults, Rickover developed a feeling for his ship. As engineering officer he knew more about her than anyone else aboard. His willingness to try his hand at any piece of maintenance, his mastery of his trade made him popular with the sailors. But even when he was promoted to executive officer, Rickover was too caustic, too much the perfectionist to make friends with his fellow officers. At sea or ashore, he was the student, the loner. He always had had a low regard for the majority of his colleagues. Since Rickover was not then, nor is he now, a man capable of keeping his opinions to himself, this became general knowledge in the small, tightly knit world of the between-the-wars submarine service, and it may have influenced the navy's decision not to give him a submarine command. Instead, he was moved to a shore job in the Office of Naval Material.

There are two interesting aspects to Rickover's career at this stage. One is that, onerous although they may have appeared at the time, all his jobs were contributing to the knowledge that later proved essential to his country. The other is that quite apart from his natural "orneriness," he was developing a distinctive cultural personality.

Clay Blair, Jr., notes that Rickover was impressed by Harold Nicolson's *Peacemaking 1919*. He was impressed by this minor classic because, Blair writes, "Nicolson's behind-the-scenes account of the workings of the Versailles treaty confirmed a fact that Rick had long suspected; all too often men in public office were unduly influenced by personal friendships and sometimes compromised their governments simply for the sake of accommodating a friend."

This analysis of Rickover's thought tells us a good deal about the man. He had become a seasoned naval officer, highly sophisticated in the technology of the day. But he apparently was naïve politically. For Nicolson's account was a simple restatement of what any mature practitioner of the political art understands from adolescence. The effect of *Peacemaking 1919,* a good but not necessarily seminal work, on Lieutenant Rickover may have had a good deal to do with his prickly, belligerent attitude toward politicians, an attitude that at times came close to blocking his progress. He had never accepted the stereotype of the charming, popular naval officer. As the years went on, he withdrew increasingly into the personal boundaries he had drawn for himself. He would superimpose his own standards upon those of the navy. He would not flatter, he would not kowtow. He would make his position known as forcibly as possible.

Rickover was a remarkable young officer. Nothing proves this so much as the manner in which he emerged from the series of arduous, unrewarding jobs to which he was assigned after his submarine experience. He was assistant engineering officer on the USS *New Mexico,* a battleship, and managed to cut her use of fuel oil and fresh water. In this phase, the peppery Rickover comes through in some respects as an intelligent version of Captain Queeg in *The Caine Mutiny:* a specialist in minutiae, a nagger, a bumptious but brilliant officer who irritated his superiors and raised hell in the hearts of his peers.

After a solid success on the *New Mexico,* Rickover got his first command, a command that might have shattered the spirit of a less resilient character. She was an ancient minesweeper on the China Station, the USS *Finch.* His record as her commander was not unlike the one he established on the S-48 or the *New Mexico.* Unremitting labor for himself and his crew. Enterprise that upset the brass. And —those were the days when the Japanese were moving into China— a strain of personal courage. But the *Finch* was not a glamorous command. Rickover must have realized that whatever miracles he might accomplish in keeping her seaworthy, there was no future for him as a ship commander. So when the opportunity came to apply for a permanent post as an engineering officer, he took it. As an engineering officer, Rickover could not be named to ships, but the position established him in the field where his peculiar genius lay.

"Rickover would have been a menace as a ship commander," Adm. Alan Kirk once told me after the war. "To my mind, he didn't have that sort of discipline. But give him a technical or organizational problem, and he was miles ahead of anyone else in the navy. In those situations, he was on his own. But commanding a ship in action, where cooperation is essential—well, frankly, no. Too much individuality."

Rickover's first job was assistant planning officer at the Cavite Navy Yard in the Philippines. The yard was a mess. Rickover, stepping on the usual number of toes—and perhaps a few more—put it right. He eliminated jobs. He banned procedures that were time-wasting. He installed programs to repair ships faster. He was cursed heartily by many and admired by the prescient few who could see the storm clouds hanging over Europe.

He returned to Washington in the autumn of 1939. The capital —with its enormous bureaucracy, interservice feuds, rivalry for congressional and executive favors and resources that could whip the world—was his proper arena. It was in Washington that he was to fight his battles and win his victories. His basic weapons were his knowledge of naval electrical apparatus and his views on how it could be improved. Soon he was chief of the electrical section, the master of a small group of dedicated officers who were ten steps ahead of routine naval technological doctrine. From the electrical systems on warships to measures to counter German magnetic mines to an infrared signaling-and-detection device, all these were part of Rickover's ever-widening sphere. He was tough on subordinates and superiors, equally hard on civilian workers and contractors. Some of Rickover's superiors were impressed by the speed and efficiency with which he accomplished his work. Others speculated, not too privately, whether the strained relations, enmities and bureaucratic disorganization that marked his successes were not too high a price to pay for efficiency.

Rickover's experience in an operational theater was short. He was sent to Okinawa in the summer of 1945 to organize a base to repair ships that might be damaged in the impending invasion of Japan. He remained there until autumn, when he was given another of those jobs that no one else seemed to want but in which he excelled: inspector general of the 19th Fleet, then being prepared for the mothballing process. Here again was a job devoid of glamour but one that had to be done. Rickover did it.

His future, like that of thousands of other regular naval officers, was in doubt. Congress was looking skeptically at military appropriations. The war was over, and the cold war that was to stimulate military appropriations had not begun. Would there be a place in the postwar navy for an energetic but rather unpopular captain? Rickover, not for the first time, displayed his flair for discovering precisely the sort of job in which he would be most valuable. He went to Washington and told his chiefs in the Bureau of Ships that he was interested in atomic energy and its application to ship propulsion and that he wished to be trained in the field. After some juggling of assignments, Rickover went to Oak Ridge. The man began his life-work.

The story of the development of America's first nuclear submarine, the *Nautilus*, has been told often. It is a long, intricate record of setbacks and minor victories, of scientists and naval officers exploring new areas of ship construction and nuclear engineering. With his extraordinary ability to drive to the heart of any question, Rickover soon realized that the principal problem was in the field of engineering. Throughout his life, he has resembled Al Smith, of whom it was said, "All Al can see is the point."

The first significant step toward the proper organization of the naval team that was to produce the *Nautilus* came early in January 1948 when Rickover formed the Nuclear Power Division of the Bureau of Ships, filling its upper echelons with officers he had come to know and trust during their joint nuclear apprenticeship at Oak Ridge. The next step, surprising and highly controversial, was the appointment of Rickover as chief of the Naval Reactors Branch of the Atomic Energy Commission, the civilian agency charged by Congress with the control of nuclear, or as they were known then, atomic, matters.

Rickover's rather odd predicament of holding equally influential positions in both the civilian and the military agencies charged with nuclear development was one of the stimulants the program required. The captain was able to preach to prominent civilians as well as to naval officers his gospel that the nuclear submarine was not some Jules Verne notion possible in the distant future but a vessel that could be built immediately.

Technical problems naturally proliferated. Rickover and his associates, military and civilian, were venturing into the unknown. There were critical shortages of metals, such as zirconium and hafnium, capable of withstanding the very high temperatures generated by nuclear reactors. Beyond all other technological questions was the major one of how to fit a reactor into a submarine. Westinghouse Electric Corporation, the contractor, solved this by placing the reactor inside the *Nautilus*'s pressure hull and by designing a reactor that required only simple maintenance for itself and for the heat-exchange machinery. Westinghouse also discovered that the coolant water for heat exchange lost its radioactivity faster than anticipated once the reactor was shut down, thus enabling earlier maintenance of the reactor's machinery.

The architecture of the new vessel presented another problem. As we saw earlier, a nuclear-powered submarine would have characteristics totally different from submarines of the past. They were surface vessels constructed to submerge for varying periods of time. The navy had never had to consider a submarine hull built for prolonged undersea duty.

Another perplexing factor was that the newer ships move faster underwater than they do on the surface because surface vessels expend their energy in two ways while submarines do so in only one. The energy of surface vessels is dissipated as they make waves and as they overcome the friction of cutting through the water. A submarine deals only with the friction of the water. Ultimately, the navy decided on a relatively simple hull rather like those of the fleet submarines, with a blunt bow that, it was believed, would give a higher underwater performance.

By April 1950, construction of the first atomic-powered submarine began. A naval officer familiar with the program commented that the preceding sentence doesn't "sound like a big deal, but my God, it was." The start of construction meant that Rickover and his associates had completed all preliminary work, had established a school to train nuclear engineers, had finished the first plans for the ship and the power plant, had won government approval of the project and had convinced both the General Electric Company and Westinghouse that they should build not one but two atomic-powered submarines.

When one considers the obstacles Rickover faced, this catalog of progress may be regarded as outstanding in the annals of naval obstruction and construction. He had overcome the inertia of an entrenched bureaucracy, the resistance of senior admirals and politicians, the doubts of eminent scientists and engineers and the "unknown unknowns" that lurk in the path of all technological pioneers.

He did it through the formula that had brought him that far: hard, unremitting work. No one labored longer, no one was more zealous in explaining, defending and proselytizing the atomic submarine. He was both bully and evangelist when the situation required. Subordinates were harried when the work lagged. They were inspired by quotations from Shakespeare: "Our doubts are traitors and make us lose the good we oft might win by fearing to attempt." Blair points out with almost English understatement that "Lack of sleep and impatience sometimes caused him to be insolent and disagreeable, traits that did not help his standing with the navy brass." Never one to go through channels, Rickover cajoled and hectored civilian contractors who were slow fulfilling contracts. He was a workhorse, a pest and a genius.

While his tactics infuriated the senior naval officers, Rickover had a different effect on some important politicians. They liked his forthright approach, his disdain for small talk, his ability to get things done. And this popularity did not endear him to the admirals. In 1951, the Navy Selection Board chose a new list of rear admirals. Rickover didn't make it. In navy language, he was "passed over." The reactionaries in the navy rejoiced. Some politicians, notably Sen. Brien MacMahon, chairman of the Joint Congressional Committee on Atomic Energy, were upset. Rickover, deep in the problems of the *Nautilus,* seems to have regarded his rejection as a minor incident. What mattered was the *Nautilus.* The navy had disclosed that her keel would be laid in early 1952 and that she would be operational in 1954. To the dedicated Rickover this was basic; far more important than whether he was Admiral Rickover or Captain Rickover.

For the project still was encountering problems. There was a shortage of the inch-and-a-quarter steel necessary for the sides of the submarine. Only three mills in the country made this special thickness of steel, which was also used in aircraft carriers and destroyers. Rickover's group figured that the *Nautilus*'s construction would consume the total United States production of one-and-a-quarter-inch steel plate for three months. Inevitably there was a clash. The Bureau of Ships looked askance at any allocation of this steel that might delay completion of the aircraft carrier USS *Forrestal.* To the navy, the carrier remained *the* weapon, and the completion of the *Forrestal* was far more important than Rickover's construction of an untried weapon. Rickover won by a typically adroit move. He got the steel by using the priority of the Atomic Energy Commission, which was higher than that of the Bureau of Ships.

The incident didn't help Rickover with the navy brass. In July 1952, he was again "passed over" for promotion to admiral. This time the outcry was heard well outside the Navy Department. Rickover had been recommended for promotion by the Secretary of the Navy, the chairman of the Atomic Energy Commission, MacMahon and several other influential congressmen and senators. Articles critical of the navy appeared in *Time* and *Life* and in newspapers around the country. At the time, the navy believed that Rickover had instigated these articles and had fed information to reporters. On the contrary, Rickover had pleaded with *Time* not to run its article, which he feared might harm his project and the navy.

The navy's second slight to Rickover may have done a lot of good by fixing public attention on the man and his work. Memories were not so short that Mitchell's long, vain fight to convince the army and the navy of the bomber's role in war had been forgotten. Rickover was compared to Mitchell. Thoughtful editors pointed out that Rickover had been passed over twice and that, since he had completed 30 years service, he would have to retire at 52. A valuable officer would be lost to the navy and a project that the editors and the public hazily understood as important to the country might be sidetracked or canceled.

In this they were correct. When the threat of retirement hung over Rickover, he would be a lame-duck boss. Would naval subordinates and civilian contractors give him the same obedience or work as hard when he was in that situation? What would happen to his authority in the months before retirement?

Rickover handled himself with restraint and dignity. While he did not criticize the selection board, he did point out that the conservative military minds of seagoing officers often operated as a brake on creative developments in the engineering branch. (Oddly enough, some of the sea officers had been those who had pressed hardest for technical innovation, particularly in torpedoes, during the Second

World War. Confident that America's victory had written the last words on technical improvement, they now resisted change.) Technical minds, he insisted, "must be allowed to operate with some freedom, you can't order a man to do brainwork."

The navy reacted to the controversy as any massive, hierarchical organization would be expected to. It planted articles favorable to its promotion system in professional journals. Influential admirals cornered influential politicians and explained that an enormous fuss, harmful to the navy, was being made over of nothing. Secretary of Defense Robert A. Lovett and Secretary of the Navy Dan Kimball became involved. Into the uproar, the Atomic Energy Commission dropped a bomb of truly nuclear proportions in the form of an official statement. This said in part that if Rickover were forced to resign, it was probable that morale in the AEC's Naval Reactors Branch would decline, that some of the captain's staff would leave and that the change in personnel would result in a delay in important work.

The impression made by this statement was reinforced by the reading on the floor of Congress of the commendation Kimball gave Rickover on July 7, 1952, which said in part that the captain "has accomplished the most important piece of development work in the history of the navy." More and more congressmen, prompted by letters from their constituents, began to ask awkward questions. One congressman wondered if "selection boards consist of human beings like all of us." Sen. Martin Jackson told a reporter, "It's really shocking what's happening to that man," warning that young naval officers might be frightened away from scientific and technological work as a result of the treatment Rickover recieved.

A great deal of heat and not much light was being generated, and the public began taking sides in the kind of argument that appeals to it most—one involving personalities. The fact that Rickover was a Jew almost automatically won him the support of liberals. That he appeared to be persecuted by exactly the type of stiff, reactionary senior officers that millions of Americans abhorred as a result of their recent experiences in uniform fed the arguments and increased the bitterness.

Sea Trials of the USS Nautilus *at Groton, Connecticut, February 4, 1955.*
(Official U. S. Navy Photo)

The Senate Armed Services Committee met to consider "the Rickover case," as it was now called. The committee heard a long report by Rear Adm. Homer N. Wallin that was the navy's account of the nuclear-powered ship program. The account satisfied the entrenched navy. It failed to make much impression on Rickover's supporters, who claimed it was misleading and contained a number of errors. One misleading passage was easy to spot. Admiral Wallin said that the AEC felt "fully confident" of its capabilities in the event of Rickover's resignation or retirement, but as we have seen, the commission had expressed grave doubts on this point.

The situation now had some of the aspects of the classic Dreyfus case in France. Appalled by the uproar, the navy moved to protect itself and made what its sister service, the army, would have called "a planned retirement." The selection board recommended Rickover's retention in the navy and also recommended that when it met the following year, it promote to rear admiral a man involved in and competent to direct work on nuclear propulsion. In July 1953, the board met under specific instructions from the new secretary of the navy, Robert B. Anderson, to "select an admiral experienced and qualified in the field of atomic-propulsion machinery for ships." It is almost unbelievable, but some admirals still balked at naming Rickover. There was a five-hour debate. Finally, however, Rickover was selected. He was a rear admiral.

The Rickover case illustrates much of what is worst and best in the navy. The promotion's opponents showed that rigid distaste for the loner, the outsider, the innovator, the nonconformist that exists in most big military organizations. Opposition to such men is always a blemish on a service in war or peace. It is doubly so when the man is bringing to fruition the greatest advance in naval construction since sail gave way to steam.

In retrospect, the navy could find some positive gains. The man at the center of the storm was an Annapolis graduate, he had come up through "the system." In public, at least, he had comported himself with discretion and inner serenity at a time of great personal trial.

It had been a trial, too, of his project. Now that, too, was over. On January 21, 1954, the USS *Nautilus* was launched, five years after Rickover and his aides had first conceived the idea.

By today's standards, the revolutionary vessel was cheap: $55 million, of which $15 million represented the cost of the atomic reactor. She was 300 feet long, capable of speeds of 25 knots submerged for a period of 50 days.

The launching of the *Nautilus* began a new chapter in the history of the submarine, a chapter that is still being written. The moment the *Nautilus* went down the ways, every submarine in the world became obsolete; the tactical doctrines so carefully worked out since the days of Holland became so much rubbish; the priority the strategists had given to the aircraft carrier came into question; the destroyer's old prey became the hunter not only of other submarines but of the destroyers themselves. A new and frightening military age had dawned.

 The naval world into which the USS *Nautilus* steamed when she was commissioned in 1955 was dramatically different from that in which an unknown Captain Rickover had gone to Oak Ridge to study the mysteries of the atom.

The duel that we call the cold war had been going on for seven years between the two superpowers and their allies. The echo of the guns of Korea still hung in the air. Guerrilla wars were being fought in Malaysia and Borneo; and the Vietnamese peace, patched together at Geneva in 1954, was slowly coming apart. From the standpoint of the Department of Defense, particularly the Department of the Navy, there had been another pregnant development. After years of adherence to a naval policy that emphasized the defense of the motherland, the Soviet Union appeared to be gesturing warily toward the projection of Russian naval power onto the seven seas. Looming overhead was the most startling strategic development of all. The United States had lost its atomic monopoly. The Soviet Union and Britain were nuclear powers. France and China (the latter at that time still a close ally of the Soviet Union) were on the road to membership in the club.

Submarines had played minor roles in the various wars that had broken the peace established in 1945. But submariners all over the world and the more open-minded admirals recognized the consequences of the *Nautilus*. For she and her sister ships entering service in the late Fifties soon demonstrated the extent of the United States's technological breakthrough. In 1960, the USS *Triton* circumnavigated the globe completely submerged. The fleet was reinforced by nuclear submarines of more than 3000 tons displacement and with underwater cruising speeds well in excess of 25 knots. There were no wars in which the new weapons could be tested, but naval exercises demonstrated their effectiveness. In 1959, the USS *Skipjack* "sank" every aircraft carrier involved in a major NATO exercise in the Mediterranean.

It was now recognized—enthusiastically by some, reluctantly by others—that naval warfare had taken on a new dimension. In 1960, antisubmarine warfare, on which the American, Soviet and other navies have since spent tens of billions of dollars, was about where it had been at the end of World War II. This meant that the destroyer-bomber team of ten years before would be almost powerless to halt attacks on convoys or battle fleets by nuclear submarines that ran faster and deeper than the current antisubmarine technology was able to counter.

The nuclear submarine was revolutionary enough in itself. But more radical changes were to come. Weapons development, especially of vehicles for nuclear warheads, had progressed remarkably in the Fifties. The nuclear missile, then of relatively short range and indifferent accuracy, rivaled the manned bomber as the principal means of delivering nuclear munitions. The marriage of the nuclear ballistic missile to the nuclear-powered submarine was the second great change in naval warfare in the latter half of this century.

The idea of firing a missile from a submarine was not new. Even before the *Nautilus* was commissioned some older American fleet submarines had been armed with a single short-range Regulus missile, and the USS *Halibut*, an early nuclear boat, was similarly equipped. These missiles, however, had to be fired from the surface, which robbed nuclear submarines of one of their major advantages. It also might be noted that the Soviet navy, then in the first stages of expansion, was experimenting with missile-firing submarines that had to surface to launch their weapons.

American nuclear missiles housed in silos on the territories of allied states—the day of the intercontinental ballistic missile (ICBM) had not arrived yet—were vulnerable to Soviet attack by air or could be overrun by Soviet ground forces, then as now superior in numbers to those of our allies. Consequently, the establishment of missile bases in Turkey and on the territories of other NATO allies could not

Commissioning ceremonies of the USS Grayback, *showing a model of the Regulus II on the submarine's deck immediately aft of the missile hangars. March 31, 1958.   (Official U. S. Navy Photo)*

The nuclear powered submarine USS Narwhal goes down the ways during her launching ceremony at Groton, Connecticut. September 9, 1967.
(Official U. S. Navy Photo)

The submarine USS Grampus surfaces during an exercise off the coast of Cartegana, Colombia. August 10, 1969.
(Official U. S. Navy Photo)

be considered a guaranteed deterrent to Soviet ambitions. As the range and accuracy of ballistic missiles increased, ICBM silos and bases were built in the north central United States from the Dakotas to Wyoming. These bases, like those that have been deactivated in Tur-

USS Ulysses S. Grant *and USS* Proteus *at Polaris Point, Guam, April, 1965.*
(*Official U. S. Navy Photo*)

Off-loading a Polaris missile in Holy Loch, Scotland. January 17, 1963.
(*Official U. S. Navy Photo*)

*An A-3 Polaris missile is loaded on board
the USS* Stonewall Jackson. *April 1965.*
(Official U. S. Navy Photo)

USS Sam Rayburn *at the
Newport News, Virginia shipyard,
1964.*
(Oficial U. S. Navy Photo)

key, suffered from growing vulnerability. As the range and accuracy
of Soviet missiles increased, the survivability of static installations
became doubtful. What the United States needed was a mobile platform for long-range ballistic missiles.

Once again, the submarine provided the answer. The USS
George Washington fired a Polaris ballistic missile from a submerged
position on July 20, 1960. This was a climactic event in submarine
history, one comparable only to the launching of the *Nautilus*. For
the submarine, already moving toward the domination of the sea,
became a general military weapon when coupled with the ballistic

missile. Henceforth, industrial plants and oil fields, cities and inland ballistic missile sites would be as much targets for submarines as were transports, merchantmen or warships.

The first 41 submarines to be equipped with the Polaris missile (and thereafter loosely but accurately termed "Polaris submarines") were a new element in global strategy. The Polaris missile had a range of 2800 miles, and by the middle of the Sixties, about 20 of the new submarines, each carrying 16 Polaris missiles, were constantly on patrol.

The United States Navy believes today that the exact whereabouts of the Polaris submarines and of the later, more modern boats carrying Poseidon missiles are unknown to the Soviet Union. At this

Chief Torpedoman's Mate Pease (right) points to an open missile compartment aboard the nuclear powered fleet ballistic missile submarine USS James Madison *as timing and cycling tests are underway. Port Canaveral, Florida, October 1970.*
(*Official U. S. Navy Photo*)

A 1500 nautical mile Polaris A-2 missile is launched from beneath the ocean from the USS Thomas A. Edison *off Cape Kennedy during test exercises. April 1964.*
(Official U. S. Navy Photo)

USS Henry Clay *launches a Polaris A-2 missile from the surface of the Atlantic Ocean off Cape Kennedy, Florida. The objects flying through the air are launch adapters designed to detach themselves automatically once the missile has left the tube. The tall mast is a temporary telemetry antenna installed for operations at the cape only. This was the first demonstration that Polaris subs can launch missiles from the surface as well as from beneath the surface. Thirty minutes earlier the* Clay *successfully launched an A-2 Polaris missile submerged. April 1964.* (Official U. S. Navy Photo)

writing, this appears a reasonable assumption. The Russians, like the Americans, have expended huge sums to perfect submarine detection systems, but the Soviets are believed to lag well behind the United States in this field. And although American progress has been steady, the "breakthrough" that technology seeks has not been achieved.

Considering the situation from the United States's point of view, the navy has established a second-strike delivery system that, because of the missile submarines' mobility and the presumed inability of the potential enemy to plot their positions, is invulnerable to

Sequence views of the firing of a Poseidon missile by the nuclear powered fleet ballistic missile submarine USS Casimir Pulaski. *August 16, 1971. (Official U. S. Navy Photo)*

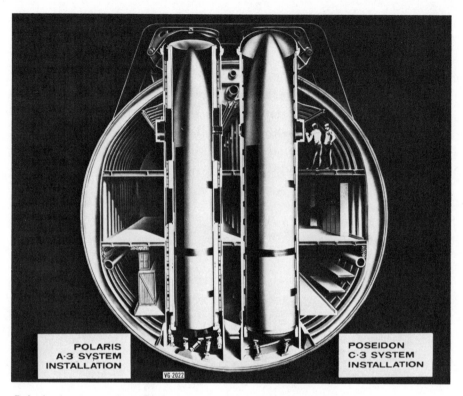

Polaris A-3 system installation and Poseidon C-3 system installation.
(Official U. S. Navy Photo)

a Soviet preemptive strike. The American SSBN (ballistic missile sub-marines nuclear) fleet has improved qualitatively if not quantita-tively. Twenty-two submarines are deployed armed with 352 Posei-don nuclear ballistic missiles, each of which has 10 to 14 MIRVs (multiple independently targetable reentry vehicles). By 1977, an-other nine submarines will be converted to carry the Poseidon. Work has begun on the Trident submarine, which will be discussed in a later chapter.

The United States's lead in nuclear-powered submarines armed with ballistic missiles did not last long. In the early Sixties, the

British launched HMS *Dreadnought,* a nuclear-powered submarine armed with conventional torpedoes, and laid down the first British ballistic missile submarine in 1964. Britain today has eight nuclear submarines classed as "attack" vessels and four SSBN nuclear submarines, each armed with 16 Polaris A-3 missiles. (The force is small, but nuclear weapons are what Damon Runyon called a revolver, "the old equalizer." Because of its awesome destructive power, a small nuclear force manned by dedicated, skilled men equalizes other nuclear forces far greater in number by giving the smaller nuclear power political leverage.)

The French began to follow suit in the middle Sixties, and the first submarine, the *Redoutable,* was operational in 1971. Three of them are now deployed. Each is armed with 16 M-1 missiles, a French development. A fourth submarine is scheduled to be commissioned in 1976, and the building of two more is under discussion.

The development of ballistic missile squadrons by Britain and France did not upset the United States. The British boats are assigned to NATO. France withdrew from military integration in the alliance in 1966, and her Redoutables are independent—theoretically at least. It is difficult to conceive of their use against the United States. But should the Soviet armies overrun France in some future war, the disposition of these submarines, like that of the French fleet in 1940, would be of paramount concern to the United States and her allies—if any.

The French, the British, the Chinese, these are not the submarine fleets that concern the United States. The American preoccupation is with the rise of Soviet sea power in the post-Stalin era, specifically underwater sea power—bearing in mind that when the most powerful land power in the world turned to the expansion of its naval power, strategic balances changed and are still changing. Viewing the spectrum of Soviet military force, nuclear and conventional, it is reasonable to believe that the development of Soviet submarines for both nuclear and conventional purposes is the single most significant threat posed to the United States by the Russians.

The Russians had been interested in underwater craft from the dawn of the submarine age. They did little with them in World War I and slightly more in World War II. In the Stalin era, submarines and the navy as a whole were considered defensive services in terms of national strategy. I recall the look of surprise on the face of a Soviet general in London in 1941, soon after the German attack on Russia, when a navy-conscious Briton asked him if the Red Fleet would send a naval attaché for liaison with the Royal Navy. The Russian shook his head in bewilderment, "The navy, the navy," he said through his interpreter, "what have the sailors to do with this war?"

There has been a significant change. Even the timing of the change is important. American naval writers cherish the theory that the Soviet defeat in the Cuban missile crisis of 1962 stimulated the expansion of the Russian surface and submarine fleets. There is little objective evidence to support this idea. On the contrary, there are indications that the Soviets began to rethink their general naval strategy, especially the role of the submarine, shortly after Joseph Stalin's death in 1953. Their reverse in Cuba undoubtedly influenced those in the Politburo who urged that the Soviet Union could not play the role of a world power without an adequate navy.

The Russians have always been interested in submarines, although until the middle of this century their industrial base was too small to enable them to build extensively. In the 19th Century, tsarist Russia produced a series of theorists and inventors: Spiridonov, Alexandrovski, Dzhevetski and Bubnov. But the corrupt and inefficient imperial governments paid little attention to their work except in times of national peril. The basic approach to the submarine as an instrument of war by both inventors and officials was defensive; they sought a cheap, efficient weapon that could guard Russia's long coasts against the numerically superior navies of potential enemies.

F.V. Bubnov gave the Russians their first true submarine. He was an intelligent and industrious shipbuilder and, apparently, a first-class engineer. In 1903, he launched a research submarine, the

Dol'fin, powered by an internal combustion engine for surface use and an electric motor for underwater power. Although successful by the standards of the day, the *Dol'fin* did not suffice. In the Far East, the Japanese and Russian empires were moving toward war, and the navy ministry in St. Petersburg turned to the United States for submarines. Several designed by Simon Lake were purchased between 1904 and 1907. One, the *Protector,* was renamed *Osetr* and commissioned in the imperial navy. In all, 16 submarines were bought abroad while Russian yards produced eight.

Ironically Russian interest in submarines gave the growing German industry a boost. The first submarine order ever given the Krupp-Germania yards at Kiel came from the Russian government. The result was a 16-ton submarine, the *Forel,* built in 1902. Three more of the Karp class were purchased in 1904.

The crushing defeats sustained by the imperial navy in the war with Japan stimulated submarine construction. The Russians needed a combat vessel that could be built in a relatively short time and that would give them some means of countering the growing strength of the Imperial German Navy in the Baltic. By 1912, Baltic shipyards were turning out a number of reasonably effective boats of the Bars class, and designers were indulging themselves in the universal national penchant of "thinking big." By 1912, the Russians had plans for a submarine-cruiser of 4500 tons, with a speed of 14 knots submerged and an armament of two 4.7-inch guns, 36 torpedo tubes, 60 torpedoes and 120 mines.

Communist propaganda has conditioned us to think of imperial Russia as a totally inefficient despotism. The tsars' political views were certainly disastrous and the regimes corrupt, but there was no lack of imagination and energy among Russia's engineers, few in number though they were. It was a Russian engineer who first hit upon the idea of using modern submarines to lay mines. As was usual, he got little help from the imperial authorities, but he persevered, and in 1908 the keel of the world's first submarine minelayer was laid. She was named *Kreb,* and her exploits in World War I are one of the few bright passages in the melancholy history of the Russian navy in that conflict. Twice she penetrated the Bosporus to lay more than 120 mines that sunk many Turkish ships.

But the overall picture was disappointing. The Russians had 28 submarines in August 1914, but only four were operational and these were deployed in the Baltic Sea for defensive purposes. They did little, and the German fleet steamed about almost at will until the British sent five boats into the Baltic in 1915. After the October Revolution of 1917, Russia's new masters bestirred themselves to overhaul and man some of the submarines. They had one success. They sank the British cruiser HMS *Victoria* during the period of Allied intervention in the civil war. Elsewhere, the Allies destroyed 13 Soviet submarines in the Black Sea and four in the Baltic.

Soviet submarine construction between the wars leaned heavily on foreign designs. The Dekabrist class, which appeared in the early Thirties, was made up of oceangoing boats copied from contemporary Italian submarines. The Leninetz boats were based on the British L class, one of which had been sunk off Kronstadt in 1919. The Russians raised her in 1928 and used her as a model for their Leninetz class, the most successful submarines they had at that time, which tells us a good deal about early Soviet submarine construction.

The rise of Hitler in Germany stimulated Russian submarine construction. Again the emphasis was on the defensive. The Russians needed a lot of submarines in a hurry for coastal patrols, so in the M class they tried mass production. Sections of the submarines were built at inland factories and then shipped to ports where the boats were assembled. But mass production remained a dream. Industrial resources, both engineers and matériel, were required for tanks and guns. The Red Army was the dominant service. The M class boats did well when the war began, but there were never enough of them.

Two larger classes appeared before the war. The oceangoing S class was copied after the elderly German 1-A boats. These had a curious history. To circumvent the Versailles treaty's prohibition on German submarines, the Nazis had had the 1-A designed in the Netherlands and had her built in Spanish shipyards under German direction. How the Russians got the plans is not known, but the available evidence points to a brilliant piece of espionage.

The final prewar boat was the K class, which appeared in 1936. These were oceangoing and were able to dive rapidly.

Those who are impressed by the present strength of the Soviet undersea fleet should keep in mind that at the outbreak of the war in 1939, the Soviet Union's submarine force of nearly 200 boats was the largest in the world. It was followed by the Italian fleet, 98; the United States, 96; France, 79; Britain, 62; Japan, 60; Germany, 45. By June 21, 1941, when the Germans invaded the Soviet Union, the Russians had 276 submarines in commission: 76 in the Baltic, 45 in the Arctic, 68 in the Black Sea and 87 in the Far East.

Despite its numerical strength and the undoubted valor of its crews, the Red Navy made a mess of its submarine operations in World War II. Commanders were forbidden to use initiative. Rigid operational rules were laid down by shore headquarters and there was no attempt by these headquarters to coordinate submarine operations. The usual method was to assign a specific sea area to a submarine and forbid the commander to move beyond it.

Of course, the Red Navy was operating under great handicaps. The German advances on the northern front in 1941 and 1942 had penned most Russian submarines and surface ships in the Gulf of Finland. Not until the Soviet armies began their long advance westward in 1943 did the submarines have their chance. When it came, they made the most of it. As an example, in January 1945, Soviet submarines sank three steamers laden with refugees from the eastern Baltic, the *Wilhelm Gustlov, General Steuben* and *Goya*. The loss of life was estimated at approximately 15,000; the highest toll ever exacted in a single submarine operation.

Russian losses were very heavy compared with the meager results. Soviet submarines sank 128 warships and merchant ships in the Baltic, Arctic and Black seas with a loss of 110 boats; a much higher ratio of losses to sinkings than that of the German navy.

At the end of the Second World War, the Soviets had about 190 submarines, including three British boats transferred to them in 1944. They also received 17 German and two Italian craft as war booty. However, Russian conquests in Germany yielded far more valuable loot. In the shipyards and factories occupied in eastern Germany, the Russians captured large amounts of matériel connected with submarine construction and, perhaps more important, hundreds of scientists, engineers and technicians engaged in the German submarine-building program. For example, in the Schichau yard at Danzig, the Soviets took over six of the new German Type XXI boats that were nearing completion there. These the Soviets finished with German help.

Indeed, the first postwar Soviet submarines, the W class, bore a marked resemblence to the Type XXI. This class was followed by a slightly larger boat, the Z class, built for ocean warfare.

The decision to expand the Soviet navy was made in the late Fifties, probably after long and serious study and heated debate. Since the end of World War II, the Russian military establishment had been dominated by the triumphant army and, to a lesser extent, by the Strategic Nuclear Forces. We can guess who led the fight for sea power: Admiral of the Fleet of the Soviet Union Sergei G. Gorshkov.

To build a major navy, to go farther and build the largest submarine fleet in the world, to envisage the use of surface warships and submarines in the projection of power across the world was an industrial and intellectual challenge the Soviet system proved able to meet. To some extent, the Russians were reversing the trends of a century. They not only were taking on, on its own ground—or water —the United States, the most formidable naval power in the world, but they also were altering their own centuries-old national strategic attitude.

"The Russians," Winston Churchill told the House of Commons at one point in World War II, "are land animals." For the Russians, military danger and military victory have always been associated with invasion by land—from Germany and Poland in the west, from the wastes of Central Asia and China in the southeast and east. The Crimean War, largely an Anglo-French seaborne operation in the Black Sea, was not a major invasion by sea but a curious revival of the 18th-Century strategy in which the enemy's pawn, in that case, Sevastopol, was seized as part of a leisurely military chess game.

There is some evidence that many Russian leaders, civilian and military, considered a major naval expansion program both wasteful and unnecessary. Vast armies protected the motherland on the west and east against the Americans and the NATO allies and the Chinese. The coming generation of long-range ballistic missiles would suffice to convey military power. The northern seas were icebound most of the year. The approaches through the Baltic were protected by existing Soviet squadrons and by those of the Polish and East German navies. None of these arguments affected the final decision. The Soviet Union plunged into the program of naval building that has made it the second naval power in the world, and in some categories of ships, the first.

If we do not know how the decision was taken, it is pretty clear from Soviet military writings why it was taken. Simply put, the Russians had to have a means of keeping American fleets, particularly the aircraft carriers and their nuclear strike planes and the missile-armed submarines, away from waters where their presence endangered targets within the USSR. The Russians could not prevent American squadrons from venturing into the eastern Mediterranean or the Norwegian or Arabian seas. They could, however, build enough submarines and surface combatants to cope with American vessels in the event of a war. This was another aspect of the expansion of Russian interests.

As Norman Polmar puts it, "The postwar Soviet navy evolved in this atmosphere of opportunity and uncertainty. The primary mission would still be defense of the Soviet state; but in a period of expansion (actual and potential), Soviet interests encompassed lands and seas far from the borders of the Soviet Union. . . . Defense of the Soviet Union—whatever its boundaries—now meant the ability to intercept U.S. warships, troopships and freighters that would try to reinforce the land battle in Europe or possibly the Middle East, or conceivably even in Asia, when and if the United States and the Soviet Union clashed."

To a limited extent, Stalin, too, had believed in the projection of Soviet sea power. But he saw the process almost entirely in terms of surface ships like the powerful Sverdlov class cruisers, not in submarines. So far as the latter were concerned, Stalin regarded them as useful chiefly for coastal defense, in conjunction with bombers and torpedo boats. This was in keeping with the defensive mentality of the Soviet Union in the prewar period. Stalin was the quintessence of the Russian "land animal." To Russian leaders of his generation, the objective was to insure security against invasion by land.

The most effective of Russian despots died in 1953. The change in the Soviet appreciation of naval power, particularly the submarine, came soon after. The doctrinal expression of the new strategy was outlined in Marshal V.D. Sokolovsky's *Military Strategy*, first published in 1962 and since rewritten and brought up to date by a group of eminent soldiers and sailors. As might be expected, the role of the army is emphasized in the book. But the first glimmering of a new naval strategy comes through.

The navy, according to Sokolovsky, will have a greater scope and a more important role in any future war than it did in World War II. But the marshal noted in 1962 that the fleet "will hardly be decisive for the outcome of the war." It is a reasonable assumption that Soviet thinking has changed since then.

As Sokolovsky saw it:

The main aim of fleet operations in naval theaters is to defeat the enemy's navy and disrupt his maritime communications. In addition, it may be necessary to deliver nuclear missile attacks on coastal targets, carry out joint operations with the ground forces, provide transport and protect one's own sea communications. . . . Nuclear submarines and naval aircraft armed with missiles will make *decisive* [author's italics] naval operations possible against a powerful maritime enemy.

Two obvious comments: The Russians, except when they are making propaganda, do not use words like "decisive" loosely. Second, there can be no doubt of the identity of the "powerful maritime enemy." It is the United States. Who else?

And how does the Soviet fleet deal with this enemy? Sokolovsky spells it out.

Like every Soviet strategist since the establishment of NATO, Sokolovsky is concerned with two elements in the West's plans for a European war arising from Russian aggression: the striking power of American aircraft carriers and American resupply and reinforcement of allied forces on the continent. According to *Military Strategy:*

From the outset, one of our navy's most important tasks will be to destroy the enemy carrier strike forces. The enemy will attempt to deploy these formations in the most important theaters near Socialist countries so as to deliver surprise nuclear strikes on major coastal targets (naval bases, airfields and missile sites) and, possibly, on targets much further inland. . . . In the center of such formations will be the attack carriers, which represent the main, *and extremely vulnerable* [author's italics], target for nuclear missile and torpedo attacks. The carriers are protected by antisubmarine surface ships and antisubmarine aircraft. Radar pickets will be deployed on the perimeter of the area. But these forces can no longer be relied upon to protect the attack carriers from missile strikes launched by submarines and naval aircraft.

The presence in our fleet of submarines and aircraft equipped with missiles allows them to engage the carrier without entering the task force's antisubmarine and air defense zone. It is essential to attempt to destroy the attack carriers before they launch their aircraft; we must destroy the protective forces, the auxiliaries and the carrier bases. It should be remembered that these forces are extremely vulnerable on passage, during refueling operations and during the launch and recovery of other aircraft. . . . The attack carrier is an extremely vulnerable target for nuclear strike.

The direction in which Soviet naval doctrine is moving is reflected in the next passage:

An effective means of combating attack carriers and other surface forces is the nuclear-powered nuclear submarine. . . . New methods of submarine operations have come to replace the former methods of torpedo attack from short distances—missile strikes from great distances and from submerged positions. Previously it was necessary to concentrate several submarines for a mass torpedo attack to destroy a surface ship. Now *any surface ship* [author's italics] can be destroyed with a single missile or torpedo with a nuclear warhead.

There are other Russian approaches to the carrier problem. But the Sokolovsky doctrine appears to be the principal basis for contemporary Soviet tactics.

It also seems to American intelligence analysts to underlie Soviet thinking on tactics to be used against an American reinforcement of Europe in a general war.

One of the navy's main tasks in a future war will be to sever the enemy's ocean and sea transport routes and to disrupt his communications. We should remember that up to three-quarters of the possible enemy's resources of men and material are on *the other side of the ocean* [author's italics]. According to the calculation of certain military theoreticians 80 to 100 large transports would arrive daily in European ports in the event of war and 1500 to 2000 ships, excluding escorts, would be at sea at any one time.

What are the weapons to be used against this enormous supply and reinforcement effort? Sokolovsky mentions the Strategic Rocket Forces and the Long-Range Air Force, but he appears to put his faith in "nuclear-powered missile submarines" directed "against naval bases and ports, against channels and narrow inlets, shipbuilding and ship repair yards; by destroying convoys and transports at sea using submarines and aircraft.

The mobile use of nuclear submarines, insuring the maximum concentration of effort against enemy communications within a limited time, will be of great significance in this context. Diesel-electric submarines, which obviously will still be used in operations against enemy communications, can be deployed as mobile screens, in systematic operations or in free search.

With one important exception, Marshal Sokolovsky's work represents the elemental Russian approach to American sea power. When he compiled his data, the first American Polaris submarine, the USS *George Washington,* had joined the fleet only recently. The Soviets reacted with a radical change in naval emphasis. As we have seen, this was not the first instance in which a new underwater weapons system had forced an adversary to alter his priorities.

In the Sixties, the navies of the two superpowers entered a complex rivalry. The Russians' concentration on submarines as a means of knocking out American carrier forces and cutting the North Atlantic reinforcement route had to be considered in conjunction with a new tactical problem, the suppression of the Polaris submarines.

The solution to this problem will and already has involved a great expenditure of money and effort on antisubmarine warfare. More than that, the Soviets have been forced to alter their naval deployments. The presence, suspected or actual, of American nuclear missile submarines in the Arabian Sea at the northwest corner of the Indian Ocean forced the Soviet naval high command to establish a squadron in the Indian Ocean. The makeup of that squadron varies from eight to ten surface combatants. It reflects Soviet preoccupation with submarines, for its composition is basically that of an antisubmarine force. The Russians have made it clear to their friends in the area, primarily India, that they are concerned that in the event of war, American nuclear missile boats in the western Indian Ocean would be able to destroy the industrial area in the Donets Basin and the naval bases at Sevastopol and elsewhere that maintain the Black Sea fleet and its offspring, the Russian squadron in the Mediterranean Sea. Obviously this is a Soviet strategic interest. But the size of the Russian submarine fleet is such that it must be regarded as a definite threat to the seaborne commerce of the West. About 90 percent of the world's merchant shipping is operated by western countries, while the Soviet Union possesses about 60 percent of the submarines built for antishipping operations. The Soviet fleet had been long on numbers but short on quality at the outbreak of World War II. German, British, Japanese and American submarines on the whole had better sea-keeping qualities and longer ranges.

The expansion of the submarine force began in the early Fifties with the Z class boats, 18 of which were built at the Sudomekh yard in Leningrad. It was the start of the most formidable submarine fleet in history, one far exceeding in numbers and power that of the Germans in 1939–1945. During the decade, more than 150 of the W class, also known by the NATO designation of Whiskey class, were launched. These were long-range, medium-sized boats, many of which were employed as experimental weapons platforms. The early Soviet cruise missiles were installed on some. These were emplaced in tanks behind the boat's fin or mounted into the boat. Compared with the attack submarines then being developed by the United States, they were not particularly impressive. They had a submerged speed of 15 knots and a surface speed of 17 knots. The largest Soviet diesel-powered attack submarine of this period was the F class (Foxtrot) of 45 boats displacing 2000 tons on the surface and fitted with eight torpedo tubes.

The Russians accelerated their development of the cruise missile as a submarine weapon and as an answer to the strike aircraft aboard American carriers. The missiles were mounted in two types of the E class, Echo I and Echo II. The former are nuclear-propelled submarines with a surface displacement of 4000 tons. They are armed with six Shaddock SS-N-3 cruise missiles. These missiles have a range of 450 miles and, when nuclear armed, a warhead yield in the kiloton range, or 1000 tons of TNT. Echo II was a larger boat, 4500 tons and 390 feet long, armed with eight tubes for Shaddock missiles.

The Russians were watching American submarine improvements very carefully. They knew the United States had developed and then discarded its own cruise missile. They were aware that the Americans still held the lead in constructing long-range ballistic missiles. The Russians' first move into the field came in the early Sixties with the deployment of 25 G, or Golf, class submarines. These are propelled by diesel engines, not by nuclear power plants; but they are armed with three Serb (SS-N-5) ballistic missiles with a range of approximately 650 nautical miles. The Golfs are not as large as the Echo IIs, only 2350 tons, and their role in the expansion of the submarine fleet is that of an intermediate boat.

The next step took the Russians into the nuclear-powered, nuclear-armed submarine in the form of the Hotel class. Intelligence sources say that about a dozen of these were constructed. They are 360 feet long and have a surface displacement of 4000 tons. Like the Golfs, they are armed with Serb missiles.

Then came the plunge into the Y, or Yankee, class boats, the first Soviet Polaris-type submarine in mass production. The Yankees displace 8000 tons and are 425 feet long. British and American naval intelligence put the production rate in the late Sixties and early Seventies at about eight a year, and the force is now estimated at about 40 boats. The submarines are armed with 16 tubes for SS-N-6 Sawfly missiles with a range of 1750 miles and a warhead yield in the megaton (one million tons of TNT) range.

Next came the D (Delta) class boats, each armed with 12 SS-N-8 missiles with a range given by NATO intelligence of 4600 miles, the greatest of any contemporary submarine-borne missile.

In early 1976, the Soviet submarine ballistic missile fleet comprised approximately 75 boats armed with 784 ballistic missiles, an increase of 92 over 1974. Intelligence estimates are that the Soviets build between six and eight of these boats a year, although some put the number at eight to ten. If we accept the lower figure, the assumption must be that the Russians will have 62 or more modern nuclear-powered, ballistic missile submarines on active duty by early 1977, scrapping or mothballing some of their older boats. In addition, a new version of the Sawfly is believed to be under test for eventual installation in the Y class, and the SS-N-13 missile with a range of 4000 miles is known to be under development.

The Soviets' submarine threat does not rest only on their ballistic missile boats. In a non-nuclear conflict, which the Russians might prefer in view of their growing preponderance of man power and conventional weapons, Soviet attack boats armed with torpedoes and cruise missile submarines would pose a serious threat to American battle fleets and seaborne commerce.

The Russians have 170 attack submarines, including 30 that are nuclear-powered. These include the V class, the Foxtrots and the Charlies, or C class. The Charlies are big, 4500 tons surface displacement, and are armed with torpedo tubes and eight underwater-launched SS-N-7 missiles with an estimated range of 25 to 30 nautical miles. The Charlies' mission, apparently, is to deal with the protecting screen around American carriers.

There are also 66 submarines armed with cruise missiles. Of these, 41 are nuclear-powered, including ten Charlies, and 25 are powered by diesel engines.

The deployment of this massive submarine force implemented by ballistic missiles, cruise missiles and torpedoes is a major factor in the naval balance of power, and its potential effect on American and NATO naval strategy will be examined later. The magnitude of the threat is expressed by a simple comparison: The Soviet Union today has more attack boats in the Mediterranean than the German navy deployed around the world at the start of World War II.

The non-Communist powers that depend on overseas imports —a group that includes the United States, its allies in western Europe and Japan—face an unprecedented situation, one that most Americans have scarcely realized. They can no longer take comfort in the thought, never entirely true, that the United States is self-sufficient. The navy estimates there are no less than 16 essential raw materials imported into this country from overseas. Considering the strength of the Soviet undersea fleet, realists must expect that the continued import of these materials in war would be hazardous and uncertain, perhaps impossible. In two world conflicts a much smaller number of German submarines came very close to breaking Britain, the geographical heart of the Allied war effort in the West. In a third world conflagration, the Russians with their much stronger fleet are likely to turn a similar strategy against the United States, their chief adversary.

One steaming August day in 1970 an oddly assorted Soviet flotilla entered the Cuban port of Cienfuegos on the island's southern coast. In addition to a conventional surface warship, the flotilla included a submarine tender, but no submarines, a seagoing tug and two barges of the type usually used to service nuclear-powered submarines.

The arrival of the barges and the subsequent appearance at Cienfuegos and other Cuban ports of Russian submarines classed as strategic nuclear weapons systems exemplifies the use of sea power, particularly submarines, by the Soviet Union to project and support foreign policy.

No one can say who ordered the submarines and other war vessels to Cuba. Nor is it possible to identify the specific policy objectives of these visits. But they cast a curious light on détente, or rather, on Moscow's interpretation of that word, and they tell us something about the Russians' attitude toward understandings with the United States.

A constant factor in this examination of Soviet policy as projected through the use of submarines is that the barges, built to dispose of the effluents from nuclear power plants, remain at Cienfuegos. The arrival of the nuclear submarine and the tender gave the Soviets a nuclear presence in the Caribbean. The Russians have also constructed shore facilities, including barracks and a water tower.

The pier has been rebuilt and moorings laid for submarines and tenders.

The Nixon and Ford administrations both believed that Soviet plans to use Cienfuegos for ballistic missile submarines had been put aside as the result of American protests in the autumn of 1970. They found consolation in a statement in *Izvestia* denying that the Soviet Union had built or intended to build such an installation. Officials reported that an "understanding" had been reached with the Russians over the basing of naval vessels in Cuba. But the wording of this understanding remains secret, although the American objective is clear enough.

Any understanding must be a reaffirmation of the United States's position taken in the 1963 agreement between President John F. Kennedy and Soviet Party Chairman Nikita Khrushchev, which dealt with the deployment of Russian ballistic missiles in Cuba. After the discovery of the two barges at Cienfuegos, a White House source declared that "the Soviet Union can be under no doubt that we would view the establishment of a strategic base in the Caribbean with the utmost seriousness" and quoted Mr. Kennedy's statement of November 2, 1962, "If all offensive weapons are removed from Cuba and kept out of the hemisphere in the future . . . there will be peace in the Caribbean." In January 1971, President Richard M. Nixon, possibly intending to clarify the situation, muddied it still further. He said that "in the event that nuclear subs were serviced either in Cuba or from Cuba, that would be a violation of the understanding. That has not happened yet."

Taken together, these statements are evidence that in the view of the United States there is an understanding. But Mr. Nixon's mention of "nuclear subs" makes it a rather cloudy one, lacking that definition that is the core of successful diplomacy.

The Russians were provided with an opportunity to test the United States. They did not delay long. On April 29, 1972, a date perhaps chosen because of the United States's deep involvement in North Vietnam's Easter offensive, a Golf class submarine and a tender put in at Bahia de Nipe. What better way to test Mr. Nixon? Golf class submarines are diesel-powered. So the visit did not come within the compass of the understanding as seen by Mr. Nixon. But Golf class boats carry three ballistic missiles with nuclear warheads, missiles that are generally believed to be designed for employment against land targets. So although the submarine was not a "nuclear sub" it *was* a strategic weapons system.

The Golf's visit was the most blatant in a series of Soviet movements in defiance of the understanding. Previously, in the summer of 1969 and in May 1970 Foxtrot, Echo II and November class submarines had been deployed in the Caribbean. The November class boats are nuclear-powered attack submarines armed with torpedoes. They joined the Soviet fleet between 1958 and 1963. Since the understanding, the Russians have sent a nuclear-powered attack submarine with a tender and a nuclear-powered submarine with cruise missiles and a tender into Cienfuegos, and a diesel-powered ballistic missile submarine and a diesel-powered strategic missile submarine into Havana.

The American inference must be that the Soviet navy places a very high value on the use of Cuba as a base for strategic weapons. The evidence is that there has been a steady escalation in the type of submarines sent there. It is interesting to speculate that the next step may be the deployment to Cuba of Yankee class strategic submarines, if the United States does no more than protest.

The advantages of a Cuban base to the Russians are obvious. The strategic submarines at Cienfuegos or elsewhere on the island would be much closer to their duty stations off the U.S. East Coast. With adequate maintenance and replenishment facilities, the submarines would be able to remain in the western hemisphere for extended periods, avoiding the long voyage to and from their bases in the Murmansk area of the Kola Peninsula, which brings them through the gaps between Britain, Greenland and Iceland, where they are vulnerable to detection by NATO's submarines, surface ships and aircraft.

Strategic nuclear submarines, however, are only one weapon of the many involved in the silent jockeying for advantageous position that goes on day in and day out between the superpowers and their allies. Attack submarines based in Cuba would be closer to their obvious targets, the aircraft carriers based at Mayport, Florida, and Norfolk, Virginia, and the strategic submarines operating from Charleston, South Carolina.

These are the military implications. But what does the ongoing Soviet use of Cienfuegos, Havana and other ports tell us about the Russian attitude toward détente? One can argue that this attitude is selective both as to time and to geography; that détente in Moscow's view applies only to Northwest Europe for a period that will be fixed by the Politburo.

To probe the limits of détente as it is understood by Americans, the Soviets have chosen the most powerful and flexible of all weapons, the submarine. If they establish a strategic nuclear base at Cienfuegos, as they have shown they are capable of doing, they will offset the advantages of United States bases at Holy Loch in Scotland and Rota in Spain.

Much has been made of the expansion of the Soviet surface fleet. Its missile-firing destroyers and cruisers are a clear threat to the American naval strategy built around carrier task forces. But it is arguable that this threat pales in comparison with that posed by the Soviet submarine force. The submarine flying the Red Flag, deployed either as a platform for ballistic missiles or as a menace to American warships and commerce, has developed into the single most potent element in the vast Russian arsenal. The submarine, in short, has reasserted its position as the key factor in war and as the most essential ingredient in any serious agreement on nuclear disarmament between the two superpowers. At present, the scenarios for the submarine's use in war are horrible.

7

The submarine's maximum impact upon man has been as a weapon of war. The major motivation behind its development and improvement has been military. But from the first inventors onward (Lake is an example), men were also driven by the concept that the submarine would permit them to explore the vast and mysterious world beneath the sea; to study at close hand the creatures of the deep, the source of so much of the world's folklore; to search for archaeological treasures and Spanish doubloons; to map the valleys and mountain ranges that they dimly perceived must run across the nether of the marine world.

The sea bottom was not a desirable neighborhood for the first submariners. To them, it was something to be avoided, an unknown country from whose bourn few travelers returned. Only when under attack by depth charges did they seek the sea floor, to wait until the crash of explosions ceased. And they did this with extreme trepidation and in extreme danger because of the effect of water pressure on the rather primitive construction materials of their craft.

They understood that the lower levels were dangerous for other reasons. The charts that guided them were often wildly and understandably inaccurate. Until the beginning of the 20th Century, the depths were of little interest to seamen. They learned through frequent tragedies that some areas were sewn with the wreckage of ships, some sunk deliberately to guard the entrances to naval bases. Prien, it will be remembered, bumped an underwater obstacle on his way into Scapa Flow.

But above all, there was that inexorable element of water pressure. At 3500 feet, a depth these pioneer submariners reached only when they were dead, the pressure on a hull is 1500 pounds to the square inch. Hulls early in this century could not stand such pressure. And neither the machinery nor the instruments for navigation at extreme depth had been built, although by the late Thirties scientists perceived that they could be fabricated. So the great underwater world waited—unexplored.

The middle Sixties accelerated change. There was a rapid expansion of undersea research and exploration around the world. The sea floor was popularized as "the last frontier." The Sunday supplements provided graphic and often highly inexact reports on the riches below the waves and the ingenious methods by which man would tap them. Congress and President Lyndon B. Johnson were equally enthusiastic about the plunge into "inner space," which was defined by scientists as the vast depths below the diving limits of existing submarines. Proponents of the study of inner space called for a program to match the space program.

Behind this movement lay both scientific curiosity and economic factors. The scientists wanted to learn more about the oceans' floors, their geography, inhabitants, currents, salinity. The businessmen, the more prescient of whom already were foreseeing the gradual depletion of natural resources on land, were thinking of the seas' reserves. The estimate in 1965 was that there was probably more oil deposited underwater than on land; an estimate not yet disproved. In addition, it was known that the ocean floor contained copper, cobalt, manganese and nickel, all metals of great importance to modern industrial countries. The government estimated that 220 million tons of fish—half the world's protein intake—could be harvested every year.

Much of the momentum for the American effort eroded during the bitter last years of the Johnson Administration, when the nation became more and more preoccupied with the Vietnam war and the civil strife it had aroused. But enough interest had been generated, enough money appropriated, to begin the exploration of inner space.

Part of their development at least had been stimulated by submarine disasters, which will be discussed later. The nuclear submarine USS *Thresher* was lost in 1963, and in 1964 the navy began to plan both a submarine research vessel that would descend to 20,000 feet and a special rescue submarine. This marked a tremendous advance over Jacques-Yves Cousteau's water-jet-propelled Diving Saucer that was capable of exploration down to 1000 feet. The navy already had purchased and put into operation the *Trieste* bathyscaphe. It had descended to the deepest known spot in the ocean— the Marianas Trench, 36,000 feet down in the Pacific—with Dr. Auguste Piccard, the Swiss oceanographer, and Lt. Don Walsh, USN, aboard.

By 1965, five nations—the United States, Japan, France, Switzerland and the Soviet Union—had 21 submarine vehicles built for basic or applied research, naval or commercial purposes in operation or under test. The majority were American.

These were submarines of a new type that were able to drop into the deepest canyons of the ocean floor or creep along continental shelves. Water jets, rotatable propellers and other innovations moved them along the bottom. Their hulls might be of fiberglass, aluminum or steel. They used mercury or shot for ballast, gasoline or hexane gas for buoyancy.

The years 1960–1965 were the pioneer days of oceanography

and deep-water engineering, and a tremendous amount was accomplished. The depths were examined and charted. Statistics on temperature, salinity and currents were assembled to provide an accurate picture of the seas. Petroleum and other mineral resources were discovered. The results encouraged further exploration and the design and development of newer vehicles for undersea exploration.

From the standpoint of submariners, military and civilian, perhaps the most significant of these novel vessels was the navy's undersea ambulance launched in 1970. But four years before, the *Star II* and *Star III*, two deep-water research craft, had been launched at New London, and 1964 had seen the launching of the *Aluminaut*, designed to descend 5000 feet and travel underwater for 100 miles. The names of other deep-water craft appeared in technical journals, the *Ben Franklin*, the *Alvin*, the *Asherah*, designed for archaeological research; even a yellow, fiberglass boat intended to search the murky depths of Loch Ness in Scotland for the resident monster.

The exploration effort was productive, but in the United States it was rather confusing because of the number of organizations involved. Although the navy spent the most, other government agencies also entered the field: the Coast and Geodetic Survey, the Bureau of Mines, the Bureau of Fisheries, the Coast Guard, the Army Corps of Engineers, the National Science Foundation, the Atomic Energy Commission. The scientists, interested in pure research, were jostled increasingly by the engineers and the businessmen, who were anxious to apply the fruits of the scientists' research. Great corporations directed their talents toward ocean engineering. In 1969, the General Dynamics Corporation proposed the building of a fleet of nuclear-powered submarine tankers to move the oil deposits of Arctic Alaska to the population centers of the East and West coasts. The *Aluminaut*, operated by the Reynolds Submarine Service Corporation, a subsidiary of Reynolds Metal Company, brought up a 198-pound slab of manganese from an undersea "road" of the metal discovered off the coasts of Florida, Georgia and South Carolina.

The *Aluminaut* and the *Alvin* figured in one of the most spectacular exploits of the new deep-sea technology. On January 17, 1966, an air force B-52 bomber collided with a KC-135 jet tanker during refueling operations over the coast of southern Spain. Four unarmed hydrogen bombs were lost in the crash. Three were recovered along the coast near Palomares and the fourth was believed to be in the sea off Almería Province.

The incident made a great noise in the world. Communist propaganda gave America's allies the impression that they could expect a rain of such weapons if the United States continued to base nuclear bombers and their payloads in Europe. Grave conclaves of scientists, editors and politicians deplored American carelessness. The usual "authoritative sources" were paraded before television cameras and across the front pages of newspapers to depict what would happen if an errant bomb went off.

The first American answer was to ship the *Aluminaut* to Spain. Launched in September 1964, she was the most impressive of the early explorers, capable of diving deeper than any other vehicle in the world. She was the brainchild of Louis Reynolds, chairman of the board of Reynolds Metals, a man who foresaw many "fascinating facets for her use," including salvage and possibly "drilling oil from the bottom" and other forms of underwater mining. In published interviews, he mentioned that there were manganese nodules on the floor of the Pacific worth $1.4 million a square mile.

General Dynamics had built the *Aluminaut*. When turned over to the navy, she weighed 75 tons, was 50 feet long, had a hull six and a half inches thick and carried a crew of three. Her true diving capabilities have never been published. The navy's cautious statement at her launch was that the depth would be in excess of 400 feet. The vessel's cruising speed was 3.8 knots and she had a range of about 80 miles. Her equipment included underwater television, lights and mechanical devices to retrieve samples from the ocean bottom.

The *Aluminaut* was loaded onto a landing ship dock (LSD) and sent to the western Mediterranean. She was followed by another deep-water boat, the *Alvin*, aptly described by John C. Devlin, an engineer, as resembling a chewed-off cigar surmounted by a helmet. The *Alvin* was named for Allyn Vine, chief scientist at the Woods Hole (Massachusetts) Oceanographic Institution. The first un-manned tests sent her down to 7000 feet at the end of a cable; so with or without a crew of two or three, she was capable of diving more than a mile. Her most interesting piece of equipment was an eight-foot outboard metal arm that was powered by six electric motors and was more flexible than the human arm. The navy boasted that the arm, whose wrist could rotate 360 degrees either clockwise or coun-terclockwise, could tie a square knot more easily than could a Boy Scout.

The *Aluminaut* and *Alvin*, a combination that to the irreverent sounded like the name of a vaudeville magic act, proved their value, but only after ten weeks of effort by Task Force 65, a naval organiza-tion of 14 ships and 2500 men.

The five-ton bomb, swathed in a parachute, lay in a 2800-foot-deep sea canyon. By March 24, the crews of the *Aluminaut* and *Alvin* were close to success. They had been frustrated for four days by choppy seas that stirred the bottom enough to obscure the bomb. Finally, the *Alvin*'s mechanical arm got a line around the bomb. The crews worked with deliberation. The first time the arm had touched the bomb, it had slid 25 feet down a steep incline to the lip of a gorge 500 feet deeper. The navy feared it would be impossible to extract the weapon from this chasm.

With the line around the bomb, the *Alvin* tugged gently, and the bomb was moved up a few feet toward a plateau some 450 feet nearer the surface, where it would be almost safe.

Then the line snapped. Accustomed to such reverses, the navy took this one in stride. The work went on. Two other midget subma-rines were added to the task force and the weapon eventually was recovered.

Two footnotes on the *Alvin*. A year later, on the rather routine duty of exploring the continental shelf off the East Coast, she encoun-tered a mishap. When the submarine was being raised to her mother ship, her arm broke off and dropped to the ocean floor in 4000 feet of water.

The tender and the research vessel *Gosnold* pinpointed the location. Then a transponder—an instrument that gives pilots a range and bearing from a fixed point—was placed on the bottom. Beacons and other sensory devices were arranged in the vicinity to provide reference points so the area could be mapped by sonar.

Once this was done, a grid was made of a two-by-one-mile region of rolling hills on the ocean floor. Enter the *Alvin* with its sonar that could locate metal objects on the bottom that could be examined by its crew. The problem was that the *Alvin*'s sonar was too sensitive. During the first two dives, it found a lot of gallon gasoline cans and plenty of smaller ones. On the third submergence, however, the missing arm was pinpointed. The *Alvin* demonstrated her versatility by picking it up with a hook fastened to her bow. The submarine's pilot maneuvered to grasp the arm and then surfaced. There, swimmers attached lines to the errant limb and the *Alvin* dropped back to the ocean floor nearly a mile below to continue her scientific work.

The *Alvin* had a near-fatal accident in 1968 when a cable between her and her mother ship, *Lulu*, snapped during a launching operation about 120 miles south of Cape Cod. With her hatch open, the *Alvin* filled with water and sank. Steps to recover her were begun immediately. The *Alvin* was salvaged by the oceanographic research ship *Mizar* and, after repairs, rejoined the fleet.

No lives were lost, but other submarine researchers were not so fortunate. On June 18, 1968, four men were trapped in the tiny *Johnson-Sea-Link* when it was caught in the wreck of the navy destroyer *Fred T. Berry*, which had been scuttled off Key West, Florida, in 1971 as part of an artificial reef. Two of the men, sealed in the small rear compartment of the minisubmarine, died. The others, who occupied the separate forward compartment of the 23-foot vessel, were recovered alive and in good health 31 hours after the boat had become entangled in cables hanging from the *Berry*'s superstructure 60 fathoms down.

The fate of the *Sea-Link* illustrates the hazards of submarine exploratory work and the "unknown unknowns" that lie in wait. Initial rescue attempts were balked by the swift current of the Gulf Stream, a factor that appears not to have been given sufficient weight by the rescuers. The *Sea-Link*'s mission had been routine: to explore the wreck of the *Berry* on American Shoals and to collect fish traps set on a previous dive. There was no atmosphere of risk; the dive was a relatively shallow one for the nine-ton *Sea-Link*, which was box-shaped, with a transparent bubble and stacks of gas cylinders attached to her hull. These appendages might have contributed to her mishap. Archibald Menzies, the pilot and commander, was steering the *Sea-Link* through the murky underwater eddies of the Gulf Stream, which at that point flows at an average surface rate of five knots an hour at that point. He was attempting to clear the *Berry*'s rusting hulk when the *Sea-Link* became ensnared in the cables, which held against the power of the small submarine's six electric engines.

The crews on the *Sea-Link* and the surface tender decided to wait for navy divers to come from Key West to free the boat. The divers, using a diving bell flown from San Diego, California, failed to clear the cables that held the submarine, and time began to run out for E. Clayton Link and Albert Stover, the two oceanographers in the aft compartment. The men in the forward section were a little better off because they were able to use the portable breathing tanks stored there.

Finally, another rescue vessel arrived from Fort Lauderdale. A grappling hook was secured to the *Sea-Link* with the aid of a remote-control underwater television camera, and the submarine was hauled to the surface.

But it was more than 20 hours before the bodies of Link and Stover could be extricated. This was because of the time it took to gradually decompress the compartment. The medical judgment was that the men were alive but unconscious when the *Sea-Link* reached the surface. The temperature of the aft section had dropped to 40 degrees, the same as that of the surrounding water 360 feet below the surface. The cold adversely affected the baralyme, an ash-soda compound stored in the compartment to absorb the carbon dioxide exhaled by the crew. To activate this substance, the two men apparently increased the air pressure in their compartment gradually, and this raised the temperature slightly and kept them alive for a while. However, by the time they had equalized the pressure with the 360-foot depth, the combination of the cold and the carbon-dioxide buildup left them numb and gasping for air. The *Sea-Link* was not raised until just before five in the afternoon; both men were still alive but unconscious. The compartment was flushed with a combination of oxygen and helium, but it was too late; the men failed to respond.

The cruise of the *Ben Franklin* had a happier outcome. She was a 50-foot, 130-ton research submarine that rode the Gulf Stream for 30 days and 1200 miles from Florida north to the coast of Maine. The Gulf Stream was the *Ben Franklin*'s only means of propulsion for the operation, conceived by Dr. Jacques Piccard, who, on January 23, 1960, had made the deepest undersea voyage up to that date. He called the *Franklin* adventure "Project Gulf Stream Drift."

The motivation for the project was ostensibly scientific. The scientists aboard were to observe and photograph marine life, listen to the noises made by fish and perform experiments in underwater sound that would be impossible in a vessel whose engines might drown out acoustical signals. Dr. Piccard also wanted to learn whether giant squid, said to be 75 feet long, existed in the Gulf Stream. Before his departure, the Swiss oceanographer reported to the impressed media representatives that the remains of a squid, 30 feet long, had been found recently on a Florida beach. This hint of a search for a sea monster was enough to win abundant publicity for the *Ben Franklin*'s venture.

The voyage, or drift, also had some military significance. Experts in antisubmarine detection had reported a "sound-scattering" layer approximately 1000 feet below the surface that deflected sound waves. Scientists guessed that the cause was a layer of tiny sea creatures called plankton, and it was Dr. Piccard's task to locate and examine it.

This submarine marked an advance over other research vessels in that she was more a drifting laboratory than a submarine. She was to make studies of the biology, chemistry and physical properties of the Gulf Stream and was equipped to draw in plankton samples.

The interior of the *Ben Franklin* was rather like a narrow Pullman car. The emergency hatch, the oxygen tank and much of the scientific installations were placed at the back of the long cylinder. A television camera was mounted above the hatch. Moving forward, there were bunks and beyond these a gallery and the pilot's console. Forward were the spherical observation area with eight portholes and the main hatch leading to the conning tower.

Nearly all the equipment was designed to be passive and thus use a minimum of electric power. The submarine's batteries had to run the motors, the scientific instruments and the lights for four weeks. Moisture was removed from the cabin by silica gel placed in cloth bags at various points. The electrically run dehumidifier was to be used only in an emergency.

The *Ben Franklin* was corked when submerged. There was no dumping of waste. Charcoal filters removed smells; and to keep odors at a minimum, no deodorants, shaving lotions, smoking or cooking were allowed. Most of the food was freeze-dried and was prepared with hot water stored in four 50-gallon insulated tanks. The water was to keep hot for four weeks.

When the submarine finished its mission, having heard among other things the whistle of porpoises in the deeps, the crew of six scientists and engineers regarded it as an unqualified success. The scientific information concerning the sound-scattering layer of plankton was promptly classified by the navy, but it is known to have contributed to the ongoing work on the detection of deep-diving submarines. The attention paid to the whistling porpoises and the plankton diverted the public from one other notable aspect of the *Ben Franklin*'s trip: Never before had men been confined in a hostile environment for 30 days without outside supplies.

While research submarines like the *Ben Franklin* and the *Sea-Link* were extending man's knowledge of the ocean floor and ocean currents, the navy had embarked on a difficult and, eventually, highly controversial project. This was the building of a submarine research vessel. By 1970, everyone knew that special submarines could dive deep; in 1968, the research boat *Special Quest* had dived to 8150 feet southwest of San Diego. But the complacent conviction that nuclear submarines were safer than ordinary boats had been shaken by the loss of the *Thresher* and, in 1968, of the USS *Scorpion*. We know now that the Soviets had lost at least one nuclear boat in the Pacific in the late Sixties, and there are reports that a second disappeared in the Indian Ocean early in this decade.

The navy called the new class of submarines deep submergence rescue vehicles (DSRV). The first of them, 50 feet long, was built by the Lockheed Missiles and Space Company of Sunnyvale, California. Its main feature was a computerized guidance and control system that would make rendezvous and docking between two vehicles as precise underwater as in outer space. The system was designed to enable a rescue craft to find and link up with a disabled submarine as deep as 5000 feet, as long as the boat was still intact. Below certain depths, the exact depth is classified, a submarine's hull caves in from the immense water pressure. The failure of the submarine to perform as planned was one of the reasons for the controversy.

The first rescue vehicle consisted of three eight-foot spheres enclosed in a conventionally shaped submarine hull. A crew of two or three occupied the forward sphere, which served as a control station. The two aft spheres were designed as passenger compartments for survivors from disabled submarines.

A bell-like skirt slightly larger than the largest submarine hatch was mounted on the underside of the center sphere. This skirt would link with the hatch of a damaged submarine. When the connection was secure, water would be pumped out of the passage and crewmen could then move between the two boats.

The rescue boat's guidance system, which is the key to its effectiveness, was developed at Massachusetts Institute of Technology on the basis of experience with the guidance and navigation systems of the Apollo moonship. MIT's Instrumentation Laboratory was the prime contractor for both the Apollo navigation system and the guidance apparatus of the new submarine.

The system consists of sensing devices that measure the rescue vessel's speed and direction of movement and a compact 70-pound computer. These are linked to the boat's sonar system, which determines the location and distance of obstacles, the sea floor and the disabled submarine. In theory, MIT believed that the pilot of the rescue craft could maneuver with only an inch or two of error, although the developers explained that docking underwater would be more difficult than docking in space. Pilots in rescue submarines must cope with darkness, pressure, shifting currents and the turbulence stirred by their craft's propellers. Astronauts, on the other hand, operate in the stillness of near-vacuum. Consequently, the rescue submarine's guidance system was designed so that even the most minute changes of the vessel's position and other navigational information would be instantly recorded and displayed in the pilot's position.

The program ran into two kinds of trouble, technical and financial. When completed, the rescue submarine weighed 68,000 pounds or 6000 pounds more than planned. The navy wanted a vehicle that could be carried in a large transport aircraft to a point nearest a disabled submarine. The added weight limited mobility. Then it was found that instead of being able to dive to 5000 feet, as expected, the submarine could go only to 3500 feet. Lockheed explained that this was because there was no way to test the craft's ability to withstand the water pressure at 5000 feet, where it is 2250 pounds per square inch.

Both the navy and Lockheed found the job a great deal more

difficult than they had anticipated. One officer who had been connected with the program commented sourly, "It's easy enough to get support if you're building a research submarine that may turn up a new oil field or a vein of manganese or copper. It's a lot different when you're working on a boat that will save human lives."

Whatever the reason, the navy discovered that there wasn't the industrial base to provide the required components and that it was difficult to interest private industry in the project because of the smallness of the potential market. The service also found costs mounting. When the project was conceived in 1963, it was estimated that it would cost $36.5 million to design and build 12 rescue boats. By late 1969, the estimate was that it would cost $463 million, including training and support costs, to build only six.

Meanwhile, skeptics in and out of the navy began to question the boats' usefulness. Most submarines lost at sea, they argued, drop below their collapse depth. The critics pointed out that there have been only one or two instances of submarines disabled at depths at which the new rescue boats would be useful. Finally, they maintained that a disabled submarine might easily break up before the rescue boat reached it. The navy's program, if a submarine was lost at sea, would be to airlift a rescue submarine to the nearest shore, place the boat aboard an LSD or a specially modified nuclear attack submarine and take it to the approximate scene of the accident. The elapsed time, the critics contended, would be too long.

Two nuclear-powered submarines, the USS *Halibut* and an early boat of the Sea Wolf class, have been converted into "mother submarines" for the deep submergence rescue program. They can move to the scene of a submarine accident with the deep submergence rescue vehicle on their afterdeck, from which the DSRV can "take off" and "land" while the mother ship remains submerged. The *Halibut* displaces 5000 tons submerged and was commissioned in 1960.

Three other diesel-powered boats are categorized by the navy as research submarines: the *Tigrone,* commissioned in 1944; the *Al-*

bacore, 1963; and the *Dolphin*, 1968. The *Dolphin*, the most elaborate of the three, is fitted with research stations for scientists.

The rescue submarine, like most research boats, is in the midst of steady development. In the end, its chief use may be as much civilian as military. More and more minisubmarines are being used for commercial research and this increases the chance of mishaps. In 1974, for example, two Americans working in the North Sea in a 10-ton, 20-foot boat were trapped for six hours at 275 feet when their craft became entangled in an anchor line. Two divers struggled for 20 minutes to free the submarine, which then surfaced under her own power. The men in the submarine were working for the Shell United Kingdom Exploration and Production Company.

The lure of untold riches on the ocean floor has helped promote the building of small boats for underwater exploration. All Ocean Industries of Houston, Texas, has developed a line of one- and two-man boats that, delivered dockside, cost $4950 for the small vessel and $9950 for the larger. The small boat is ten feet long, three feet wide and five feet high. The larger is 15 feet long, but its other dimensions are the same. They are not fast, four knots submerged for the small boat, two and one half knots for the larger. Both work off 12-volt battery-powered motors that drive a six-inch propeller. The continuous life of the battery is rated at two hours, but the submarines can stay submerged for as long as four hours and can operate at a depth of 150 feet.

Buyers may range all the way from underwater treasure seekers to workers on offshore drilling platforms and pipelines. The boats also can be used for underwater photography because they have a bottom view port. Special equipment—a rotating searchlight, a mechanical arm for lifting or retrieving objects—can be added as optional extras. The boats are far more sophisticated than the one- and two-man submarines developed by the Japanese and Italians in World War II. Several safety features have been built in to allow for underwater escape. In appearance, the submarines are a queer throwback to the Holland boat of 75 years ago.

Mermaid II, *a German submarine now owned by an American company, International Underwater Contractors of New York. 1975.*

The industrial submarines' usefulness in examining underwater pipelines, cables and oil rig foundations has fostered their development by European as well as United States builders.

In 1975, an American company, International Underwater Contractors of New York, added a German submarine to its fleet of submersibles. This was the *Mermaid II*, designed and built by Bruker Physik AG of Karlsruhe as a general-purpose workboat. She carries a crew of two to 1000 feet, is all-hydraulic in power operations and, according to the American company, has "extraordinary maneuverability for a boat of her size."

This maneuverability is due to her ability to change attitude without forward motion, like a helicopter rather than an airplane.

IUC has modified the boat slightly to improve its inspection and work capabilities by adding a 36-inch domed forward view point, by increasing the power output 50 percent and by adding a remote-control manipulator arm of American design and construction.

Closed-circuit television with remote pan and tilt and video-tape recording facilities permit continuous recording of an inspection. Obstacle-avoidance sonar and a sophisticated navigation system complete *Mermaid II*'s electronics.

Other ships in IUC's fleet are the *Beaver Mark IV* and the PC-3B *Techdiver*, submarines that can dive to a maximum depth of 2700 feet and have made pipeline and cable inspections around the world.

Experts are divided over whether there is a market for such boats. Those who believe there is forecast a rapid increase in interest in underwater exploration as a result of recent discoveries of treasure and artifacts. Others argue that the commercial companies that would buy these submarines have purchased all the boats they need and that private individuals have neither the money nor the endurance to go fortune-hunting in one-man boats.

It is unlikely that midget submarines will rival snowmobiles in popularity. But we clearly have not reached the limits of their use, as the 1969 Loch Ness experiment, although unsuccessful, demonstrated.

Dan Taylor, an oceanographer from Atlanta, Georgia, took a 20-foot, one-man boat to Scotland, hoping to dive deep enough to get a look at "Nessie," as the resident monster is familiarly known to the Scots. His intention was to get a sound-wave fix on Nessie, take pictures and then, with a dart fired from a harpoon gun, get a sample of the monster's flesh for analysis. Unfortunately for zoology and the Sunday supplements, Mr. Taylor didn't get far. His submarine sank in five feet of water. Earlier it had suffered a broken instrument panel, a leaking hatch and a mishap to the main motor. The locals considered that Nessie's magic was working overtime.

In the meantime it was discovered that the loch is at least 820 feet deep at one point instead of the 754 feet given on the charts. This was found by yet another monster-hunting submarine, the *Discus*, a boat built by the Vickers shipbuilding organization of Britain to operate at a depth of 3000 feet.

Interested groups—the navy, the shipbuilding industry, oceanographers, scientists—hope that the next ten years will see a saner, more methodical approach to the use of submarines for exploration and research. While a great deal has been learned in the past ten years, the consensus among naval officers and oceanographers is that mankind has only plucked at the curtain that hides the oceans' secrets. Continued effort appears inevitable. As man on earth consumes his mineral resources, he will have to go under the sea to find new ones. As the world's population mounts, new sources of food protein must be found in the seas. And despite the show business aspects of some research of the past ten years, at least the door has been opened. If the world wishes to use that door, it would do well to forget Captain Nemo and Spanish doubloons and concentrate on discovering and developing the resources of the planet's seas.

A submarine disaster has a certain horrible fascination, perhaps because it takes the ordinary citizen, watching television or reading a newspaper, into another dimension of fear. He has never known anything like it—the opaque and frigid depths, the darkness, the gasping for air, the cold denial of hope by the trapped realist, the frantic struggle for survival by the fool. These are the worst of death's guises.

For the sailor, the technician, the builder, the scientist, it means something else: The loss of a proud vessel and old friends, the professional wonderment at what went wrong, the gnawing suspicion that something in the construction was not quite right, the scientist's groping return to first principles in an effort to correct whatever did go wrong.

The loss of a submarine in peacetime is also a political event

176

of the first magnitude. Ministries of defense have spent so many millions, senior admirals have pledged their professional reputations. The repercussions are far-reaching. Congressional committees meet. Questions are asked in the House of Commons—and perhaps in the Politburo. The cause of the disaster becomes the prime target of intelligence agencies, friendly as well as hostile. Even in the Communist countries there are murmurs in the elite when a submarine is lost.

In the nuclear era, the United States has sustained the unexplained loss of two nuclear-powered submarines, the USS *Thresher* in 1963 and the USS *Scorpion* in 1968. The word "unexplained" is used advisedly. Theories have been advanced about the causes of both losses, but submarine accidents are unlikely to provide objective evidence.

Before we examine these two disasters, it is worth recalling that from the time the first submarines were deployed, they have had a record of mysterious disappearances. French, Russian, British, German, American and Japanese boats left port and were never heard of again. Submarine service in the early days was hazardous in peace as well as in war. Long before World War I, submariners were a special breed not unlike the RAF fighter pilots of 1940 or the Special Forces of the Fifties.

The United States Navy, like all forward-looking navies, has spent a great deal of effort and money on the prevention of submarine disasters and the rescue of crews caught in disabled boats. The most spectacular and effective such operation in submarine history was accomplished by the navy on May 23, 1939, when 33 seamen were extricated from the forward torpedo room of the USS *Squalus*, a diesel-powered boat. The McCann rescue chamber was used, and four trips were necessary down to the escape hatch of the *Squalus*. But 29 men trapped aft were drowned.

The McCann chamber has been improved since, but essentially it is the same mechanism that saved the men on the *Squalus*. It is ten feet high and eight feet in diameter, weighs ten tons, and if there are favorable surface conditions, which is a very large "if," it now can operate at a depth of 800 to 850 feet. There is another important condition in addition to a relatively calm sea. A stricken submarine must be disposed in such a way that the rubber-gasketed skirt at the bottom of the McCann chamber can link with the submarine's escape hatch.

There had been other losses in the Twenties and Thirties. The 0-9 sank with a death toll of 33. Submarines had collided with each other, had run into rocky shores. Abroad, HMS *Thetis* had gone down in the Irish Sea with a toll of 90 lives in June 1939. A French submarine had sunk in a collision with a Greek freighter. But no event so shocked both the American people and the navy as the loss of the *Thresher* in 1963.

The ascertainable facts—that is, facts that would stand up in a court of law—are stark. Sometime between 9:14 and 9:17 A.M. on April 10, 1963, the USS *Thresher*, on a test run, imploded some thousands of feet below the surface of the Atlantic Ocean off the New England coast, taking the lives of all 129 men on board.

The *Thresher* was something special. She was the lead ship of the navy's latest class of nuclear attack submarines and thus was the first nuclear-propelled boat to be sunk by an accident. All that the navy and American shipbuilding could put into a submarine at that time had been put into the *Thresher*. She had the new tear-shaped hull, a Westinghouse S5W reactor plant and a single propeller driven by a geared turbine. The navy saw her as significantly in advance of all other submarines "in the areas of performance, depth, quieting and sonar" and claimed that she was "a true submarine independent of the surface with unmatched submerged maneuverability and speed" and "our country's best ASW defense." (ASW stands for Antisubmarine Warfare. It is a branch of the navy that includes detection of hostile submarines and the means of destroying them. It is one of the most expensive and extensive of naval activities.)

There are critics of these claims, notably John Bentley in his detailed investigation, *The Thresher Disaster*. But it is clear that the submarine was presented to the nation as the most modern attack submarine and that the admirals and politicians who backed that presentation believed it.

The loss of a nuclear submarine sets up shock waves not associated with the disappearance of diesel boats. When the navy announced on the night of April 10 that the *Thresher* "appeared to be lost" after a deep test dive, concern spread over the prospect of "nuclear contamination" to shipping in the area. Adm. George W. Anderson, chief of naval operations, gave his assurance that there was "no chance of nuclear explosion in the submarine." But this did not quiet all the fears about nuclear effects among the general public. For the navy, the basic question—never completely answered to this day—was how one of its most modern submarines, 278 feet long with a beam of 21 feet and displacing 3700 tons, could be destroyed so quickly. She had cost $45 million, but the navy's grief could not be measured in dollars and cents. It was grief for men and for the destruction of a fine and lovely submarine. It is unlikely that the public, then or now, would understand what Admiral Anderson called the "sad occasion when a ship is lost."

The loss of the *Thresher* led to a public controversy whose echoes have not died yet. The navy has been abused and vilified. It has, of course, put forward a defense, but one constrained by security requirements. The *Thresher*, after all, as the lead ship of a new class, was equipped with some novel devices. But reading the pages and pages of testimony at the congressional inquiry and the transcripts of the navy's inquiry, one has the impression that the service presented a poor case, especially in view of the widespread public ignorance of the navy. This ignorance applies not so much to what the navy is as to what it stands for. I have never been in the navy or any other service; but as an outsider, it strikes me that one of the major barriers between the public and the service is the former's failure to grasp the distinctive quality of the navy's attitude toward itself and its country.

Professional naval officers are affected drastically by two conditions that generally do not bear upon their counterparts in the army. The first is that they spend much of their lives at sea, which means that they are outside the mainstream of American society. The navy, for example, took years to realize the changed status of blacks in that society, something the army had recognized in the Fifties. Secondly, the navy, in one of its favorite phrases, is "hardware oriented." Ships, submarines, naval aircraft, data systems, antisubmarine devices are the core of the navy's being. The public admission that a piece of its hardware, from an aircraft carrier to a sonar system, is deficient in any way is a matter of the gravest concern within the service. The loss of a ship under any condition is a calamity.

Granted these characteristics, the navy is a poor witness in cases like that of the *Thresher*. It hems and it haws. It seeks asylum in torrents of technicalities, or as the British army puts it, "blinds 'em with bullshit." It pulls rank. And, far more effectively, it pulls security. Also, even under its most enlightened leaders, the navy almost invariably displays a gentlemanly inability to understand why anyone, including the American public, should pry into its secrets. The navy, then, is not at its best in affairs like the *Thresher*, and it is unlikely that it ever will be.

The navy mounted the greatest search in its history for the *Thresher*.

By April 12, then 39 hours after the receipt of the last garbled message from the lost submarine, six destroyers, two submarine rescue vessels, a salvage ship, two submarines and the spanking new research ship, *Atlantis II*, were in the search area. Aircraft from two navy squadrons were overhead, while other planes already had been searching the area for 24 hours. According to department records, the navy augmented this force with the USS *Rockville*, a radar patrol craft carrying a special high-precision fathometer; the USS *Redfin*, a specially equipped diesel submarine; and the USS *Hazelwood*, a destroyer carrying deep-mooring buoys, special personnel and instruments from the Woods Hole Oceanographic Institution. The *Atlantis II*, which had been on the spot for some hours before the rest of the armada arrived, had busied herself taking water and bottom samples to test for radioactivity. Not a trace was found beyond normal background radiation.

The *Thresher*'s last message had been received from 41° 44' north and 64° 59' west. When her wreckage finally was located on the sea floor, it was 41° 45' north and 64° 56' west; only one minute north latitude and three minutes west longitude of the original coordinates that governed the search.

This is not an inquiry into the loss of the *Thresher*, the search for her shattered remains or the causes of the disaster. But the event provides some insight into what happens to a modern submarine when it is lost and the technology employed to find it.

So far as the facts of the disaster are concerned, it appears that the *Thresher*, from causes that are unknown to this day, suddenly plunged to the bottom at a very high speed.

Enter the *Trieste*. This bathyscaphe has been mentioned as the vehicle that had made the deepest dive on record. The search for the *Thresher* showed that the *Trieste* had other uses besides setting records. When the *Thresher* was lost, the *Trieste* was at the Navy Electronics Laboratory at San Diego, California. She was ordered to prepare to aid in the *Thresher* search and was shipped to Boston aboard an LSD.

But the *Atlantis II* was over the presumed site of the disaster with her trailing cameras. They photographed a mass of debris over an area 1000 by 4000 yards, and her dredge did even better. On June 24, it brought up a battery plate identified as belonging to the *Thresher*.

The *Trieste*'s part in the search is worth detailed description. First about the craft herself. Originally designed by Prof. Auguste Piccard, she had been bought by the navy in 1958. The 50-ton vehicle is made up of two separate units. One is a large floating gas tank, 60 feet long; the other is a steel sphere seven feet in diameter that hangs amidships beneath the tank. The tank holds approximately 35,000 gallons of fuel. A seawater ballast tank is located at each end. These are flooded to reduce the craft's natural buoyancy. Two large vented ballast hoppers are located forward and astern.

The sphere, or as the navy calls it, the gondola, is round because this is the shape that best withstands underwater pressure. In the record-breaking dive in the Marianas Trench, the sphere and the gas tank had withstood a pressure of 16,940 pounds per square inch. The sphere is packed with electronic and photographic equipment and has two small portholes made of a special plastic material. Two very powerful lights can illuminate the surrounding sea area for the *Trieste*'s high-speed cameras.

When the *Trieste* prepares for a dive, the seawater ballast tanks are filled. This makes the craft neutrally buoyant; that is, it weighs almost as much as the water it displaces and has enough floatability to keep it from sinking. The fore and aft ballast hoppers are then filled with steel pellets packed in 22-pound bags. The *Trieste* begins to sink, and the water pressure increases, with two results. The gasoline in the tank is compressed, reducing its mass and increasing its weight. The drop in temperature caused by the cold of the surrounding water compresses the gasoline still more. Its mass is further reduced and its weight increased. The lower the *Trieste* sinks, the more pronounced the cycle becomes. The rate of descent is about three feet per second.

The same factors, in reverse, apply to the ascent. Steel pellets are jettisoned. As the bathyscaphe rises, the seawater temperature increases and the water pressure decreases. The gasoline expands and regains its volatility. Specific gravity is reduced and a more positive buoyancy generated. When the surface is reached, the seawater ballast tanks are pumped out.

The *Trieste*'s mechanical arm is a useful tool in underwater exploration. Lt. Comdr. Don Keach, the *Trieste*'s captain, had her fitted with one before her second series of dives after the *Thresher*. It was thought that the arm would extend the *Trieste*'s search because visibility from the sphere is restricted and the vessel moves very slowly across the ocean floor.

The *Trieste* sighted some debris, presumably from the *Thresher*, on her first series of dives, but it was not until August 28, on the third of her second series of dives, that she hit what Keach described as "an area like a large automobile junkyard," with dozens of pieces of metal lying around on the ocean bed, some up to 20 feet long. He decided to bring something to the surface and hooked a section of brass piping almost five feet long. For 15 minutes Keach worked the remote-control mechanical arm to grasp the piping. Finally satisfied that it was secure, he began the ascent. It took nearly two hours, but it was worth it. Stamped on the piping was "593 boat"; 593 was the *Thresher*'s navy number. On September 5, Secretary of the Navy Fred Korth announced that "The location of structural parts of the *Thresher* on the ocean floor having been positively confirmed by the bathyscaphe *Trieste* . . . I have today directed that the associated operational aspects of the search for the nuclear submarine *Thresher* be terminated." That was the end of the search but not the end of the controversy. The official navy statement on the *Thresher* inquiry reads:

It is most likely that a piping system failure had occurred in one of the *Thresher*'s saltwater systems, probably in the engine room . . . that in all probability affected electrical circuits and caused loss of power.

Norman Polmar in his *Death of the Thresher* considers that "the initial minor difficulty was more probably the loss of propulsion. With the loss of forward motion, the *Thresher* began to sink deeper and deeper as a result of her heavy water ballast, which it was decided to expel. However, before the downward motion of the submarine could be halted—and before she reached her collapse depth—the increased pressure ruptured one of the numerous pipes penetrating the submarine's pressure hull. This water drove the submarine still deeper."

Capt. Dominic A. Paolucci, USN (Ret.), veteran submarine officer writing in the *Naval Institute Proceedings*, considers the Polmar account "consistent with the facts" and "probably correct."

The reader will note the emphasis on probability in all statements. Under the circumstances, nothing could be proved.

The subsequent row centered on the *Thresher*'s preliminary tests, and especially on the testing of her silver-braze joints. In a congressional hearing, Sen. Bourke B. Hickenlooper jumped on this point like a fox on a pullet:

The thing that has been intriguing me throughout the hearing is that I have not seen one word of criticism of any higher authority or commanding officer or anybody else who failed to explain why, when they discovered 14 percent deficiency in the silver-braze joints of that ship . . . they did not test the rest of them. No criticism of anyone who failed to see whether this blow system would work at depths, even though it was equipped to work at such depths.

Adm. William A. Brockett's view was that "the 14 percent deficiencies below standard do not mean that these were bad joints in the normal sense. They were tight joints and they held 150 percent of the normal working pressure. . . . These hydrostatic tests were made."

John Bentley, the most trenchant critic of the navy over the *Thresher* affair, condemns the admiral's sophistry. Another American writer on naval affairs, who is highly reliable, believes the navy knows the cause of the disaster but will not make it public until all those concerned in the inquiry are dead or retired. My object is not to condemn or excuse, but to employ the *Thresher* affair to illustrate that for all their supposed safety, nuclear submarines are as much prey to mechanical failure as any other machine and that size, speed and lethality of weapons are no guarantee against malfunction. The *Thresher* disaster, like the ineffective torpedoes and their detonators on the World War II boats in the Pacific, carries its warning; great organizations can err, the gods of the machines are not infallible, the Republic is best served when a skeptical approach accompanies courage and loyalty.

The *Thresher* affair was still reverberating through the Pentagon when, on May 27, 1968, the navy reported that the nuclear-powered attack submarine USS *Scorpion* was overdue. The *Scorpion* had been engaged in an exercise with the Sixth Fleet in the Mediterranean and was due in Norfolk on the 27th after a three-month cruise. There were 99 officers and men aboard.

The grim drama was reenacted. The wives of the *Scorpion*'s crew said they were hopeful. A task force was assembled to search for the lost boat. A Naval Court of Inquiry was convened. The research ship *Mizar* photographed the wreckage, lying at 10,000 feet on the sea floor 400 miles southwest of the Azores. Congressmen gave weighty statements. Editorial writers wrote equally weighty editorials.

This time, however, there was an additional factor. The *Thresher* had disappeared during a test run. The *Scorpion* had been lost after she had been exercising in waters frequented by Soviet submarines and surface craft. Was there even a suspicion that her loss had not been the result of an accident?

The navy's seven-man court of inquiry met for 11 weeks and heard 90 witnesses. But even before the court reported its findings, the pictures of the sunken boat had convinced most navy experts that foul play could be eliminated. Rather, the pictures suggested that some accident within the boat had led to the *Scorpion*'s loss. If the submarine had been hit by a torpedo or scraped or rammed by a surface ship, the navy experts said, identifiable damage would have been seen on the hull.

This view was reinforced by the court of inquiry's finding that "No evidence of any kind to suggest foul play or sabotage was found by the court."

But the court added that "The certain cause of the loss of the *Scorpion* cannot be ascertained from evidence now available." Photographs released at the same time as the court's report showed that the submarine's superstructure or "sail" was intact but evidently had been torn from the hull and was lying on its side approximately 100 feet from the bow. The bow itself appeared to have sunk partway into the sand and the nuclear reactor was not visible in any of the photographs.

Two possible causes for the disaster were dismissed by the court. The *Scorpion* could not have hit an undersea mountain, a theory entertained by many; and as a result of expert testimony, the court was convinced that the nuclear power plant could not have failed to function properly.

Much of the court's report was negative.

The loss could not be attributed to any delay in the completion of the submarine's "subsafe" program, which involved safety improvements. The *Scorpion*'s condition was called "excellent," and none of her pending maintenance requests were of a nature that would affect her safety.

The crew was well trained, especially for such emergencies as flooding or control failure that would cause a drop into crush depth.

The photographs gave no indication that a torpedo had exploded. Witnesses told the court that the torpedo crews were well trained in safety precautions.

There was no evidence of a collision with another submarine or with a surface ship.

Finally the court came to the human factor, the x factor that can affect any highly technical operation. Navy departments the world over are concerned with this, especially when the manning of nuclear submarines, with their tremendous potential, is under consideration. One undetected psychotic could start the holocaust.

In the case of the *Scorpion*, the testimony established that the crew was able and mature. There was not the slightest indication that any officer or seaman was other than fully reliable. According to the court, the evidence did not establish that the loss of the *Scorpion* and her crew was caused by "the intent, fault, negligence or inefficiency of any person or persons in the naval service or connected therewith."

"Of their bones are coral made," but the mystery persists. The mystery of the *Scorpion* is deeper than that of the *Thresher*. Was the court right in dismissing some of the suggested causes for the disaster? There are authorities outside the navy who argue that the *Scorpion* was not an open-and-shut case.

For example, the cause might have been control failure. If the submarine was running fast and deep and her diving mechanism suddenly locked in a dive position, she could have gone below crush depth before corrections could have been made. The counterargument is that unless the submarine was proceeding near her maximum depth, the correction could have been made by a highly trained crew. It is well to remember, however, that once a submarine starts to dive, she goes down very rapidly.

Then there is that perennial danger of leakage from small cracks. Some witnesses before the naval court testified that the *Scorpion* had tiny cracks in her hull and around her propeller shaft. If she had been proceeding at depth, the cracks might have forced a breach and the breach brought about disaster. But the *Scorpion* had been cleared for the long voyage to the Mediterranean. If there were cracks, they were not regarded as significant by the inspectors.

Some cling to the theory of a malfunctioning torpedo. Submarine history is full of instances of the accidental activating of a torpedo. There are procedures to deal with such a situation and a well-trained crew would know how to carry them out. The photographs showed no evidence of an explosion outside the *Scorpion*, and this would seem to rule out the possibility that she was hit by one of her own "fish." It does not, of course, rule out the possibility of the internal explosion of a torpedo.

The *Thresher* and *Scorpion* disasters are the most grievous and best known of modern—i.e., nuclear—submarine history. We know that a Soviet nuclear boat was lost in the Pacific in the Sixties and that an expensive, complex and ultimately unsuccessful effort to raise her was made by the Central Intelligence Agency and the navy. It is the only known Soviet mishap. The British used to call the submarine branch "the silent service." The description could be extended to all the navies of the world today. For as modern submarines run deeper, their losses will be more difficult to explain and, granted the sensitivity of admiralties to publicity, perhaps more common than we know.

We have considered principally the submarine forces of the superpowers and to a lesser degree those of secondary military states. But in addition to the British, French and Chinese, other governments are building or buying submarines. As the number of boats multiplies, the chance of further accidents increases. And accidents can be more than an occasion for national controversy, as in the case of the *Scorpion*.

Some of the sea-lanes of the world run through narrow waters, in which submarines as well as surface ships must move. What happens if, despite modern sensors, a Soviet submarine under way from Cienfuegos to the Gulf of Mexico, a customary patrol route, is run down by an American merchantman? What is the result if an American submarine bumps a Soviet cruiser in the Greek islands? Little imagination is needed to foresee the crisis that would arise; we have not gone so far in détente that the loss of 100 or so lives could be smoothed over by diplomacy, no matter how adroit.

These are the circumstances under which submarines must be considered not only a major weapon of war but, as their number increases, a potential for causing wars. Imperial Russia and Britain were very close to war during the Russo-Japanese conflict early in this century when the Russian fleet, en route to its dire rendezvous at Tsushima, fired on a few British trawlers that it mistook for Japanese torpedo boats. What would happen today if an American or Soviet submarine, believing itself under attack, loosed its torpedoes at a presumed enemy?

The submarine, whether or not it is engaged in military operations, has a political significance, passive as well as active. The prudent course would appear to be an agreement among maritime powers to advise on the paths their submarines were taking, at least when the boats were passing through crowded waters. The United States and the Soviet Union have reached a rough understanding governing the movement of surface ships. But submarines today, especially nuclear missile submarines, are ultimate weapons, and their movements are far too important to be signaled even in the most general way to a potential enemy.

The dour conclusion is that the world must expect more disasters comparable to those of the *Thresher* and *Scorpion*. For there is no limit to the submarine's scope, and because of its power, nothing that will induce its masters to restrict its operations.

 We know a great deal about the Soviet submarine fleet. Satellite photographs, electronic intelligence gatherers and covert operations have produced a rich harvest. The size, speeds, operational depths and armaments of Russian boats from the relatively small Bravo class to the Deltas and Yankees are known to the United States and other NATO navies. When, however, we enter the field of Soviet submarine strategy and tactics in the event of a war with the United States and its allies, the ground is less firm. This is an area of speculation, although the speculation is based on Russian military writings and on the careful analysis of Soviet surface and submarine forces in such major naval exercises as Okean 1975, the largest maneuvers ever carried out by the Russian navy. The assessment of Soviet strategy and tactics has to be applied to the two main types of conflict: conventional war and nuclear war. Ever since the atomic bomb was dropped

on Hiroshima, the public has been conditioned to think of the next war in nuclear terms. But it is arguable that as Soviet military power increases and its nuclear arsenal approaches or reaches parity with that of the United States, the Russians may be tempted to use what they consider their superior conventional strength to fight limited, conventional wars.

Michel Tatu of *Le Monde* has pointed out that "Landings of the type carried out by the United States in Lebanon in 1958 and in the Dominican Republic in 1965 would be more hazardous, if not entirely out of the question today" should the Soviets seek to oppose them. On the other hand, he continues, "A landing by Soviet marines to support some 'progressive' regime, to help some minority faction in a power struggle is no longer inconceivable."

Former Supreme Allied Commander Atlantic Adm. Ralph G. Cousins commented to the writer that in a global confrontation with the United States, the Soviets might initiate an undeclared submarine war, with merchant ships, particularly tankers, the principal targets.

It is a step, albeit a long one, from these two types of minor conflicts to a short and violent global war fought without recourse to nuclear arms, in which the Soviets would depend on their present superiority in men and weapons and the political divisions within the allied camp to produce victory. The two elements in such a victory would be the defeat of the NATO armies in Northwest Europe and of allied attempts to ferry men and supplies to Europe and to support ground operations there with fleet aircraft. Having accomplished these objectives, the Russians would reckon that the United States would not wish to enter a strategic nuclear war that would involve the destruction of its own society as well as that of the Soviets. The Russians also would count on America's allies in Europe (those of them, that is, that still would have organized non-Communist societies) to violently oppose such a strategy.

In this context it is well to remember the admonition of Adm. Thomas E. Moorer, former chairman of the Joint Chiefs of Staff, to the effect that an attack by the Soviets in Europe would not result in a purely European war, because Russia is a Pacific power as well.

The Soviet submarine force will play a major role in whatever type of conflict erupts. Ever since Nikita Khrushchev, in one of those off-the-cuff comments that so infuriated his colleagues, said that cruisers were useful only for carrying senior officials on state visits, there has been a growing emphasis in Soviet naval thinking on the employment of submarines in a war with the "imperialist aggressor."

As was pointed out earlier, the Soviet reversal over Cuba did not generate Russian naval expansion. But there is abundant evidence that it did stimulate both the production of submarines and the study of how best they could be used against the United States and its NATO allies. The Cuban missile crisis in 1962 developed into a situation in which only Soviet submarines could have been effective. But the Soviet submarines of that day were not up to the job. The Navy Department later reported that American antisubmarine forces had found all the Russian boats moving toward the Caribbean in the first two days of the crisis. One destroyer, the USS *Cecil*, located and made contact with a Soviet submarine for 36 hours. The Russian commander tried every known ruse to escape. In the end, conscious that he was faced with superior surface and air opponents, he came to the surface, and the submarine was identified.

Although the navy recalls this exploit with relish, it understands that conditions have changed. The Soviet submarines launched since 1962 run deeper and quieter, and by 1966 the first of the second generation of Soviet nuclear submarines, the Victors, the Charlies and the Yankees, had been deployed. The Russians, however, have not yet achieved qualitative superiority.

As Admiral Rickover commented, "Numerical superiority, however, does not tell the whole story. Weapons systems, speed, depth, detection devices, quietness of operation and crew performance all make a significant contribution to the effectiveness of a submarine force. From what we have been able to learn during the past year [1970], the Soviets have attained equality in a number of these characteristics and superiority in some."

The Russians' expansion of their submarine arm has been facilitated by an extraordinary increase in shipbuilding facilities. The first Soviet nuclear-propelled submarine was built at the Severodvinsk yard in 1960. Its launching was followed by those of similar submarines at Komsomolsk in the Pacific. About a decade ago, three other yards—the Admiralty and Sudomekh yards in Leningrad and the Gorky yard inland—were altered to build nuclear submarines, and in 1970 all these yards were producing 12 to 15 nuclear-propelled submarines a year. United States intelligence estimates that the Russians have the capability to build 20 submarines a year on a single-shift labor program and approximately 30 on a three-shift program. According to Admiral Rickover, the Severodvinsk yard alone has a greater capability than all American submarine-building yards combined.

Navies by their nature are technology-oriented. But behind the ships, the submarines, the missiles and the torpedoes are men. The Russian achievement of training a naval force of 470,000 officers and men to operate the most sophisticated equipment is remarkable, especially when it is considered that the standards of technological education in the Soviet Union are lower than in the United States. This is a situation, however, that we cannot expect to continue.

The Soviet military system is based on national conscription, so the Russian navy is assured of a regular annual intake. It does not have to worry, as does its American counterpart, about recruiting. The length of a Russian's active naval service is two or three years, depending on the sailor's special field.

The young Russian who enters the navy or other services is likely to have had some prior military experience either in the Young Communist League (Komsomol) or in the Voluntary Society for Cooperation with the Army, Aviation and Fleet, popularly known by its Russian acronym of DOSAAF. This organization has a naval section called DOSFLOT, which trains teen-agers in naval discipline, seamanship and communications. Most of the DOSFLOT establishments are located near naval bases and seamen from the fleet lecture at the DOSFLOT clubs. The youngsters get an opportunity to visit

Soviet ships in port. There are no newspaper editorials protesting that the military is corrupting Russian youth.

With this preservice training, the Russian naval conscript finds it relatively easy to move into his formal program. He starts ashore, where great emphasis is placed on shipboard simulators and other advanced training aids. Then he is assigned to an operational ship, shore installation or naval air station, where he begins a cycle of advanced training programs. The Russians employ stimulants to excellence comparable to those used by the United States Navy. Each year, one submarine and one surface ship are singled out as the best of their types in the navy.

Officers follow a roughly similar route as ours. Most are graduates of one of the several naval colleges, which means that after a short basic course officers go through four years of instruction in military and political fields and, of course, "the science of Marxism-Leninism." Both the seaman and the potential officer are liberally dosed with Communist indoctrination. An article describing the S.O. Makarov Pacific Ocean Higher Naval School at Vladivostok, base of the Pacific Fleet, notes:

In party work, particular importance is attached to instilling in the youth *a hatred for the imperialist aggressors* [author's italics]. The future lieutenants are often visited by merchant sailors who have traveled to capitalist countries. These sailors, who while on distant ocean voyages visited areas such as Southeast Asia, Africa and other places in which the consequences of an imperialist 'civilization' are still visible, furnish the officers with very rich materials and stories.

The young officer goes from his naval college to a ship or air unit. Like the conscript, he will be sent to various specialized courses to further his technical education. Unlike his American opposite number, he will also attend political courses.

The Russian navy regards its system of education as superior to that of the army chiefly because, as an expanding service, it has many officers who are relatively young but high in rank. These, it believes, appeal more to youth than the elderly veterans of World War II who lecture the army's recruits and young officers. Admiral Gorshkov is almost complacent about the navy's personnel training program.

His comments in *Naval Digest (Morskoy Sbornik)* are revealing.

Soviet navy men . . . do not want to be satisfied with their motherland occupying the position of a second-rate sea power. They are well aware of the importance of sea power in strengthening the international prestige of our country, in its military power, in the defenses of the immense maritime boundaries and in the protection of the state interests of the Soviet Union on the seas and oceans, hence [they] are constantly seeking ways in which to strengthen its military might.

It is brutally evident that Russia is no longer "a second-rate sea power." Much of the credit must go to Sergei G. Gorshkov. As is true of most Soviet civilian and military leaders, we know little about him. But we know enough about his work to realize that he is an innovator and organizer of the highest rank. Like Admiral Rickover, he has exerted a deep influence on his country's navy. But Gorshkov's field was wider. His efforts encompassed not only the building of ships and the production of weapons but the entire naval philosophy of his country. His success in these fields has been such that in the eyes of today's naval world he stands as a combination of two of the West's naval geniuses: Admiral Lord Fisher, who rebuilt the British fleet before World War I, and Adm. Alfred Thayer Mahan, who expressed and developed a philosophy of naval strategy for the United States and Britain.

The West may not know much about Gorshkov as an individual. But it knows more than it did about Gorshkov the strategist. Four years ago, articles by the man who has commanded all the fleets of the Soviet Union for the past 20 years began to appear in the Soviet professional press. The 11 articles in the series were published under the title *Navies in War and Peace.* Although they contained a high percentage of the usual Communist propaganda, much of it arrant nonsense, the articles did disclose some significant points about the admiral's strategic thinking, particularly on the use of submarines in a future war. The publication of the articles also was important for another reason. Their appearance in the closed society of the Soviet Union indicated the admiral's high standing within the Communist system. Publication of the country's senior naval officer's views on strategy could have been permitted only if the officer had the confidence of the Politburo and his writings had the endorsement of that body.

Consequently, Admiral Gorshkov's views on naval affairs are of the most urgent interest to all Americans. As is true of many Soviet writers, Gorshkov discusses contemporary ideas in the context of comments on past events. Writing about the Soviet navy in World War II, in which it cut a somewhat sorry figure, he notes that the service before the war sought "To achieve superiority of forces over the enemy in the main sector and to pin him down in the secondary sectors at the time of the operation means control of the sea in a theater or a sector of a theater; i.e., to create such a situation that the enemy will be paralyzed or constrained in his operations, or weakened and thereby hampered from interfering with our execution of a given operation. . . ." In the Second World War, the Soviet navy never approached these goals until just before the end of the hostilities.

The admiral comments that it is precisely this interpretation of sea control that is the basis for the employment of naval forces in war.

The implications of this statement are vast when the size of the Soviet submarine fleet and the number of its targets are considered. For the Russians equate control of the sea with submarine activity, and undersea operations against an enemy's seaborne commerce are a key element in their submarine strategy.

The internal evidence may be found in Admiral Gorshkov's reflections on the role of the submarine in World War II. After reporting the number of Allied and Japanese ships sunk by German and American submarines, he concludes that "submarines were the main force in the battle with enemy shipping," hardly an original statement. But he follows it with a more revealing comment.

British and American antisubmarine warfare forces, he concedes, played an "important role" in checking the operations of German U-boats, but the German reverse was accomplished only by an inordinate concentration of Allied naval and air power. "For each German U-boat there were 25 British and U.S. warships and 100 aircraft, and for every German submariner at sea there were 100 British and American antisubmariners," he writes.

Admiral Gorshkov continues, saying that "the question of the ratio of submarine to antisubmarine forces is of great interest *even under present-day conditions* [author's italics] since, if antisubmarine warfare forces, which were so numerous and technically up-to-date (for that time), possessing a vast superiority, turned out to be capable of only partially limiting the operations of diesel submarines, then what must this superiority be today in order to counter nuclear-powered submarines, whose combat capabilities cannot be compared with the capabilities of World War II era submarines."

The Soviet naval leader's final conclusion is that "it is clear that in World War II submarines were the main means of combating enemy shipping, and they are *even more important* [author's italics] in today's context." No one on the NATO side therefore should have any doubts as to the prime target for the Soviet submarine fleet.

But Soviet strategy extends far beyond the NATO area, which is limited to Northwest Europe and the Mediterranean Sea in terms of practical operations. As Admiral Moorer has reminded us, a NATO war would be a Pacific war also, one that would involve Japan. Every extension of Soviet naval power in the western Pacific represents a potential threat to the Japanese, who today, as in 1941–1945, exist as an industrial power by virtue of imports of raw materials and exports of finished goods across the seas of the world.

Shortly after the final defeat of South Vietnam, a respected western intelligence service reported that the Soviet Union had asked Hanoi for the use of Camranh Bay, in what was once South Vietnam, as a naval base and anchorage in return for "favors rendered." At this writing (April 1976), we do not know Hanoi's answer. But the news of the Russian request elicited two striking comments from Vietnam's (and Russia's) neighbors in the western Pacific.

A Chinese official of great experience conceded that a Soviet naval presence—"especially submarines"—at Camranh Bay would represent a serious threat to his country's maritime security.

A Japanese official was even more to the point. Russian submarines in Camranh Bay, he said, would be in a position in time of war to intercept and sink the stream of tankers, merchant ships and smaller craft that ply between Japan and the countries to her south and southwest. The official hazarded a guess that in a crisis, the Russians would not wait for war.

"They might pick off a few of our ships as a warning," he said, "in order to impress upon us the necessity of throwing the Americans out of their bases in Japan."

The United States Navy has not missed the significance of Admiral Gorshkov's remarks on submarines. In a commentary on the article quoted above, Rear Adm. J.C. Wylie (Ret.) said that "Admiral Gorshkov is very strong on submarines as the predominant weapons system for upsetting the other fellow's maritime commerce, his economy and his war-support capability."

Admiral Wylie also notes that the Soviet admiral appears to be less than impressed with antisubmarine warfare, past and present, and that "with this point of view, combined with the relative internal self-sufficiency of the Soviet Union in terms of resources, we can see very good reason for the size of the Soviet submarine fleet today, and we can infer that the prospects look good for continuation of the attention given to these ships."

Developments in submarine weaponry reinforce the existing threat of undersea craft to surface ships. The new conventional weapons make the submarine a far more efficient hunter of warships and merchantmen than it was in the last great war, and these new weapons are bound to impose drastic changes in antisubmarine warfare tactics.

In the opinion of many western naval officers, the antiship guided missile and the wire-guided homing torpedo must lead to an early and extensive revision of traditional antisubmarine warfare tactics. Naval warfare is about to witness a practical demonstration of Admiral Mahan's dictum that changes in weapons force changes in tactics.

In an article in the *United States Naval Institute Proceedings,* Capt. W.J. Ruhe, a retired American submariner, put the new and alarming developments in the perspective of anticommerce warfare:

The accurate attack ranges which are afforded the nuclear submarine by its antiship missile and wire-guided homing torpedo are so great as to require excessive numbers of antisubmarine warfare units for protection of even a small number of merchant ships—with present methods. Changed antisubmarine warfare tactics and an economical technology to support such tactics are needed to meet the new threat.

Submarine weapons have come a long way from Whitehead's first experiments in imperial Austria nearly a century ago. What is the significance of the two new developments?

The long-range, wire-guided, terminal-homing torpedo fired from a nuclear submarine is likely to get hits at 20,000 rather than 2000 yards. The torpedo's guidance comes from sound bearings taken on the noise of a target ship's rotating propellers. The torpedo can be fired from a comfortable depth, so the submarine need not surface in the encounter. To further reduce the prospect of detection, the torpedo can be programmed to remain deep during its run. The weapon is regarded as accurate—Captain Ruhe says "even at ten miles"—and can be set to explode under a target's hull. This torpedo costs less than a guided or ballistic missile. Its major limitation is that because it is wire-guided, only two, preferably one, can be fired at a time.

The submarine-launched guided missile is a weapon of comparable capability. According to Captain Ruhe, a semisubmerged submarine can fire an antiship missile at ranges of well over 100 miles on the approximate bearing of a target. Self-contained, mid-course guidance in the form of an autopilot or an inertial system keeps the missile on the course of its previously set bearing. The missile then begins a homing search, commencing at a previously set range, using radar, radiation or infrared detectors. Once the missile is locked on to its target, it may attack from just above the surface of the water at just under sonic speed or from several thousand feet up at supersonic speed.

"For either type of attack, the problems of defense are quite similar," Captain Ruhe comments, "in that warning time is measured in seconds."

The employment of both weapons, say in a combined attack by two submarines, is bound to upset existing antisubmarine tactics. To spread a convoy and so reduce a submarine's prospects will only decrease the prospects of missile defense. On the other hand, pulling ships together to improve the defense against missiles will present a submarine commander with a group target.

The submarine's advantage over the merchant ship in convoy, which was reduced in the Atlantic during World War II by the Anglo-American "hunter groups," is likely to be restored by the new weapons. Both can be fired at hitherto unprecedented ranges. This means that a boat can approach a convoy deliberately. The day of "seeing a submarine before it attacks" is done, Captain Ruhe comments.

Nuclear submarines will not provide the "giveaways" of the past in the form of masts or periscopes. The long-range missiles and torpedoes will increase the hazards of forward picketing by escorts. Indeed, the electronic antisubmarine measures employed by escorts are likely to give a submarine captain valuable information about his prey while he keeps his craft out of range of his trackers.

Other advances in weaponry over the past decade have increased submarine effectiveness. Perhaps the most important of these advances is the development by the United States of a long-range cruise missile (LRCM) that can be fired from a surface vessel or from the less vulnerable submarine.

A cruise missile is essentially a pilotless aircraft propelled by an air-breathing engine and carrying either a conventional or a nuclear warhead. The LRCM under development for the navy will be fired from torpedo tubes, with its wings retracted. The projected range is 1300 to 2000 nautical miles. General Dynamics Corporation, which is working on the seaborne missile, will fit it with an entirely new guidance system that can be refined to the point where fairly small targets can be hit.

When the LRCM is given to the fleet late in this decade, it will further enhance the submarine's military importance. Even when this weapon was in its first stage of development, those in the navy who knew its capabilities were predicting that it, like the new torpedoes, would further limit the wartime deployment of major surface units. Secretary of State Henry A. Kissinger thought enough of its potential to suggest at the Vladivostok meeting with the Russians that the LRCM be counted as a weapon comparable to the new Soviet Backfire bomber that has figured in the SALT II talks.

Commenting on the cruise missile, a navy captain described it as part of "the revolution in weapons" that has affected all military services "but none more so than the navy." He continued his assessment by saying:

We are ahead on the LRCM, but the Russians are sure to catch up or, with their penchant for doing things big, overtake us. By 1985, both submarine fleets may be armed with these long-range missiles, as well as with new sophisticated torpedoes. The carrier task force is already vulnerable to standoff missiles and modern torpedoes. How much will the task force be worth if it has to account for LRCMs as well?

The layman will recognize, as does the expert, that these new weapons increase the lethality of submarine forces. The assumption is that both the American and Russian navies, and perhaps the British, will employ them in an East-West war and that their use will alter present basic antisubmarine tactics.

This is a hard assumption for some to swallow. Some experts in this form of warfare cling to the idea that the principle of the concentration of forces—that is, convoys closely escorted by a strong complement of warships—will apply against the wire-guided torpedo and cruise missile. Others, Captain Ruhe among them, suggest that new types of convoy vessels must be developed to counter the submarines. One of the captain's proposals is for a new form of Q-ship carrying concealed or camouflaged VSTOL (very short takeoff/landing) aircraft, to prevent detection by submarines or reconnaissance aircraft.

Debates on such subjects among naval tacticians and strategists would be of more than academic interest to Americans. These discussions would show that at the moment, the edge is with the attack submarine. It is an edge that in war would be applied against American overseas commerce. It cannot be emphasized too often that this commerce is essential to the United States and that the American position in this respect is in marked contrast to that of the Soviet Union. The United States is no longer a self-sufficient continental power, but an island power relying on essential imports.

Adm. James L. Holloway III, chief of naval operations, outlined the dimensions of the American problem in a report to the Committee on Armed Services of the Senate in February 1975:

Recent statistics indicated that the U.S. imports about 30 to 40 percent of its current oil production. The "blueprint analysis" for

Project Independence has predicted that in five years—and even under the most optimistic assumptions—this dependence will be at 25 percent. (Under pessimistic assumptions, and during the same period of time, our dependence would continue rising to 48 percent.) Over 15 percent of our oil imports come from the Persian Gulf area. Over two-thirds of western European oil consumption in 1973 came from the Persian Gulf, while at the same time Japan was importing 76 percent of its energy needs from that area.

In view of these figures, the navy's concern over Soviet submarine activity in the Arabian Sea and over the activity of Russian minesweepers in the Persian Gulf is understandable.

Oil is not the only resource involved. Admiral Holloway pointed out that America "depends upon the sea for the import, in whole or in part, of many strategic materials (including 98 percent of cobalt, 70 percent of manganese, 74 percent of bauxite and 93 percent of chromite requirements). In 1973, U.S. seaborne commerce represented over one-fifth of the more than three billion metric tons that moved across the oceans of the world."

Freighters carrying these imports *to* the United States would not be the Soviet submarines' only target. In a war crisis or in war itself, the West's position would depend to a considerable degree on the maintenance of sea-lift programs across the Atlantic. "Primary emphasis is placed on the ability to support a NATO mobilization contingency," Admiral Holloway told the Senate committee. There must be, he emphasized, "assured surface pipelines to replenish stocks and build up levels adequate for high-intensity combat."

Developments in ground warfare have increased the importance of ship-borne reinforcements and, consequently, the importance of the submarine as the chief enemy of such reinforcements. In the Middle East War of October 1973, the rate of equipment destruction was greater than even the most pessimistic logistics experts had contemplated. Between October 6 and October 22, the Egyptian and Syrian armies together lost more tanks than the United States Seventh Army bases in Germany. Dueling tanks in World War II scored only one shot in ten; the ratio was one in two in the Middle East. One final statistic to emphasize the need for rapid resupply: American projections had estimated that a division would use 350 tons of supplies a day; the Israelis consumed 500 tons.

Land war has reached the point where war theater stocks of fuel, ammunition, reserve weapons and spare parts will be expended at an unprecedented rate. The burden on the navy to provide safe conduct for the ships ferrying supplies to American forces and those of our European allies will be immeasurably heavier. For, as Admiral Holloway sees it, "The sheer volume of ammunition and petroleum products consumed by modern military forces can be provided on a sustained basis only by sea transport."

On the one hand is arrayed the growing Soviet submarine fleet with its increasingly lethal weapons. On the other is the navy's belief that a credible capability to utilize and protect the Atlantic and Mediterranean sea-lines of communications remains the essential ingredient in NATO strategy. Or as the admiral put it, "To the extent that NATO's sea-lines of communications are perceived as vulnerable, the credibility and psychological cohesion of the NATO alliance will be eroded."

The Soviet submarine and, to a lesser but still important degree, the Soviet missile-armed surface ship already are influencing NATO strategy and to some extent NATO credibility among European peoples. The situation is bound to worsen if the alliance's position in Southwest Europe is weakened.

"It will be difficult enough with existing facilities to get men and supplies to Europe," a Canadian navy commodore said. "It will be close to impossible to get them there if Portugal goes Communist or turns neutral and gives the Russians facilities."

Here is a major political element in the submarine vs. commerce match. Portugal's defection from the Atlantic alliance would mean the loss of air bases and naval anchorages in the Azores and of the NATO base near Lisbon. In all probability, a Communist Portugal would mean Soviet use of the Azores and Lisbon. The Portuguese capital is on roughly the same latitude as New York. Soviet submarines based there and in the Azores inevitably would force Atlantic convoys farther north where, as the Canadian said mordantly, "they would meet the other Russian submarines coming south from the Norwegian Sea."

The NATO outlook in a conventional war is dark unless some significant advance is registered in antisubmarine detection. Basically what we have is a contest between a large, well-armed submarine fleet and merchant convoys whose escorts are likely to find that the tactics of 1943–1945 no longer suffice against the new submarine weapons. We know from our surveillance of the Soviet naval exercise Okean 1975 that the Russian submarines practiced attacks on merchant convoys (their own) in the course of the maneuver, and it is assumed that the Soviet naval high command is as aware as is NATO of the importance of transatlantic convoys to the western cause in the event of a war.

However, before we Americans hand the ball to the Russians and go home to watch television, we should recognize that the Soviet submarine fleet and the entire Russian navy suffer certain obvious handicaps.

The most obvious is that the main submarine bases in the Kola Peninsula, in Sevastopol, Leningrad and near Vladivostok are distant from the boats' most probable theater of operations. A complementary factor is that the routes in and out of these bases are well known and are watched constantly. This is particularly true of the exits from the Baltic and Black seas through Danish and Turkish waters and the passage around northern Norway traveled by all Soviet ballistic missile submarines.

A submarine fleet following a forward strategy, sitting for example off the American East Coast to prey on merchant traffic, requires support from tenders. Until very recently, the Russians had not paid much attention to tenders, perhaps considering that their vulnerability in war made their use too risky. Now they are building submarine tenders, but the undersea fleet's principal means of being serviced appears to be by overseas bases like Cienfuegos in Cuba and Conakry in Guinea. In war, these bases might prove untenable very early in the game.

Another Soviet weakness is that once their submarine fleet ventures outside the range of shore-based Russian naval aviation, the boats are half-blind. The Battle of the Atlantic in World War II demonstrated the importance of the Condor bombers' reconnaissance to the German U-boats and of the lift given antisubmarine warfare by the inclusion of small carriers in the hunting forces. Since then, radar, sonar and other devices have extended the operational range of both submarines and their enemies. If submarines have no aircraft to scout for them, convoys can escape detection by using the vastness of the seas.

The final Soviet handicap is intangible. For all the boasting in Admiral Gorshkov's essays and in the navy newspaper, *Red Fleet*, the Russians have no significant naval tradition. Military historians note that they have had only two major sea victories in almost a thousand years of national history: at Gangut Point in the Baltic Sea against the Swedes in 1714 and in the Black Sea against the Turks in 1770. As Norman Polmar has pointed out, the drive for "warm water ports" by both tsarist and Communist Russia did not reflect any deep appreciation of maritime problems. Such ports were necessary to the expansion of the economy. They were not viewed as bases for the expansion of Russian naval power until very recently.

In the past five years, the Soviet submarine fleet has gained ample experience in oceanic exercises. But it has no experience in oceanic submarine warfare. Some American, British and West German naval officers believe this will place the Russians at a significant psychological disadvantage in a war. This may be a deciding factor in the final equation. But it would be unwise for the Soviet Union's potential adversaries to count too heavily on it. The history of the past 50 years has demonstrated the folly of believing that because the Russians were unable to do things previously, they would be unable to accomplish them in a present crisis. Some comfort may be taken from the geographical limitations of the Soviet submarine fleet and from the lack, for the present at least, of long-range air cooperation with submarines. But if war ever comes, we may find the Soviet submariners teaching the maritime powers a trick or two.

On balance, therefore, the Soviet submarine fleet, considered only in a conventional weapons role, must be regarded as probably the most dangerous element in Russia's general purpose force; dangerous alike to the commerce of the United States, to the warships that would escort the merchantmen on "their lawful occasion," to the fleets that would seek to control such vital sea areas as the North Atlantic and, finally, to the general war plan for supporting NATO forces in Europe.

The United States, British, French, Canadian and other NATO navies have expended billions of dollars on antisubmarine warfare, a subject to be discussed in connection with the American navy's submarine warfare doctrine. At this point, all that need be emphasized is that although the navy believes it is ahead of the Russians in underwater detection and in some classes of antisubmarine weapons, no breakthrough has occurred. This fact is of transcendent importance in relation to conventional submarine warfare. It is even more important when we turn to the ultimate question of how Soviet submarines would be used in a nuclear war.

II

A mild tremor ran through the Pentagon in the first week of June 1975. A Soviet Yankee class nuclear submarine, armed with 16 nuclear missiles with a range of 1500 miles, had been detected within 350 miles of Cape Cod, Massachusetts, and about the same distance off Norfolk, Virginia, home of the U.S. Navy's Atlantic Fleet. This was about 1000 miles closer to the coast than Y class boats usually patrol.

No one knew the reason for this change in Russian tactics. But the theories put forward by naval intelligence provide much insight into the way the intricate and potentially deadly game of nuclear maneuvering is played, even in what is supposed to be a period of détente.

The first explanation was that the boat's operations were being carried out in cooperation with those of another Y class boat stationed in the Pacific. The object, if this scenario was correct, was to establish the conditions for "optimum target coverage" of the continental United States. The deployment of Soviet submarines at that distance from both coasts would provide such coverage; there would be no target in the country beyond the range of the Yankees' SS-N-6 Sawfly missiles.

This is an obvious and a simple explanation. We enter the dark and devious world of intelligence ploy and counterploy when a second theory is examined. This is that the boat's operation was part of a military deception plan, a field in which the Soviets are very active, intended to spur the United States Navy to take some action that would add to Russian information on American submarine detection and the steps by which the detection of a hostile boat would be developed into an attack.

According to a third theory, the Russians might have been testing their antidetection capabilities. By moving that close to the East Coast and the very heavy North-South maritime traffic, the commander of the Y class submarine might have expected that her passage would be missed by sosus (sound surveillance undersea), the American submarine detection system along the coast, because of the presence of so many other ships in the area. The Yankee boat could rely on any one of the scores of Russian surface ships plying those waters, including Soviet AGI intelligence-gathering ships disguised as trawlers, to check whether this new tactic was successful in confusing the underwater detection devices that the AGIs carry—and therefore, hopefully, it also would be successful in confusing sosus. The navy does not know the AGI verdict. It does know that American detection devices picked up the boat.

A fourth and more prosaic explanation was that the submarine might have been in some mechanical difficulty or had a seriously ill crew member. In either case, the boat might seek the assistance of Russian surface ships better equipped to handle the situation.

There is a final explanation. The Russians, well aware that American submarines have been used for electronic espionage in the past, may have been interested in merely "rattling the cage" and reminding the United States that they too have submarines that can move close to American coasts. The navy's story is that no American submarine has been nearer than three miles to Russian shores, a story that qualified American observers and European experts on submarine espionage take with more than a grain of salt.

Such missions are secondary to the primary role of the nuclear submarine in an all-out war between the two superpowers. If Yankee class missile submarines were deployed in the Pacific and Atlantic, the survival of the United States would be threatened by sea for perhaps the first time since the War of 1812.

A Soviet Delta class nuclear powered submarine underway in international waters. 1973. (Official U. S. Navy Photo)

While the threat to the United States from the Yankee class submarines is extremely serious, it pales in comparison to that posed by the new Delta class boats. According to an intelligence service that is not badgered by wool-hat congressmen, the Soviets are producing these submarines at the rate of six to eight a year. The prestigious International Institute for Strategic Studies in London put the number of Deltas at nine at the end of 1974, and one informed guess was that there would be 14 deployed by the middle of 1975 and perhaps 20 by the time the United States celebrated its Bicentennial. Under the SALT agreement, the Russians are to have 62 "modern" nuclear submarines, boats of the Yankee and Delta classes. The IISS estimates that the Russians are aiming at a ceiling of 744 of the most advanced submarine-launched ballistic missiles. The Russians also are testing a new short-range (400 miles) variation of their SS-N-13, which may be ballistic, and a new version of the SS-N-6.

There are two types of Delta class boat. The first is armed with 12 SS-N-8 missiles, with a range of 4600 miles and a warhead yield in the megaton range. The second type may have 16 missiles. The missiles have a longer range than any yet used in the submarines of

A Soviet Z IV class ballistic missile submarine in port. 1973.
(Official U. S. Navy Photo)

A Soviet N Class nuclear powered submarine which appears to be in distress in the Atlantic Ocean. A Soviet merchant ship stands by. 1970.
(Official U. S. Navy Photo)

An aerial view of the amidships and stern of a Soviet Victor class fleet submarine underway in the South China Sea. 1974.
(Official U. S. Navy Photo)

either superpower. Until now (April 1976), the Deltas have been cruising the Barents Sea. Late in 1975, intelligence reports indicated that the Soviets were building a "stretched Delta" that would carry more than 16 missiles, possibly 24.

The potential of the Soviet submarines has never been fully recognized by the public. Politicians and editors talk of "the nuclear threat." Translated into everyday terms, the seaborne threat is of a general attack on United States targets by nuclear submarines whose missiles on a depressed trajectory have a flight time to target of less than 15 minutes. As long ago as 1970, Grant L. Hansen, then the Air Force's assistant secretary for research and development, reported to the House of Representatives that "the toughest job" facing the Safeguard antiballistic missile system and the early warning system was "to warn against and intercept a warhead which is launched from a Russian submarine."

Since then, a more extensive and accurate long-range radar warning network has been built. But the alert period is still uncomfortably short. The Soviet boats' capabilities have forced major rearrangements in the American defense establishment. The B-52 bomb-

A Soviet F class submarine and the Destroyer USS Jonas Ingram underway in the Mediterranean. 1973. (Official U. S. Navy Photo)

A Soviet G-11 class ballistic missile submarine. 1970.   (*Official U. S. Navy Photo*)

ers, the air arm of America's nuclear Triad, have been dispersed in small groups to many military and civilian airfields in the hope that an effective number would escape a submarine attack on Strategic Air Command bases. This move naturally forced the rearrangement of the SAC logistics and security systems and compounded the communications problems between the command and the alert elements of the B-52 forces.

Nuclear submarines also could be targeted on another arm of Triad, the intercontinental ballistic missile force based mainly in the northern Middle West states.

Soviet submarine-launched ballistic missiles might be fired to detonate over ICBM silos. As far as is known, the SS-N-6s do not have sufficient accuracy to take out individual silos. The American reasoning is that enough missiles would be gotten off by the submarines to delay the launching of American ICBMs, whose warheads and guidance systems might be damaged by the submarine fusillade. This would give Soviet ICBMs, which are being improved in throw weight and in the number of MIRVs each missile carries, the advantage. While he was secretary of defense, Melvin R. Laird feared that the Russians would increase the accuracy of their missiles to the point where, by using MIRVs, they would be able to destroy upwards of 80 percent of American Minuteman ICBMs in their silos.

A Soviet H class nuclear powered ballistic missile submarine apparently disabled 600 miles northeast of Newfoundland. February 1970. (Official U. S. Navy Photo)

A Soviet F class large attack type fleet submarine underway in the Mediterranean. 1971. (Official U. S. Navy Photo)

Therefore, the prudent assumption is that Soviet nuclear missile submarines as we now know them are capable of inflicting severe damage on two arms of Triad: the ICBMS and the B-52 bomber force. The introduction of the B-1 bomber sometime in the Eighties will not alter this situation drastically. The B-1 will not require as much time to become airborne as the B-52, but it still will be vulnerable. Clearly, the only element of Triad not open to attack by Soviet missile submarines or ICBMS is the American missile fleet.

(It is useless to discuss the tactics of a strategic nuclear war. Gen. Carl A. Spaatz, commander of the Eighth Air Force in World War II, remarked of a third war that "once it starts, if it does, nothing, I mean nothing, will count but hitting as fast as you can and as hard as you can." His words are all the more weighty in view of the Russians' failure to distinguish, as the West does, between tactical and strategic nuclear weapons. If Soviet military writers mean what they say, the United States must assume there is a good chance that a single low-yield nuclear bomb or shell detonated in Europe would invite the holocaust.)

The advent of the newest Soviet nuclear ballistic missile submarines—and of the American Tridents, which will be discussed later—gives submarine warfare a new dimension. The public should not be chided unduly for failing to grasp the complexities of naval nuclear warfare, although it has been slow to grasp the extent of the Soviet threat. For it is quite evident to American naval commentators that, as Admiral Gorshkov's writings show, the Soviets have been unable to solve the problems posed by ballistic missile submarines. One problem, which runs through the gamut of nuclear weapons, is that while ballistic missile submarines exercise a deterrent power, no one, American or Russian, knows accurately the effect of a nuclear exchange on hostile fleets.

Vice Adm. James F. Calvert, USN (Ret.), commenting on Gorshkov's essays on naval warfare, noted that the Soviet admiral clearly has been unable to master "two great factors in naval theory," the "nuclear war at sea and the ballistic missile submarine." Gorshkov, Calvert wrote, was "honest enough to reveal that the dilemma posed by these two factors in the structuring of his navy has given him deep pause. As he attempts to come to grips with the nuclear exchange and the ballistic missile submarine, he talks increasingly about 'presence.' For all its importance 'presence' can never be a major purpose of a navy. It can be a convenient auxiliary use but, almost by definition, never a central one."

From the foregoing it is evident that the Soviet submarine in itself is a greater threat to the United States than any weapon in history. The problems arising from its deployment are outweighed by its awesome striking power. The possibility that antisubmarine detection may improve is balanced by the likelihood that hostile submarines would be able to launch their missiles before they were attacked. To take only one point: It has robbed America of her insularity. However much we may wish it, and many do, there can be no such thing as Fortress America under modern conditions. In a nuclear war, Main Street would be the front line. In a conventional war, attack submarines could frustrate the carefully thought-out military programs for supporting American and other NATO forces in Europe and sever the maritime lifelines on which the United States increasingly depends.

For a generation, the carrier task forces of the United States Navy have commanded the seas. Like every other form of American maritime power, they are now in danger. The problem confronting American naval planners and builders is how the maritime establishment can adapt to this situation. Much depends on how successfully they can solve the problem. An American lead is necessary if our allies in Europe and Japan are to feel reasonably secure when the Soviet Union begins to employ its submarines and new missile-armed surface craft to reinforce the more aggressive diplomacy that is sure to develop when the Politburo believes that it has extracted all the dividends possible from détente.

Let us examine the American posture: our navy's answer, active and passive, to Soviet submarine strength.

> All weapons of war are
> expensive.
> Cheap weapons will not win us
> a war.
> And, if we cannot win a war,
> there is
> no sense in spending money on
> weapons
> at all.
>
> Adm. Hyman G. Rickover

 Future historians will notice a curious paradox when they study American history in the years from 1965 to 1976. For well over half of that period, the United States was engaged in a great military effort in Vietnam that involved almost every conventional weapon in our armory. Yet during that same period, our military strength, especially our naval strength, declined sharply in relation to that of the Soviet Union. On January 1, 1976, the American navy had fewer ships in its inventory than on September 3, 1939, when World War II began.

This ebb in American naval power coincided with the rise of Russian sea strength, a process that was qualitative as well as quantitative. The Soviets, for example, slightly reduced the number of their submarines but dramatically increased their undersea fleet's quality. During the same period, they completed and sent to sea a large number of destroyers and two helicopter cruisers expressly designed to hunt down and destroy American submarines. The construction of three 40,000-ton aircraft carriers also was begun.

The process of arresting the American decline has been very slow getting under way. This is not only because it takes years to build the simplest warship but because of other factors. Inflation sent cost estimates rocketing. In a period of recession, shipyards were more interested in civilian than in military contracts. The power of pressure-group politics was arrayed against many procurement programs, among them the Trident program, which may be the most important of all.

The Trident submarines, so called because they will be armed with Trident missiles, represent the ultimate in American undersea weaponry. No one can say with complete confidence that the Trident, or any other type of armament, is the maximum deterrent to a nuclear first strike by the Soviets. What can be said is that once the Tridents are on station, the penalties for such a strike will be catastrophic. Because of their importance to the future and of the controversy that has surrounded them, the Tridents are worth the most careful and critical analysis.

The Trident submarine is America's third generation of nuclear-powered boats. When the first Trident is deployed (the navy believes in 1978 or 1979), the oldest ballistic missile submarines on duty will be nearly 20 years old, or near the end of their useful service life. Soviet production of Yankee and Delta class boats started later. Consequently, the Russian undersea fleet is more modern and will continue so until the Tridents appear.

The new submarine will be 560 feet long, or 135 feet more than the largest Poseidon submarine now in service. She will probably be about 18,700 tons displacement, submerged. She will travel faster, run quieter and be able to remain at sea longer than present boats. These qualities are important in an era of intense antisubmarine technology development.

But the Trident's principal advantage over the Poseidon will be in its firepower. Each submarine will carry 24 missiles instead of the 16 on the Poseidon. The missiles will have a far greater range. The navy admits to 4000 miles with a full payload, instead of 2500, but some foreign intelligence estimates put the range at 4400 miles. The initial missile will be called Trident I or C-4 and will be designed to the same dimensions as the Poseidon missile so it can be fitted to existing Poseidon submarines. Improvements in solid propellants, electronics and material give the missile its greater range. The payload is made up of MIRVs. A Trident II missile, taking advantage of technological progress, also is under development. This missile will have a range of more than 5000 miles.

The navy is planning to modify Poseidon submarines to accommodate the Trident I during normal refits. This will improve the service's nuclear capability without interfering with shipyard schedules.

The Trident submarine will not only be faster and quieter than present boats, it also will have greatly improved sonar and other equipment that the navy expects will increase its prospects of surviving against antisubmarine devices that may emerge in the next 30 years.

"We cannot guarantee their [the present missile submarines] invulnerability in the future," Admiral Holloway told a congressional committee, "especially in view of the increased Soviet interest and efforts in antisubmarine warfare. For this reason, we are continuing the development and procurement of the Trident system with its quiet, mobile submarine platform and long-range strategic missiles."

Another Trident advantage over today's boats is that its patrols will be longer, 70 days, and its refit periods shorter, 25 days. The systems designed for the new boat, coupled with a procedure for progressively renewing, repairing or replacing equipment or piping, will permit longer operating periods between overhauls. A support site is being built at Bangor, Washington, to refit, supply and maintain both submarines and missiles. (The maintenance program will decrease time spent in port by crew training and drydock arrangements peculiar to the Trident. The Trident will be fitted with larger hatches, which will facilitate the replacement of parts and other maintenance work and thus reduce the time spent in port. Similarly, the Trident, although larger than earlier ballistic missile submarines, has benefited from the previous experience in crew training, and the time necessary to train its crews is expected to be shorter.) Additional support provisions will be established at Cape Canaveral for demonstration and shakedown operations and at the Pacific Missile Test Range for training shots.

The navy believes the Tridents will be able to cover more of the ocean patrol area because they will be much quieter at high speed and so have a much greater patrol range. Quiet-running Tridents will be able to venture undetected into areas where the noisier Poseidon and Polaris boats would be picked up by hostile sonar. Under present plans, the Tridents will be sent to the Pacific Ocean.

The placement of the Tridents in the Pacific has a strategic significance. Although the Soviet Union is a Pacific power, with one of the largest of her four fleets, the Pacific Fleet, based at Vladivostok in Siberia, the Soviets have comparatively few air and sea bases in that area compared to the Atlantic. There, they have the use of Cienfuegos in Cuba, Conakry in Guinea, and should the worst happen, they will be able to use Portugal's Azores islands, Madeira and bases in Portugal itself for air surveillance of the American Poseidon and Polaris submarines in the Atlantic, whose missiles are targeted on Soviet missile sites and other military targets. The Soviets in 1975 also gained access to naval and air bases in Angola and Nigeria and, according to British intelligence reports, are building a new air-naval base near Conakry.

Intelligence officers believe that the Russians' knowledge of American plans to station ten Tridents—the number in the present program—in the Pacific may have accounted for their request to Hanoi in May 1975 to use the former U.S. anchorage and air base at Camranh Bay. Parenthetically, Soviet utilization of Camranh also would have the most serious strategic consequences for China.

Living conditions for Trident crews, as for all the men on the newer submarines, will be spacious in a way that submariners of the first and second world wars, immured in their sweating steel cigars, could not have imagined. Life on those earlier submarines was arduous, uncomfortable and likely to be short in war. To begin with, there was the ever-present danger, even in peace, of grave mechanical problems and consequent disaster. Seamen and officers served in craft that were the scientific marvels of their age, but the crews lived in greater discomfort than surface sailors, in conditions as bad as those endured by the men of Nelson's ships of the line.

Existence was circumscribed by sweating steel walls. The air was usually foul and sometimes poisonous. Clothes absorbed the moisture in the air and clung to dirty, sweating bodies. The food was the routine rations of the service, distributed without consideration

Holy Loch, Scotland. cdr. Thomas A. Jewell (center) directs men of the nuclear powered fleet ballistic missile submarine USS John C. Calhoun *as they bring the boat into port to end the one-thousandth undersea ballistic missile submarine patrol. Captain Jewell is commanding officer of the* Calhoun. *May 1972.* (Official U. S. Navy Photo)

Apra Harbor, Guam. cdr. Raymond E. Engle, commanding officer of the nuclear powered fleet ballistic missile submarine USS Ulysses S. Grant, *stands by the periscope of his submarine. March 1969.*
(Official U. S. Navy Photo)

Arctic Ocean. Crewmen aboard the nuclear powered submarine USS Whale *stand watch at the ballast control panel. April 1969.*
(Official U. S. Navy Photo)

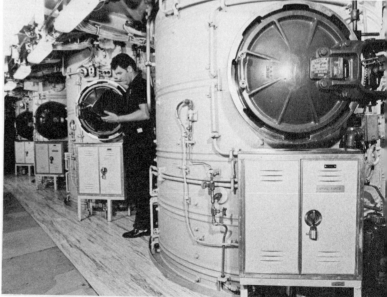

USS Lafayette *interior. April 1969.*
(*Official U. S. Navy Photo*)

Launch operating panel in missile compartment aboard USS Lafayette.
(*Official U. S. Navy Photo*)

Atlantic Ocean. Torpedoman's Mate Third Class Robert W. McLelland makes a systems check in the Polaris missile compartment on board the nuclear powered fleet ballistic missile submarine USS John Adams. *December 1969.*
(*Official U. S. Navy Photo*)

for the extraordinary conditions of submarine life. In war, crews looked forward to the "breather" on the surface at nightfall. But often the sea was too rough to permit even a few minutes on deck. Occassionally the weather was so bad that the captain, commanding from the conning tower while the crew remained below, had to be lashed to the railing with a steel belt.

The introduction in the Fifties and Sixties of much larger boats, including the nuclear-powered submarines, changed conditions. The submariner of pre-World War I days would be as astonished by life in a modern submarine as a cave dweller would be by a Manhattan apartment. Even so, the seaman might be shaken by the thought of nine or ten weeks at sea submerged in a ballistic missile submarine.

Living quarters aboard submarine; view of the bunks. (Official U. S. Navy Photo)

Atlantic Ocean. Crewmen on board the nuclear powered fleet ballistic missile submarine USS John Adams *sit down to a meal of spaghetti with meat balls, garlic bread, salad, milk and ice cream. December 1969.* (Official U. S. Navy Photo)

Navy personnel officers and psychiatrists have labored over the problems that arise when a crew of more than 140 men—the complement of the Trident class submarines will be much larger—is confined underwater for long periods. No men in naval history ever faced such a trial. When Grant Garritson was executive officer of the *James Madison* ballistic missile submarine, he reported he was "amazed at how well these men with landlocked background adapted to the extremely isolated conditions."

Garritson pointed out that there is no two-way communication with families and friends once a ballistic missile submarine begins its patrol. Families are allowed to send up to five "Family Gram" messages on each patrol. The messages are limited to 20 words.

The tedium and anxiety of long patrols are met by a full schedule. A typical officer probably works 14 to 16 hours a day. The crewmen manning the missile system and nuclear power plant can count on about six hours of duty plus training programs, study for promotion to higher ratings and constant occupation with preventive maintenance. Yeomen, corpsmen, storekeepers and cooks work a normal 10 to 12 hour day.

The submarines patrol specific areas, areas that are within range of assigned targets. Missile-firing drills are part of the daily routine. But in addition to these drills, the submarine has to be prepared to take evasive action if strange ships or submarines are detected.

These duties are made easier by the relative expansiveness of the new boats. The crew's bunks are scattered throughout the ship, and there is an exercise area for seamen and officers. The crew's mess area is large. It serves as a movie theater and recreation hall and as a study center. There is one stateroom aboard, the captain's.

Food is the main topic of conversation and to some, the chief pleasure—hence the exercise area. Provisions consumed on an average patrol include approximately 4000 lbs. of beef, 3000 lbs. of sugar, 1200 lbs. of coffee, 120 lbs. of tea, 2000 lbs. of chicken, 1400 lbs. of pork loin, 1000 lbs. of ham, 800 lbs. of butter, 3400 lbs. of flour and 900 dozen eggs.

Menus often feature ethnic foods. The dinner menu included below was selected from a dozen and has an Italian flavor.

BREAKFAST
Chilled fruit   Fruit juice
Assorted cold cereal and hot Farina
Eggs grilled to order
Broiled sausage links
Minced beef with toast
Hashed brown potatoes
Breakfast pastry
Jam, jelly, butter
Coffee, tea or milk

LUNCH
Baked stuffed pork chop
Brown gravy
Steamed spinach
Creamed peas
Applesauce
Assorted breads with butter
Sweet potato or French apple pie
Coffee, tea or milk

DINNER
Baked Lasagna and Baked Ravioli
Boiled Spaghetti with sauce
Broccoli Polonaise
Seasoned wax beans
Hot garlic toast
Assorted breads with butter
Peanut butter cookies

Ice cream with assorted toppings
Coffee, tea or milk

According to most submariners, boredom is not a problem aboard ballistic missile submarines on long patrols. The work is exacting and difficult, and the navy's educational program eats up any spare time. The average age of a crew is about 24. Most of its members are high school graduates or have had a year or two of college, and the majority are taking courses that will move them toward a commissioned rank or, if they leave the service, qualify them to enter or finish college. For those who don't want to study there are movies, talent shows and sing-alongs.

The military question that arises from this schedule is similar to that posed by the professional army and air force: Will enlisted men so carefully nurtured in peace be prepared for the hazards of war? Will tomorrow's Trident submariners be prepared for the equivalent of entering Tokyo Bay or diving under the submarine nets of the Dardanelles?

The officers' firm, expectable answer is an unequivocal "Yes." They emphasize that military life always has alternated between long periods of bordeom and spasms of intense, and it is hoped, effective action. They see no reason to believe that the present generation of submariners will fail in its duty. In fact, as the oldest officers survey their present crews, they believe that they have better material than ever before and that the men would do better in war.

The Trident, then, is the latest and newest in ballistic missile submarines—a true underwater craft with the tonnage of a heavy cruiser and the length of a destroyer. If the need arose, Tridents could reach out from the Pacific to destroy cities in the Urals and ports on the Black Sea. But despite its virtues, the submarine has had a stormy history. Those who criticize its critics would do well to remember the navy's submarine record in World War II—the torpedoes that didn't hit, the detonators that didn't explode.

The Trident story starts in 1967. A Department of Defense

study, called STRAT-X, provided the concepts for research on an undersea long-range missile system, promptly translated by the navy into the acronym ULMS. Two years later, Admiral Moorer, then chief of naval operations, issued an Advanced Development Objective giving ULMS a 1-A priority. After another two-year interval, David Packard, then deputy secretary of defense, directed the navy to begin the engineering design of a new long-range missile to be ready in 1977 and a new ballistic-missile-firing submarine scheduled for 1981.

Toward the end of that year, Secretary of Defense Melvin R. Laird accelerated the program. The first new submarine-and-missile unit was to be ready by late 1978, and the missiles were to be installed in existing Poseidon-Polaris boats starting in 1977. Early in May 1972, the acronym ULMS was dropped, and the project was rechristaned Trident.

The name Trident, the navy decided, would be applied to the class of submarines, the missiles they carried and to the support facility in Washington. Individual submarines would be christened for states. The keel of the first, the USS *Ohio*, was laid at Groton, Connecticut, on April 10, 1976.

In 1975 the navy decided to install Trident missiles only in submarines equipped with Poseidon missiles and not in the older boats armed with Polaris.

On May 26, 1972, the SALT I agreement limited the United States to 41 ballistic-missile-firing submarines and 656 missiles, with the option of substituting three more submarines and 54 missiles for 54 aging Titan land-based missiles. The Soviet Union was permitted to increase its sea-launched ballistic missile force to 62 boats and 960 missiles.

In the middle of 1972, the Trident program began to encounter opposition. The story from that day onward is rather like that of the campaign to build the first nuclear-powered submarines, with the notable exception that in the Trident's case there has been no figure of Admiral Rickover's stature to fight for the new boat; although as we shall see, the admiral did his best.

At any rate, in the summer of 1972, the Senate rejected, by a vote of 47 to 39, an amendment by Sen. Lloyd Bentsen to cut the funds necessary to speed up the Trident program. President Nixon followed the Senate's action by according the highest industrial priority to the program in December of that year.

By now, the admirals and the Defense Department hierarchy had approved the proposed characteristics of the Trident submarine. But the program was still fighting for its life. In July 1973, an amendment by Rep. Robert L. Leggett to reduce the Trident program by $832.3 million was defeated, and in August the Senate Armed Services Committee announced that it had voted, eight to seven, to approve the $1.527 billion requested for the Trident by the Defense Department. A month later, the Senate rejected an amendment that would have cut $885.4 million from the budget request and would have delayed completion of the first boat until 1980.

Constant congressional pressure on the Trident program was reaching a notably unimpressionable White House. Mr. Nixon's budget for 1975 called for ten Tridents—the navy had once dreamed of 20 or 30—in an annual production sequence of 1–2–2–2–2–1.

Congress was not the only element in the opposition, however. In April 1974, a group of citizens gathered in the Silverdale High School, Silverdale, Washington, for a public hearing on the proposed siting of the Trident support facility at Bangor. Three months later, a Final Environmental Impact Statement on the site was filed with the Council on Environmental Quality.

Despite this, the program moved methodically. That same month, July 1974, a fixed-price incentive-fee-type contract to construct the lead Trident submarine was awarded to General Dynamics' Electric Boat Division. Options for three other boats were included in the contract.

The environmentalists struck their first major blow in August. A lawsuit was filed in the United States District Court for the District of Columbia to block the development of the Trident and the construction at Bangor. The suit was filed by counsel representing various groups entitled "Concerned About Trident," "The Hood Canal Environmental Council," "Friends of Earth," "The Washington Environmental Council," "The Wilderness Society" and others. Nevertheless, a contract was let in October for site clearing, excavation work and laying the foundations for the Bangor training establishment.

The complex will cost at least $600 million and will have an estimated population of more than 50,000 people. But the tract on which it is to be built in the northwestern corner of Washington borders on the Hood Canal, a deep marine estuary leading off Puget Sound. Local environmentalists were convinced, apparently with some prodding from like-minded folk farther from the scene, that the base would destroy the area's natural beauty. They hired David Sive, one of the country's leading environmental lawyers, and attacked the navy for siting the base at Bangor, claiming that the service had failed to file a proper environmental-impact statement, a document that the National Environmental Policy Act requires of all government agencies before they decide to undertake construction projects.

The battle was joined. The navy declared that it had presented a statement—in five volumes. The environmentalists rejoined that the statement had been written after the decision to build the base had been taken, and that in any case, it completely avoided the effects of the new construction on the people of the area. Where, for example, were the new inhabitants to get sewers, extra police, schools and roads?

The Pacific Legal Foundation, a California "public interest" law firm, then entered the fight. Its public interest was business. It supported the navy's arguments, which are that the promotion of national defense has priority over environmental law and that an executive branch decision on so important a matter as the one to build the Trident is not subject to judicial review because of the constitutional doctrine of separation of powers.

Mr. Sive, striking an attitude not unfamiliar in the last five years, said that what was at stake was the simple question of whether the military was above the rule of law.

The first legal judgment in the case came from Judge George Hart of the United States District Court in Washington, D.C., who declared that it would not be in the public interest to halt the construction of the base and refused to grant a temporary injunction that would have done so. The environmentalists had sought the injunction to stop the work until a trial could be held on whether the base should be built.

Mr. Sive told the judge that the injunction would have meant only a slight delay in the construction schedule.

"Oh, slight, my foot," Judge Hart responded.

The environmentalists, however, are not the only, and perhaps not the most potent, enemies of the Trident program. While Judge Hart was telling off Mr. Sive, it was learned that problems in the shipyards could force a delay of almost three years in the completion of the Trident fleet.

A report released by the General Accounting Office in January 1975 raised the prospect that the last of the fleet may not be finished until August 1985 instead of December 1982, as the navy had hoped. The delay may come about because General Dynamics' shipyard at Groton, Connecticut, where the navy is building the first four Tridents, is overloaded. Eighteen nuclear-powered attack submarines also are being built there.

The problem is not a new one. In 1973 and 1974, it became apparent that shipyards were not particularly interested in naval contracts when easier and more profitable work was available on tankers and merchantmen. The navy's answer was to expand the Groton yard. This seemed reasonable, but unfortunately for the service, it did not translate into practical terms. In December of 1974, the GAO found that the construction of additional facilities, designed to accommodate four submarines at a time, was at least six months behind schedule. The navy had hoped it would receive the first Trident by December 1977. It now fears that the first boat will not join the fleet until a year later.

This short history of the Trident program's tribulations is a good example of why, in peace, the Soviet Union can outbuild the United States on a specific important project. The navy, the environmentalists, the shipbuilders—each has a case. But the historian 50 years hence may judge that the defense interests of the people of the United States have received little real attention.

Other problems of the program are financial and strategic.

If the Trident lives up to the navy's forecasts, it undoubtedly will be the ultimate nuclear missile submarine. It also will be one of the most expensive pieces of hardware in military history. In January 1976, Secretary of Defense Donald H. Rumsfeld reported that the planned funding for the Trident I missiles, submarines and bases would be $1.935 billion for fiscal 1976; $606 million for the transition period; $2.933 billion for fiscal 1977; and $3.383 billion for fiscal 1978. The navy ascribes the increase to three factors: the abnormal rate of inflation in the years since the program began; the projected rate of inflation for future years; and the program's stretch-out, directed by Congress. Inflation already has eaten into the Trident missile program in two ways. The budget for research, development, testing and evaluation was exceeded by the development costs of the Trident I missile. In view of the overrun, the missile program had to be altered. Then the appropriation within the navy was insufficient to fund the ships authorized for construction in fiscal 1975.

The navy has been as nervous as a whore at a church social about the unit cost of the Trident. "A billion-dollar submarine," the taxpayer says, "forget it!" The navy is worried because of a recent experience. The approximately $15 million it paid for each of its F-14 fighters shook public opinion. Critics of defense spending have seized upon the Trident as an example of a military budget gone mad and as a prime expression of the military-industrial complex's profligacy.

The navy's answer is that the first Trident will involve several "one-time costs" unique to a lead boat. Even with these, it argues that the construction of the first ship will come to about $800 million not $1 billion, while similar expenses for the next nine boats will be about

$490 million each. When the tab for their 24 Trident I missiles is added in, these nine submarines will run approximately $700 million a copy.

With that air of pained expertise that animates a service department in a debate with laymen, the navy also has pointed out that the accusation of "the billion-dollar sub" lumps into one sum the research, design and development costs for both the submarine and its missile, the design and purchase of training equipment, the purchase of land and the building of the Bangor base.

"If you put all these costs or similar ones into the estimated price of a single weapons system," an admiral said, "you artificially inflate the cost. I'll bet the tab for the army's first new tank would be $5 million, if you figured it that way."

The navy argues that the Trident program will cost less than that of the Minuteman ICBM, that it will be comparable to those of the Poseidon-Polaris programs and that it will use a significantly smaller portion of the American gross national product than those programs did.

The clamor over the Trident's cost, the problem of delays in its production and the environmentalists' agitation all have obscured what may be the real questions about the submarine. When it is launched will it represent the strategic advance that the navy claims? Or isn't it probable that in the meantime, the breakthrough in submarine detection on which the navies of the world have been working for a decade will be achieved and that the qualities that make the Trident so attractive will be balanced by the consequent improvement in antisubmarine warfare? Finally, is it not arguable that the Trident's missiles represent an expensive form of overkill, that the present Poseidon-Polaris fleet has sufficient nuclear capability?

The navy's answer is that submarine and antisubmarine warfare always has been a duel between developments and counterdevelopments, with the balance swinging between the submarine and its hunter after major breakthroughs in tactics or technology.

The admirals argue that the United States, faced with the

prospect of nuclear war with its national survival at issue, cannot allow the balance to move toward the hunter even for a short period. There is a ten-year lag in American knowledge of Soviet submarine and antisubmarine developments and the navy must do all it can to impede Russian antisubmarine warfare progress. In the navy's view, the Trident system is not an overkill against Soviet antisubmarine capability during the Trident's lifetime, but a reasonable assurance that we will maintain an acceptable margin of survivability.

What are the prospects for a breakthrough in antisubmarine warfare, particularly in the primary field of detection, that would reduce the Trident's combat effectiveness? The author has been assured by the senior officer of the naval department dealing with the subject that the United States has not made any significant advance in this field and that he was "absolutely certain" that the Royal Navy, which yearly has devoted a high percentage of its dwindling budget to its antisubmarine program, has also failed.

Nevertheless, there are some disquieting signs. As long ago as September 1962, Admiral Rickover told a congressional committee that "It is my considered opinion that it is only a question of time before all submarines will be more easily detected" and that consequently the much larger operating area of the Trident "is one of its decisive features." Admiral Rickover, at that time, was talking of the Trident in a conceptual sense and as an advocate of larger submarines. The Trident project, then called ULMS, did not take shape until five years later.

The Trident submarine's greater range, he added, "permits us to operate anywhere in the world, so that even if we are detected—and I think ultimately all submarines will be detectable—we have a much better chance of retaining our capacity to deter a nuclear war."

The Russians, the admiral pointed out, already are establishing a widespread antisubmarine surveillance system "presumably aimed at locating our Polaris-Poseidon submarines. . . . The Soviets have made great strides in naval capability which may in the future pose a threat to our submarines."

The admiral emphasized that one of the best antisubmarine weapons is the submarine itself, and that the Red Navy has nearly three times as many submarines as the United States Navy. In addition, he reported that the Soviets are making "notable strides in quieting their newer submarines and this also contributes to their ASW capability."

The underlying rationale for the Trident was stated by the admiral as only he can:

The basic advantage of seaborne missiles, since they are mobile, is that they cannot be pretargeted for a preemptive missile attack. An attack on land-based missiles would not destroy a seaborne deterrent force. This is a simple concept and the public understands it. As long as we have seaborne ballistic missiles left which cannot be destroyed by a surprise attack, the attacker knows he is vulnerable to being destroyed himself. Therefore, this becomes *the best deterrent we have* [author's italics]. But for them to remain a credible deterrent we must assure that the antisubmarine warfare capability of a potential enemy never becomes good enough to make a preemptive strike against our sea-based missiles. Since we cannot stop his technical developments, we must have adequate numbers of submarines able to operate beyond the range of his ASW forces and still cover their targets.

Critics of the Trident program also have suggested that since the Trident I missile can be fitted into Poseidon boats, the navy's deterrent capabilities can be enhanced without the cost of building Trident submarines.

The navy's answer is that the Polaris-Poseidon submarines embody the technology of the Fifties and Sixties. This is an argument that every service makes. The air force made it about the F-4 Phantom fighter when it was seeking funds for the F-15 and about the B-52 when it asked for money for the B-1. The army has made it about a new main battle tank to replace the M-60. Repetition of the argument, however, should not blind us to its validity. Technology does advance. The older submarines in the American nuclear force lack the speed, quietness, improved sonar and the various underwater detection and tracking systems that the Trident will embody and that are a hedge against Russian technological development. Nor will a program to back-fit Trident I missiles into Poseidon submarines replace the aging hulls of those boats.

Granting all the unknowns in the Trident program and conceding that all the arguments against it are made honestly, it still appears that the Trident is necessary in the national interest. What concerns the author, and what must concern anyone familiar with the Russian military building program, is that the delays in the program will result in a period of two to three years in which the Soviet Union and not the United States will possess a submarine of this class.

The manifold difficulties it has encountered have led the navy to investigate the possibilities of a less expensive submarine that would be complementary to the Trident. Smaller, and with fewer missile tubes, this submarine would be a less costly replacement for the Polaris-Poseidon boats when their age makes their deployment uneconomical or unsafe or when advances in antisubmarine warfare reduce their credibility as a nuclear deterrent force.

At present, the navy sees the smaller submarine as an option —a class of boat that would become available in the Eighties not as a substitute for the Trident but as an additional submarine weapon. It would represent a marked improvement in survivability over today's boats. Its design would feature a propulsion plant based upon that of the attack submarine *Narwhal*, advanced sonar and the incorporation of the latest quieting devices. It would be closer in size to the Poseidon than to the Trident; its cost would be more than the boats now deployed but less than the Trident's. The new class would carry about 16 Trident I missiles and would have a submerged displacement of 10,000 tons, compared to the Trident's 18,700 tons. But if such submarines are to be ready in the Eighties, design must start now.

Progress on this project depends upon a variety of factors, ranging from the state of the economy to what can be gleaned of the Soviet advance in antisubmarine warfare. In his annual Defense Department Report in March 1975, former Secretary of Defense James R. Schlesinger said that the nation "must continue our search for technology that will provide less expensive alternatives for use in future SLBM [submarine launched ballistic missile, now classified as SSBN—fleet ballistic missile submarines, nuclear propulsion] systems. Accordingly we have established a new program element, 'SSBN Subsystem Technology,' to focus attention on this essential effort." About $2 million for this purpose was included in the budget for fiscal 1976 and $1 million in the transition budget. The department will request an authorization of about $4 million in fiscal 1977.

Thus, in 1976, exactly 76 years after the navy purchased the 53-foot, 74-ton USS *Holland* from that stubborn and farsighted Irishman, John Holland, it is building submarines with a submerged displacement comparable to that of its largest cruisers and a weapons system that can reach from the Pacific into the heart of Soviet Central Asia. It has under research a smaller submarine armed with similar missiles. Holland dreamed greatly, but he never dreamed of anything like the Trident.

The missile submarines have attracted so much attention and aroused so much controversy that the public has lost sight of a program that would be equally important to the United States in the event of a conventional war. This is the attack submarine program.

One natural reaction is to question the need for an extensive fleet of attack submarines. As we have seen, the United States and Nazi Germany found ample opportunities to use their submarines against the merchant shipping supplying the island empires of Japan and Britain. But the Soviets, occupying a vast land mass, would be independent of seaborne supplies in the event of war, or so the argument goes.

In the early Seventies, the Shipbuilding Council of America estimated that the Soviet Union had 2140 oceangoing ships of 1000 gross tons or more and that the Russian merchant fleet's deadweight tonnage was 15.4 million tons. The expectation is that in war, most of these ships would scurry back to harbor or be used in the far north along the Siberian coast during its ice-free months. Therefore, the American attack submarines' prey would be the Soviet surface fleet and, more important, the Russian submarine fleet.

According to Mr. Schlesinger's frank statement to Congress, "nuclear submarines are a highly effective component" of America's antisubmarine warfare forces. Because these boats can operate covertly, they can establish ASW barriers and conduct other missions in waters controlled by enemy surface and air forces, where it would be difficult, perhaps, impossible, for other American ASW forces to operate.

"Most modern Soviet submarines," according to the former defense secretary, "are stationed in the Murmansk area; the remaining modern units are stationed in the Vladivostok and Petropavlovsk areas with the Pacific Fleet.

"We believe that, in the event of war, we should have sufficient 'first line' SSNs [nuclear attack submarines] to establish ASW barrier lines across the Soviet submarine routes from those areas into the Atlantic and Pacific oceans."

The navy estimates that it would be necessary to deploy SSNs in the Mediterranean, where the Soviets maintain a strong peacetime submarine force and where in war there would be a "high probability" of hostile submarine concentration. It is thought that in war, American and NATO surface antisubmarine forces in the Mediterranean would be at a disadvantage because of the proximity of land-based naval reconnaissance and bomber aircraft in the southern Soviet Union and Bulgaria, a Warsaw Pact ally.

As Captain Ruhe pointed out in the article cited earlier, new submarine weapons have reduced the effectiveness of surface warships as convoy escorts, a mission on which they are now employed by NATO navies. In a war with the Soviet Union, both surface war-ships and convoys would be liable to attack by submarines, land-based aircraft and surface ships. The navy is now studying the use of SSNs to protect high-value merchant ships and troop transports. There are obvious difficulties, including those of coordinating the escorting submarines' oprations with those of NATO surface ships, American and allied, in a combat situation.

The navy estimates that it needs a force of approximately 90 nuclear attack submarines. These, together with surface and air ASW forces, should be sufficient to fulfill essential wartime tactical requirements. By the end of 1976, the navy will have 64 nuclear attack submarines and 12 diesel attack boats.

Urgently needed are the 26 boats of the 688 class, none of which has been delivered. These submarines have a length of 360 feet, a beam of 33 feet, displace 6900 tons, are nuclear-propelled and are armed with a submarine rocket and ASW Mark-48 (Mk-48) torpedoes —the wire-guided, acoustical homing torpedo designed primarily for use against other submarines. The navy classifies the speed of these boats but *Jane's Fighting Ships*, the standard British publication, puts it at 30 knots-plus, submerged.

Like the Tridents, the 688s have encountered difficulties, al-though none so serious as those facing the missile boats. The lead ship, the *Los Angeles*, originally was scheduled to be commissioned in August 1974. She was delayed for 15 months, due to the late delivery of equipment from a contractor and to the slow expansion of the work force at the Newport News, Virginia, yards where she is under construction. The *Los Angeles* should be delivered this year, with the other 25, according to Mr. Schlesinger, joining the fleet by the end of 1981.

These submarines are expensive but, again, not in the Trident class. The budget for fiscal 1976 and for the transition period, during which the start of the fiscal year is pushed back to October 1, included $1.01 billion for the SSN-688 program. Another $815 million probably will be requested for 1977. The cost of a SSN-688 in 1976 is estimated

A Soviet Echo I class nuclear powered attack submarine underway. 1975 (Official U. S. Navy Photo)

at approximately $225 million, and the navy, in Mr. Schlesinger's words, "is examining the feasibility and desirability of building a new class of SSNs" less costly than the 688s.

These newer vessels may be armed with antiship tactical cruise missiles, giving them an improved capability for attacking the more advanced Soviet surface ships such as the Kara class cruisers, probably the most heavily armed warships of their size in the world. The Russians arm their Charlie, Echo I, Echo II, Juliet and Whiskey class submarines—the first three, nuclear-propelled boats—with cruise missiles and are reported to be developing a new class, named by NATO the Papa or P class, that will be larger than the Charlies and armed with eight cruise missiles, probably of the SS-N-7 type or an improved version of it.

Admiral Rickover is one of the strongest advocates of the nuclear-propelled, cruise missile submarine. He believes it "could successfully engage and neutralize typical Soviet task forces" and that "in neutralizing such a force, the United States submarine need never approach within range of the enemy's ASW capability because the cruise missile extends the SSN attack range beyond any foreseeable surface ASW sonar range."

The admiral concluded that "consequently, the cruise-missile-firing submarine's survivability is significantly greater than any other platform that could engage a modern Soviet task force."

The cruise missile submarines would be equipped with approximately the same antisubmarine sensors and weapons as a 688, or *Los Angeles,* class boat. But they might be larger because they would have to carry cruise missile launching tubes and missile control equipment in addition to other gear. No decision has been reached on the ultimate range of the missile, but General Dynamics Corporation, developer of the Tomahawk cruise missile, puts its present range at better than 1500 miles and its cruise speed at about 550 miles an hour.

All new navy attack submarines will benefit from the experimental work done on two test boats, the *Glenard P. Lipscomb* and the *Narwhal.* The former was built to test a new nuclear propulsion system and various kinds of quieter machinery. The noise level produced by an operating submarine is an important factor in its ability to remain undetected by an opponent's passive listening devices and in its own ability to detect an opponent. The *Narwhal* was built with the prototype seagoing S5G Natural Circulation Reactor. According to Admiral Rickover, this reactor "offers promise of increased reactor plant reliability, simplicity and noise reduction due to the elimination of need for large reactor coolant pumps and associated electrical and control equipment by taking maximum advantage of natural convection to circulate the reactor coolant." Natural convection eliminates the requirement for primary coolant pumps, the noisiest component of a pressurized-water propulsion system after the steam turbines.

The emphasis placed on these new submarines may give the impression that the navy is without attack boats. On the contrary, there are 37 nuclear-powered attack submarines of the Sturgeon class in the inventory. These are smaller boats than the 688s being built —4630 tons, submerged—and slower. The Sturgeons are the largest navy submarine group built to the same design and were commissioned between 1967 and 1975. They are intended as antisubmarine boats and are armed with antisubmarine torpedoes.

Behind the Sturgeons is the smaller Permit class of 13 boats and the Skipjack class of five submarines. All are nuclear-powered, but their technology is that of the middle Fifties. There are also four Skate class boats and the Triton, originally built as a radar picket submarine to operate with aircraft carrier task forces.

The war effectiveness of these antisubmarine boats will depend a lot on that of their missiles. The navy places great reliance on the Mk-48 torpedo that, although designed basically for use against enemy submarines, also is reported to have an excellent capability against surface ships. Procurement of the Mk-48 began in 1972, and the navy bought 425 in fiscal 1975 and plans to buy 175 in fiscal 1976 and 150 in fiscal 1977.

Just as the Mk-48 torpedo is the primary weapon of the attack submarine, so the AN/BQQ-5 sonar is its principal sensor. This is a new digital, multibeamed system with both hull-mounted and towed acoustical arrays. It is being installed in the 688 class and is being back-fitted into all Sturgeon and Permit class boats during regular overhauls.

This system operates with attack boats. In its continuing and very expensive antisubmarine warfare program, the United States is developing and improving two key undersea surveillance systems, the fixed sound surveillance system (SOSUS) and the surveillance towed-array sensor system (SURTASS). The navy is discreet about the progress made, but it is understood that SOSUS was remarkably accurate in picking up the Soviet submarine that ventured close to the East Coast in June 1975. But the service believes that SURTASS is needed to supplement SOSUS. The tactical towed-array surface ships in the latter system would have computers to evaluate contacts with submarines. Specially armed helicopters or other aircraft would follow up the contacts. Tests at sea and laboratory analysis have shown that towed arrays would make a significant contribution to the ASW effectiveness of surface combatants.

The navy believes that SURTASS is ready for full-scale engineering development and has begun the design and construction of a model that will be used in sea tests.

When discussing navy hardware, it is easy to forget that submarines, torpedoes and sensors cannot be employed effectively without officers and sailors capable of using them and of hammering out a doctrine for their use in war. The young captains and commanders of the submarine service appear reasonably confident that they have the right weapons to carry on an antisubmarine campaign in the event of war with the Soviet Union. Their watchword is "balance." By this they mean a proper balance of all antisubmarine forces—aircraft, surface warships and submarines. (Naturally, they regard the last as the most important element of the team.) Submariners noted repeatedly that Germany lost her submarine war in 1943 because the force lacked balance; she fought her undersea war without sufficient cooperation from air and surface forces.

The new weapons—the Mk-48 torpedo and the Harpoon missile, which can be launched from a surface ship or a submarine—were cited as reasons for confidence.

"The Russians are ahead in cruise missiles at the moment," one captain in the Pentagon said. "But the Mk-48, the Harpoon and the cruise missile we are developing will give us a superior position. If we use submarines as they should be used, in coordinated operations with air and surface forces, I have no doubt that we can deal with the Soviet submarines."

He and other officers believed that the United States is definitely ahead of the Soviet Union in the quietness of submarines and in underwater detection systems. The Russians, they said, have no fixed surveillance system like SOSUS, which gives the United States "a great advantage." In the field of submarine tenders, they said that the Russians lag. Tenders remove the need of overseas bases, but they are expensive. They cost the United States about $200 million each. The Russians have 15 submarine support ships, but six of them are old Don class vessels.

The United States Navy is on the verge of a leap forward in sophisticated submarines and sensors. The Tridents, the 688s, SURTASS, the Mk-48 torpedo are some assurance that by the end of this decade, the Soviet submarine threat will be reduced and American deterrent power enhanced. During the same period, the commissioning of two more nuclear-powered aircraft carriers and guided-missile cruisers, destroyers and frigates will strengthen the surface fleet.

There is, however, one very large question mark. Will the navy of the Eighties have the capability of establishing and maintaining control of the seas over which American and allied supplies will move? It may be that the strategy of destroying Soviet attack submarines before they put to sea, the strategy discernible behind Secretary Schlesinger's careful comment, will suffice. But what if the nations drift into war and the first shots are exchanged when the Soviet submarine fleet is at sea?

By their nature, these questions cannot be answered now. But we have seen enough of the modern submarine, Russian and American, to recognize it as the most important weapon in any future war.